Vietnam . . . Can't Get You Out of My Mind

Propaganda mural at purported location
of COSVN headquarters

Also by Jim Jones

A Little Dam Problem: How Idaho Almost Lost Control of the Snake River

VIETNAM . . .

Can't Get You Out of My Mind

A Journey Through the
Vietnam War and Its Aftermath

Jim Jones

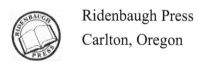

Ridenbaugh Press
Carlton, Oregon

VIETNAM ... Can't Get You Out of My Mind
Copyright ©2019 by Jim Jones

For more information, contact Ridenbaugh Press, P.O. Box 834, Carlton OR 97111.
Printed and bound in the United States of America.
First edition May 2019
10 9 8 7 6 5 4 3 2 1

Library of Congress Cataloging in Publication Data

Jim Jones

VIETNAM ... Can't Get You Out of My Mind

Bibliography

1. Biography. 2. Idaho Politics and Government.

I. Jones, Jim. II. Title.

ISBN 978-0-945648-46-8 (softbound)

Front cover designed by Brian Florence of Steamroller Studios in Boise.
Back cover photo courtesy of Kelly Jones (who is impressed the uniform still fits after fifty years).
Maps 1 and 2 are courtesy of Brian Florence, Steamroller Studios, Boise.

Ridenbaugh Press
P.O. Box 834, Carlton OR 97111
Phone (503) 852-0010
www.ridenbaugh.com
stapilus@ridenbaugh.com

Contents

Dedication

This book is dedicated to the 58,220 U.S. service personnel who lost their lives serving their country in the Vietnam War, including the 251 with connections to the State of Idaho; and to all of the others who answered their country's call to serve in that unpopular conflict. Regardless of how individual Americans view that war, we, as a nation, owe our veterans thanks and appreciation.

The book is also dedicated to the almost 300,000 members of the Army of the Republic of Vietnam, our ARVN friends, who lost their lives in the war; to the many thousands more who suffered terribly as a result of America's failure to honor its promises of supplies and air support in their time of need; to the hundreds of thousands of Vietnamese civilians who perished as a result of the conflict; and to the many more who suffered, or were displaced or orphaned by the war.

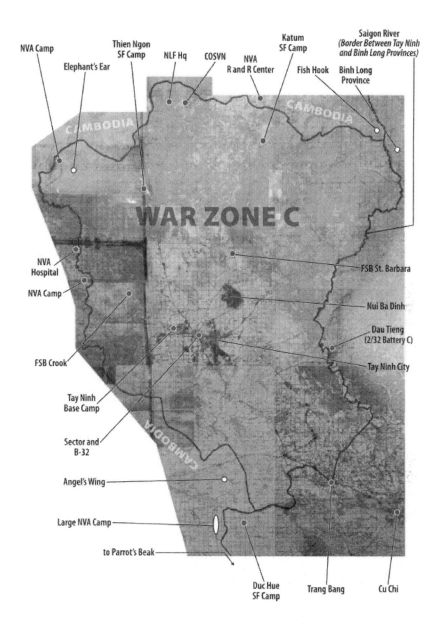

NVA Camp

Elephant's Ear

Thien Ngon
SF Camp

NLF Hq   COSVN

NVA
R and R Center

Katum
SF Camp

Fish Hook

Saigon River
(Border Between Tay Ninh
and Binh Long Provinces)

Binh Long
Province

CAMBODIA

CAMBODIA

WAR ZONE C

NVA
Hospital

NVA Camp

FSB Crook

Tay Ninh
Base Camp

Sector and
B-32

Angel's Wing

Large NVA Camp

to Parrot's Beak

CAMBODIA

FSB St. Barbara

Nui Ba Dinh

Dau Tieng
(2/32 Battery C)

Tay Ninh City

Duc Hue
SF Camp

Trang Bang

Cu Chi

Nui Ba Dinh   FSB St. Barbara

| Cao Xa | Trang Sup | Tay Ninh | Sector and | Cao Dai | Cao Dai |
| Village | SF Camp | Base Camp | B-32 | Orphanage | Holy See |

Map #2

Introduction

This is not a typical book about combat. It is a recollection of my path to the Army, my service in Vietnam, and the indelible impression that service left on my life.

Wartime service is generally a defining experience in the life of any veteran. For the majority, it is probably the most significant and important thing they have done in their lives—to take up arms and risk life and limb for an important cause. There can be nothing more noble.

Although my father did not serve in World War II, many men from my small Idaho community did. It was the thing you did, unless you were growing food for the troops. And, it was a grand and noble cause. Our nation's future was at risk.

Our troops won the war and came home to a thankful and grateful nation. While many of the veterans suffered physical and psychological problems after the war, they could reflect on the fact that they had helped protect the country from an existential threat.

For those who served in Vietnam, the cause was not so clearly noble, the result was calamitous, and thankful countrymen were few and far between, at least for many years afterwards. That left many Vietnam veterans with the same physical and psychological problems suffered by veterans of other conflicts, but with the added feeling that it was all for naught and that their service was either not appreciated or actually despised by their countrymen. As a result, a significant number of returning troops had a difficult time readjusting to civilian life. And, they did not receive the help they needed and deserved.

I was always proud of the fact that I volunteered for service in Vietnam, even though I could easily have gotten out of it. I never did anything particularly heroic, was not traumatized, and have had no serious service-related problems since then.

But I had the opportunity to see and do things that many others did not, like going to a Vietnamese wedding, being saved from oblivion by a poker game, observing a large enemy camp just across the border in Cambodia, working with an orphanage, having an audience with the Pope of the Cao Dai Church, watching earth-shaking B-52 strikes from an airborne box seat, and defending U.S. soldiers in court martial proceedings.

I got to Vietnam on July 19, 1968, about six months after the Tet Offensive. I served 407 days in a heavy artillery unit just outside of Tay Ninh City, which is located about 55 miles northwest of Saigon. During most of my tour, I lived among and worked with soldiers of the Army of the Republic of Vietnam (ARVN) at Tay Ninh Province Headquarters. Tay Ninh Province was the terminus of a main branch of the Ho Chi Minh Trail, so the Viet Cong (VC) and North Vietnamese Army (NVA) had a substantial presence there. I was the officer in charge of a 4-person liaison unit whose job was to clear all artillery fire and air strikes in the Province.

We worked with our ARVN counterparts to make sure that no ARVN units or civilians were in the target area before authorizing a strike.

My additional duties were serving as artillery support for B-32, a U.S. Army Special Forces B Camp, and acting as an aerial observer, or artillery spotter, in Tay Ninh Province. This gave me an opportunity to get acquainted with the entire Province from the air, flying at about 800 feet above ground in a small two-seater "Bird Dog" airplane. The Bird Dog was a World War II aircraft with one seat behind the other, sometimes called an L-19 (Army) or O1 (Air Force).

The ARVNs with whom I worked were Catholics or Cao Dais. The Catholics came from Cao Xa, a nearby village of religious refugees who moved south to avoid Communist persecution when Vietnam was partitioned in 1954. There were numerous Cao Dais in the area because the headquarters and Holy See of the Cao Dai Church are in Tay Ninh City.

My ARVN counterparts were wonderful people, who I trusted with my life. Although I had frequent interaction with them, I regret that I did not get to know them better and learn to speak their language other than just a few phrases. I suppose the regrets stem partly from my feeling that we left them in the lurch in 1975 and that many or most suffered mightily at the hands of the Communists when their country fell.

I also had the opportunity and privilege to work with an orphanage operated by the Cao Dai Church. It gave me an appreciation of the plight of victims of war that I still carry with me today. Had I known how our Vietnam venture was going to turn out, I might have tried to take some of the kids home with me.

When I left Vietnam in August of 1969, I was convinced that Communist forces would lose the war. Much of the VC in my area had been eliminated in the Tet Offensive and the NVA had suffered grievous losses. The Cao Dai Church, which had largely remained neutral after its own army was disbanded in 1956, had gravitated toward the government's side. I did not have first-hand information as to what was happening elsewhere in the country, but based on what I had heard from other service members and learned from the news, I thought we were on the path to winning the war.

I should say that this book is not about the wisdom of our country going to war in Vietnam. Even after having half a century to mull over that question, I still can't settle in my own mind whether it was right to get involved in the first place. Certainly, it came to a disastrous conclusion as a result of bad strategies and political blunders. How the war was prosecuted does not answer the question of whether it was in the national interest to become involved.

The principal concern at the time was whether the failure to confront the Communists in Vietnam would be seen as a lack of resolve in the Cold War and cause the countries in and around Indochina to move into the Soviet orbit. The domino theory had some surface appeal when viewed in the context of the numerous proxy wars being engaged in between the U.S. and the USSR. The Soviets were continually starting conflicts in various countries around the world, causing the U.S. to rush to the trouble spot to counter them. This particular conflict was not necessarily started by the Soviet Union, but the Soviets strongly supported Ho Chi Minh all along.

The main problem with the domino theory is that it did not particularly take into account the cultural history of the region, the long-standing enmity between China and Vietnam, and the fact that China and the USSR did not constitute one monolithic entity. Each of those countries had its own strategic objectives at the time.

Regardless of the wisdom of the war, the Vietnam experience has played a large role in my life. My service gave me a level of confidence that was very helpful in my legal and political endeavors. It provided useful perspective in dealing with difficult problems and gave me a world view that could not have come from any other source.

It clearly demonstrated to me that war is an ugly proposition to be avoided at all costs. In that regard, we have learned so very little. During the build-up to the war in Iraq, it was very obvious to me that we were headed for the same kind of disaster. We had no compelling national interest at stake. The political and military leadership had little idea of the culture of the country we were proposing to invade, or the potential consequences of an invasion, or that there would almost assuredly be in insurgency, or how to deal with a guerrilla war.

To this day, political leaders throw around the concept of going to war as if it is something to be taken lightly. They do not consider the toll it takes on veterans and their families or on the civilian populations of conflict areas. The politicians just want to show how tough they are by kicking ass, without regard to whether any vital national interest will be served or what it will cost in American lives.

I do not consider myself to be a military expert. But, I have had a life-long interest in foreign affairs, particularly since my service in Vietnam, and consider myself as being fairly well versed on foreign policy, including military affairs.

My purpose in writing the book is to tell about what happened in my world during the war and how that has affected my life ever since.

When I got home from Vietnam, it did not take long to learn that the experience was almost impossible to relate to someone without wartime experience.

Partly because of that, and also because I am basically an introvert, I have rarely spoken in any detail about what I did in Vietnam, other than my experiences with the orphans and my ARVN friends.

During most of my tour, I kept a journal of some of my thoughts and experiences and it has been helpful in reconstructing events. My hooch was destroyed on April 11, 1969, so any contemporaneous notes for the first three months of 1969 went up in smoke. A lot of the stuff in the journal is crap—bravado and the like—and that has been discarded.

I have included a number of pictures but must apologize for their quality. I generally used an old Canon point-and-shoot with color slide film. Either the camera was not as good as I thought it was at the time or the slides were deteriorated by the time I scanned them decades later.

It should be said that my observations regarding military policy during my Vietnam tour were based upon information provided through my chain of command.

One friend has indicated a different understanding of the rules of engagement along the Cambodian border. I never researched the actual rules issued by higher headquarters, but followed the rules as related to me through my battalion.

The book is based upon my own recollections and the background information available to me at the time.

Jim Jones
April 2019

1 ● The plan comes together

I had not given much thought to military service during my high school years. Actually, my interests centered around living for the moment, doing such important things as dragging Main Street in Twin Falls, Idaho, in my 1956 Mercury Medalist that was about three inches from the ground at both ends. Thinking about the future was not high on the list, although it was my assumption that I would go into civil engineering. That was because my uncle "Ranny" Martens, who was kind of my hero, was a civil engineer. He and his wife Carole had lived in Afghanistan in the nineteen-fifties, where Ranny had been working on dams. It sounded pretty exciting.

When I was growing up in good old Eden, Idaho, which then had a population of 452 souls, I was not aware of any military tradition in my family. A number of men from my parents' generation had served in World War II but a lot, like my father Henry Jones, had been exempt from the draft because farmers were considered essential to the war effort—growing food for the troops. My Dad's brother, Robert, had been in the Army Air Force and died on a training mission in a bomber, but that is about the extent of what I knew about any family military history until the just before the turn of the century.

There may be some latent military tradition in my genes from my Dad's side of the family. His mother's maiden name was Tracy. Family lore is that the first Tracy, Ramion or James, came to the country along with a contingent of French soldiers in about 1779 to fight on the American side in the Revolutionary War. I was skeptical for many years about the claim of his French origin because Tracy seemed to be of Scottish or Irish derivation, rather than French. During the late nineties, I learned that the ancestor of a Tracy family in Bourbonnais had immigrated to France from Scotland in 1420 and that the family had produced a number of French military officers. In addition, a number of Scotsmen went to France around that time to serve as mercenaries fighting against England. This appeared to support the family lore.

In any event, Tracy was wounded in fighting at Charleston, South Carolina, in the spring of 1780 and left for dead on the battlefield. A local lady found him still alive, nursed him to health and married him. No reason to waste a good Frenchman if you have a use for him. There is no further known history of military service by ancestors on either side of my family.

My family was just like most others during the early fifties in that we gathered around the radio to listen to radio programing, including news reports. We heard lots of reports about fighting in Korea and then many more about peace talks at a place called Panmunjom, including arguments about how the table at the talks should be configured. The fighting stopped in the summer of 1953 when I was 11. One afternoon, I heard a loud ruckus in the sky and looked up to see a formation of about 12 bombers flying overhead. It scared the heck out of me but then I felt some relief when they didn't drop any bombs. That led me to believe they must be friendly planes, instead of Russian bombers. Like every other kid who grew up during the early part of the Cold War, I learned how to hide under a school desk in the event the Russians were to drop an atomic bomb in the vicinity, although it never seemed to me that there was anything around Eden that was worth bombing.

I recall hearing radio broadcasts in 1954 about the desperate situation of French troops at a place called Dien Bien Phu, where they were besieged by Communists, but I couldn't have told you exactly where that was. Although I was interested in geography and was vaguely familiar with Indochina, the word "Vietnam" was unfamiliar. I do recall hearing that the French had lost their battle, which brought that war to an end.

Eden was a nice town and good place to grow up, although I never quite figured out how the town had gotten its name. It didn't look like paradise to me but it was okay. It had a number of thriving businesses, including three grocery stores, a couple of bars, a barber shop, a meat locker, a theater where you could go to a movie for 25 cents, several churches for a variety of faiths, a lumber yard, at least three gas stations, and, most importantly, a drug store where I squandered my money on comic books.

As far as the military went, I was enamored with war planes in grade school and wrote to every defense contractor that made them to get pictures of every plane they made. I would love to have flown in one of them, either a jet like the F-86 fighter, or a propeller-driven fighter like the P-51 Mustang, but I was not particularly chomping at the bit to run off and join the Air Force.

Coming across Alfred, Lord Tennyson's poem, The Charge of the light brigade, did make a lasting impression. As I read "Cannon to the right of them, Cannon to the left of them, Cannon in front of them," thoughts of glory and heroism raced through my mind. What a way to go. It was not until well after my Vietnam service that I read historical accounts of the conflict between Britain and Russia in Crimea. It turned out the charge was pretty stupid and pointless. They were actually charging the wrong objective. That deflated the thoughts of glory, but by then most of that kind of thinking had been purged from my head by the actuality of war.

As I grew into my teenage years, driving the 13 miles to Twin Falls to drag Main and chase girls (without much success) pretty much occupied my thoughts. While I was a good student in high school, I didn't particularly apply myself to getting the best grades in my class. My relaxed attitude toward life changed fairly dramatically in the fall of 1959, just as I was starting my senior year.

One nice fall evening, my steady girlfriend and I were watching the stars on a stretch of Eastland Drive in Twin Falls that had been barricaded off for construction purposes. Just as things were getting interesting, another car impolitely drove around the barricade and was headed our way. I decided it was time to go but, unfortunately, was driving stupidly fast when I went around the barricade at the other end of the closed-off stretch of road. The car bounced, slammed down violently and for some reason I could not see a thing. It felt like the car was skidding so I remember turning into what seemed to be the direction of the skid. The next thing I knew, the car was upside down and I was pinned between a couple of solid objects.

There must have been a light on in the car because I could see finely powdered windshield glass floating like a cloud all around me. I managed to pull myself free and noticed a bulge in my jeans just above my left knee, where there should not have been one. My right leg was wobbly below the knee so I figured it was broken. The strange thing is that I did not feel any pain—must have been in shock. My girlfriend said she thought she was OK, which I figured was a miracle since things were really jumbled up inside the car.

The 1958 Chevrolet Bel Air that belonged to my Dad and which I often drove, had hit a utility pole that had just been installed that very day and snapped it off at the base. The pole came squarely through the windshield from one side to the other, clamping us to the car seat just like a seat belt (photo #1) Had it not been for the good American steel in that Chevy, the pole would have crushed us against the floor of the car. As it was, the steering wheel was practically buried in the driver's seat. Both of us must have been thrown to the passenger's side at the time of impact. Thinking back, it is hard to figure out how we survived.

Luckily, I only ended up with two broken legs and she with a fractured collar bone.

After spending 14 weeks in Magic Valley Memorial Hospital in Twin Falls, flat on my back with my left leg in traction and right leg in a cast, I was sent home. The reason it took so long is that my bones did not seem to want to heal. They thought the answer was to fill me full of calcium, so I got milk at every meal, plus milkshakes and eggnog twice a day, plus calcium shots in my butt every day. Lying in one position on your back for 14 weeks can cause some serious bed sores and when you add a painful calcium shot to the butt, it can be quite uncomfortable— something like a medieval torture technique. When I pointed this out to the hospital staff, they kindly agreed to give the shot in my arm and that helped a lot. All of that calcium did not seem to speed up the healing, but the massive amounts of milk products did not do any favors for my complexion for many years to come.

The worst part about the hospital stay was that I could see all of the teenage dragsters right out of my window. The Town and Country Drive-in was just across the street and it was the western turn-around for those who spent their evenings dragging Main in Twin Falls, which was the major activity of teenagers back then. It was painful to see everyone having fun right outside of my window. On the other hand, it was my easiest semester in high school. All I had to do for an A in English was to diagram a couple dozen sentences and I got an A in math for doing a couple of pages of problems.

After several weeks at home, I started back to school in a wheelchair and gained an understanding of the barriers facing people with mobility problems. By graduation day, I was using crutches and soon got lessons from a physical therapist on how to walk again. You do tend to need a refresher course after a six-month hiatus.

I soon found myself moving sprinkler hand lines during that summer. The work was not too bad on hay ground but not much fun in the potato ground, with mud up to 4 inches deep and swarms of gnats trying to crawl into every opening in my body. My Dad often commented years later how proud he was that I got back on my feet and was working hard so soon. As I recall, I was not given any other option.

During my extended recovery, there was plenty of time to reflect on my misspent earlier years. As a result, my view of the world and my future in it took a sharp turn toward reality and practicality. It was time to get serious about life and what I was going to do with mine.

After graduating Valley High School in 1960, I went to Idaho State University in Pocatello to learn how to be a civil engineer. I enjoyed chemistry, physics, math, English, and almost everything else. The only exception was engineering drafting. At that time, it was all done manually, as computers were only something that offered promise for the future. The class was pure drudgery with all of the detailed drawing and it raised the specter of slaving over a drafting board for years into the future. I was particularly ripe for a change in my career ambition. And then, John Kennedy, the newly-elected President of the United States, gave his inaugural address. When he said "ask not what your country can do for you —ask what you can do for your country," I was struck to the core with inspiration. I knew I had to do something to serve my country.

What stood out was the fact that the 1960 presidential contenders had served in the United States Senate. Both Kennedy and his Vice President, Lyndon Johnson, had been Senators, as had their opponent, Richard Nixon. The Senate was described as the greatest deliberative body in the world. Many Senators were doing bold things at the time and it seemed to me that being a U.S. Senator would be the worthiest goal imaginable. So, I decided that I would ditch engineering drafting and do what it looked like people generally did when they wanted to become a Senator – get a law degree, get a war record, and run for office.

So, I switched my major to political science, transferred to the University of Oregon, which had a good political science program, and set my goals on getting a law degree and going into politics. The transfer to Oregon was facilitated by the fact that my girlfriend was, as John Wayne said in one of his movies, beating me over the head with a preacher. She was a wonderful person and we had been through a lot together, but I could see that my ambitions for the future were very different from hers. I'd been driving home from Pocatello every weekend to see her and it looked like some distance might be helpful. And, it turned out that it was. We broke off our relationship by Thanksgiving in 1961.

As with most state universities, the University of Oregon had a compulsory ROTC program. However, my automobile accident posed a major roadblock to getting into the service because I was pretty much 4F—physically unfit for military duty. When my left femur, which had sustained a compound fracture just above the knee, came out of traction, it was three-quarters of an inch shorter than before the accident. My right leg, which had sustained a fracture of the tibia and been in a cast for about 16 weeks, was bowed out at about 10 degrees more than before. Dr. Woodson, my orthopedist, had to rebreak the tibia at about six weeks because it was growing together crooked. He also wanted to remove my right kneecap for some reason, other than just because it was squishy and noisy when I moved it. I told him nothing doing. That was a good call because it eventually got better. I have to admit that my injuries were not as grievous as those suffered about the same time by a future U.S. President—apparent bone spurs in one foot or the other—but still enough to have kept me out of the service. In any event, I was determined to move forward with my plans regardless of the leg issues.

I had been exempted from ROTC at Idaho State because of the leg injuries, but I assured the ROTC folks at Oregon that everything was fine and they agreed to let me combine the first and second year ROTC programs in my second year of college. Everything went well until ROTC summer camp at Fort Lewis, Washington, in 1963. During my physical, the doctor raised questions about the squishy noise coming from my right knee but I assured him that it was fine and not a problem. Captain Temp, an

ROTC instructor from the University of North Dakota who was in charge of my group, expressed concern about my slow speed through the part of the obstacle course where you drag yourself through a trench of mud under barbwire. He told me he wasn't sure I was physically fit to stay in the program. I figured it was a limitation brought about by the leg injuries but did not tell him so. However, when he saw me leading a small unit maneuver exercise and gave me high marks for it, his concerns disappeared.

The maneuver tactics training was interesting because it highlighted the need to be flexible when approaching a problem. Instead of just using a head-long frontal assault, you often have better success by going at the objective from several angles. As you move toward the goal, you should examine all aspects of the problem, find the opponent's weak points and focus your effort on those vulnerable areas. And, when the first plan does not work, figure out how you can come out best with an alternate plan. In the years since, I found this type of approach to work well in practically any setting, including the legal and political realms.

My Mom pinned my Second Lieutenant bar on me at the commissioning ceremony following graduation at the U of O in 1964. At that time, I had reached the first milestone on the way to the Senate—military service—but it didn't look like there was a war that would provide the basis for a war record. There was news out of Vietnam that the U.S. was providing advisory assistance to the South Vietnamese forces but it looked as if that would not last very long because we were told the South Vietnamese were on their way to victory. On the other hand, it seemed like the U.S. never had trouble finding a war to get involved in, so the prospects of some kind of conflict being in existence when I finished law school was not too remote.

Upon completion of ROTC, I needed to select a combat branch for my commission. My ROTC advisor suggested artillery because I was good in math. So, artillery it was. I was kind of thinking of switching to the Judge Advocate General (JAG) branch when I finished law school, but that was down the road.

J.R. Klonoski, my favorite political science professor, suggested that I apply to Northwestern School of Law in Chicago, saying that it took a more progressive approach to the study of law. I followed his advice and spent my next three years at Northwestern, getting my Juris Doctor degree in 1967. Each year, the Army required that I get an extension of my active duty date and it was generous enough to grant one each year. There was never any indication that I needed to do any reserve training or service and it didn't seem advisable to volunteer for any.

During the summers of 1965 and 1966, I performed intern work in the office of former U.S. Senator Len B. Jordan of Idaho. This piece of my resume would actually come in handy during my military service. Jordan was an outstanding person—intelligent, thoughtful and dedicated to doing the right thing. In 1964, I began trying to get a position with any of the Idaho Congressional offices in order to get my feet wet in politics but had not been able to get a position. When I applied to all of the offices for the summer of 1965, they were either not hiring or had already filled any available intern positions. Senator Jordan's office advised me that it did not look like the Senate would be in session during the summer so no intern hiring was anticipated. I jumped on a plane to Washington to speak with the administrative assistant, Gwen Lewis, who expressed regret that the office would not be hiring. When I got back to Chicago, I got a call indicating that there would a position open during the summer and that it was mine. I worked in the office that summer, as well as the next.

During those three years in law school, it was clear that the war in Vietnam was increasing in intensity, that U.S. forces were shouldering a greater burden, that American casualties were rising, and that resistance to the war was growing at home. The news media covered the anti-war demonstrations and campus unrest, but there was probably more favorable war coverage at that time.

I can recall reading a story in Time magazine in the fall of 1967 about a Combined Reconnaissance and Intelligence Platoon (CRIP) operating somewhere in Vietnam. The officer in charge looked to be about 17 years old, but the story made their work sound exciting.

Another article spoke of splattering Viet Cong attackers with flechettes fired from a 105mm howitzer. Flechettes are tiny little metal darts designed to tumble when they hit a person, causing massive internal damage. Scads of them were crammed into a cannister called a beehive round. The beehive round would be fired at advancing hordes of enemy fighters at point-blank range. The article explained this all with great bravado.

Lots of patriotic stuff was being published to build support for the war and for the troops fighting in it. *The Green Berets*, A book written by Robin Moore, which was released in 1965 and later made into a John Wayne movie, had gotten lots of romantic coverage in the press. I was revved up and ready to get in on the action.

Many law school classmates were also making plans, but generally of another kind. There was a lot of discussion in the 1966-67 school year about the draft and how to avoid it. One fellow had gotten married during our first year in hopes of avoiding the draft but marriage was soon removed as an exemption. He then fathered a child to get deferred, but that exemption was also eliminated. Quite a number of classmates were looking to sign up with National Guard units since they had not generally been called up. Guard units in Texas and New Mexico seemed to be willing to open their arms to recruits from around the country.

It did not really bother me that people were trying to dodge the draft, so long as they were not high-tailing it for Canada. And, that does not bother me anymore.

After graduation in 1967, I took a bar exam cram course at the University of Idaho, passed the bar exam, and was sworn in as a member of the Idaho State Bar. By that time, the decision as to whether to switch over to the JAG branch became fairly easy to answer. The Army had increased the length of a JAG commitment from two years to four years, whereas the commitment for a combat branch remained at two years.

It was an easy choice—two years in the artillery. My orders to report for duty came shortly after graduation.

I needed to be at Fort Sill, Oklahoma, at the end of November to start the artillery officer basic course—how to become a cannon cocker.

2 ● In the Army now

I spent the next four months at Fort Sill, learning how to be an artillery officer. It was interesting to learn that so many factors went into the job of accurately getting an artillery round from the gun to the target. You needed to take into account the wind direction and velocity, the temperature and humidity, the elevation, and the earth's rotation, among many other things. All of these factors were crunched into a computer called the FADAC (Field Artillery Digital Automatic Computer), along with the coordinates of the target, to get the round where it needed to go. That was all very exciting.

I found some of the subjects to be rather boring, like learning how to survey a piece of land. Yes, surveying was important in order to get a cannon, or a battery of cannons, properly positioned. One guy would operate the transom and another guy would take a tape measure out. When he arrived at the proper distance, he would position a plumb bob over the desired point. At that time the guy at the transom would yell "stick" which was the signal to drop the plumb bob. When the plumb bob fell and stuck into the ground, the person who had dropped it would yell "stuck." I'm sure this seemingly simple-headed procedure was justified by some bad experience. In any event, it seemed to work. Motor pool was not all that interesting, either. Terrain features class was fairly simplistic—we learned that a hill is a feature that when you are standing on top of it, the ground slopes down in every direction. That was a real revelation.

Fort Sill is located in the eastern desert land of Oklahoma. Some people would say it is wind-swept, God-forsaken desert. Having come from desert lands in southern Idaho, it wasn't all that bad. What struck me is that the weather could change practically on the spot. Sometimes it was exceedingly hot, which I thought was unusual for the winter, but then it could turn exceedingly cold. One thing that I vividly remember was an ice storm where rain turned into ice when it landed on something. A thick coat of ice built up on vehicles, buildings, power lines, and even people who stood in one place too long. It was really odd to see power lines drooping all of the way down to the ground, weighed down by many pounds of ice, which caused some of them to snap.

Lawton, Oklahoma, was the nearest town. Lawton was dry, except for beer. However, you could find hard liquor at what were called "private clubs." You walked in and saw liquor bottles that were all labeled with somebody's name. If you wanted a Canadian Club and water, you looked around until you saw "Joe's" bottle of Canadian Club and ordered a bit of Joe's whiskey.

One of my favorite places was the Saddle Bar. The barstools were actually saddles and you just mounted up and ordered a beer. If you had too much to drink, there was always a saddle horn to hang onto.

One thing that offended me was when I went into one saloon to order the chili that was advertised as the very best in the area. They brought a bowl full of chili that had no beans. Whoever heard of chili without beans? Apparently, that is how they serve it in Oklahoma and vicinity.

The student body at artillery school consisted primarily of newly-minted Second Lieutenants, mostly Army, but also a few National Guard officers, and three Marines. There were two First Lieutenants, including me. The three Marines were really neat guys who had served for years as enlisted men but then taken officer training and gotten their Second Lieutenant bars. There was a fourth Marine who had a PhD from MIT and had apparently been promoted to Captain during his schooling. His rank made him the class leader.

I can't remember our Captain's name, but he took his job much too seriously. I hate to use the word martinet, but that's kind of the way he acted and people didn't much appreciate it. It wasn't like he was leading a unit into battle, since we were all pretty much in the same boat—just officers learning how to shoot cannons. It got to the point of being a bit irritating to just about everybody. The highlight of my time at Fort Sill was when everybody was loaded on a bus one day to drive out to the artillery range. Our Captain had not yet appeared, so I got to the front of the bus and started giving out orders in a Charlie-Chaplinesque fashion. Just about that time our Captain entered the bus behind me and everything got very quiet. You could immediately see that he was not happy with my mimicking. He invited me off the bus to have a bit of a discussion, whereupon I struck first, telling him he was not particularly appreciated by his troops and that he needed to chill out and take it easy. It actually worked out pretty well because he did just that.

Other than that, I can't recall anything that particularly stands out about artillery school. I do believe that it was during school, or perhaps just beforehand, that the Army asked me where I would like to serve. I thought it was nice that they would ask. There were a number of places you could choose, and I selected Southeast Asia. That seemed to be where the action was.

The news of what was happening in Vietnam was mixed. The Communists had launched a major offensive during the Tet celebration on January 31, despite having agreed to stand down, and heavy fighting was reported across the country. Over the next several days, U.S. and South Vietnamese (ARVN) forces had gained the upper hand. The news portrayed it as a major defeat for the Commies. I remember seeing a picture of a captured Viet Cong guerrilla being shot in the head by an ARVN general. The press made it sound as if we were on our way to victory. Sometimes, it is hard to see how something is actually going to play out.

When we received our grades, I believe I had placed second in the class. My downfall was motor pool. I had piddled around with my Mercury for years, taking pistons out and then putting them back in and stuff like that, but couldn't get much interest up in the motor pool arena. However, finishing second in the class should have given me an entrée to an artillery unit in Vietnam. When the orders came, I learned that I had been assigned to a transportation unit in Okinawa. That didn't seem to make a lot of sense, but things are often hard to explain in the Army. Graduation took place on March 8, 1968, and I was to fly to Okinawa later that month.

When I reported for duty in Okinawa, I learned I would be the executive officer of a transportation battalion that was responsible for loading and unloading ships at the Naha Port. What that meant is that I would have lots of administrative duties, including responsibility for the mess hall, vector control (which I soon learned was to control rats, mice and bugs), counseling soldiers about their debts and other problems back home, trying to get people to put some money in savings, and a variety of other things that didn't sound too interesting.

The battalion commander was Captain Dietmar W. L. Zurell, a German national who was apparently earning his U.S. citizenship by serving in the Army. He was a neat guy and I enjoyed working with him. He was married to an Okinawan woman, who was also a good person. We had a Second Lieutenant, Gary Peters, who reminded me of Lieutenant Fuzz in the Beetle Bailey comic strip, and a Chief Warrant Officer, Bob Cole, a good time guy who became my drinking buddy.

I was told that our unit consisted primarily of enlisted men who had been busted out of other branches and that we had essentially inherited a bunch of dysfunctional individuals. They didn't actually seem too bad but many of them kept coming before me for counseling, including Sergeant Brake, who had numerous unpaid debts, domestic problems, and no apparent solutions to any of those problems. It was not very enjoyable work. At times, I felt like a social worker or debt counselor. It seemed like all of those who needed to be counseled for past due accounts had gone to the same gyp joints to buy jewelry, stereos and the like.

Not long after getting settled in, I was assigned the defense of a court martial—my very first legal case. My client was charged with possession of marijuana and a straight razor, following a locker search. I spent a fair amount of time researching the law regarding locker searches and put on a lengthy defense for my client. I got him off of the marijuana charge, but he was convicted for having the razor. The court martial board did a pretty conscientious job, not the kangaroo court I had expected.

I could immediately see that this would be a mind-numbing job, so I told Captain Zurell I was going to request reassignment to Vietnam. He said he understood and would be happy to help. I put in my request for reassignment and expected that it would be acted upon expeditiously. As I understood it, there was a big call for officers in the combat branches in Vietnam because President Johnson was continuing to build up U.S. Forces there.

To a degree, the request for reassignment was motivated by resume building toward a run for the Senate—it might not look too impressive to have been overseeing a unit of misfits when a war was going on in the general region. But, the work was pure drudgery and the prospect of fighting in a war for my country was hard to resist. It seemed like we were doing a noble thing— fighting for the freedom of the South Vietnamese people. I wanted to be where the action was and that certainly was not Okinawa.

After several weeks, Captain Zurell told me that I had received a call from a Major in the Pentagon who wanted to speak with me about my request for reassignment. The Major had said he needed to speak with me before approving my request. I calculated the time difference and caught him in his office at the Pentagon. He immediately said, "You don't have to go." That was a bit of a surprise because I did not expect to get employment counseling. I said something to the effect that I would probably have to go to Vietnam at some time and wanted to go while I was still a First Lieutenant. That would give me a chance to get some experience before making Captain and being assigned to command a firing battery. That seemed to satisfy the Major and he indicated he would approve the transfer.

It didn't occur to me until many years later, but there may have been an element of white privilege involved in the assignment process. It was apparent from my record that I had a law degree from a good school, and it could be that the people responsible for making assignments wanted to be just a bit protective of similarly privileged individuals. That would explain the Major's comment that I did not have to go, because I certainly thought he was encouraging me to reconsider. That factor may also have been at play when I did not get sent to Vietnam straight from artillery school. I suspect that if I had been a kid right out of high school or from the inner city, my orders would have been for Vietnam from the get-go.

On May 10, I was saddened to read in *Stars and Stripes* that one of my Marine friends from Ft. Sill had died in Vietnam. Second Lieutenant Carl Gibson, a fellow who I described in my journal as always cheerful and full of life, was from Radford, Virginia. Carl died in Quang Tri Province on April 30, just 12 days after arriving in-country. I salute him.

One of the remarkable things about Okinawa at that time was that practically everything for sale on the local economy or in the military exchanges was less than half the price of the same items at home in the U.S. I took advantage of the price differential by stocking up on items I might need in Vietnam and buying things that I would probably need in the future when I went home. I got all kinds of electronic items including a Teac tape deck, a Sansui receiver, a couple of Canon cameras (what more appropriate brand for a cannon cocker), and other miscellaneous items. The household goods included a nice set of Noritake china that I still have, several carved gemstone figurines, a set of pewter mugs that remain to this day in the same unopened box that they were in when I sent them home, and a wide variety of decorative items, some of which I still have. Okinawa was a buyer's paradise.

Things have changed substantially since then because the dollar does not go even half as far.

Since the various military services were crammed together on a relatively small island, we had frequent contact with the Navy and Air Force. One day I was invited by a naval officer to take a tour of a nuclear submarine. It was very impressive, until I saw the tiny little morgue-like bays where the sailors were expected to sleep. My thought was that it was a floating crypt. That may be a result of my having grown up on a farm where a person felt it essential to have good solid dirt underfoot.

The Naha Base was not very far from Kadena Air Force Base, where there were a number of reminders of the ongoing war in Vietnam. There were scads of B-52 bombers and they were often seen leaving the air base and heading toward the west. Their large black tails that loomed 40 feet into the air were impressive but rather intimidating.

One day I saw an aircraft take off from Kadena that left me awestruck. It was the most beautiful plane I had ever seen. The plane was all black and I don't recall seeing any markings on it. It was long, slim, and looked as if it had come out of a science fiction magazine. Not long after, I saw an identical plane take off from the air strip. Both were headed west. I would learn many years later that it was an SR-1 Blackbird, a spy plane capable of speeds exceeding Mach 3. Since the Russians routinely had spy boats of one sort or another along the route between Okinawa and Vietnam, I'm sure they well knew of this fantastic aircraft long before the American public.

One of the big sports on Okinawa was a habu-mongoose fight. The habu was by reputation a very venomous snake. It was said that a person would drop dead after three steps if bitten by a habu. I have to admit I was not too keen on the idea of watching such a fight, but the spectacle was generally held to support various military charities. So, I went to one for the benefit of charity. It was quite a vigorous fight. Everyone had expected the mongoose to prevail because of its ferocious representation, but the habu won, causing the poor mongoose to stagger and die. The record should show that the mongoose took quite a few more than three steps before giving up the ghost. I had heard that the Okinawans also had bullfights where two bulls were pitted against one and other. I passed on attending one of those.

After my Vietnam orders came in, I was ordered to attend a five-day Vietnam orientation course at Camp Hardy, located toward the north end of the island. We learned a bit about Vietnam, went through a simulated combat course, threw a grenade, and fired several weapons, including an M-16 and an AK-47. The ranking people at the course were me and another First Lieutenant. Since more was expected of us, we got the more difficult routes in the compass course. We were told to go through a shallow valley of the thickest foliage I had ever seen. The foliage was slightly higher than an elephant's eye. It was suggested that we make a little noise to chase the habus away. I started out doing that but after several hundred feet it became clear that I would not have to make any noise in addition to the thrashing around caused by just trying to get past the prickly bushes. At one point, I forced my way through some foliage and relatively short trees and found myself suspended over a 30-foot drop but, because I was firmly in the grasp of several thick bushes, I didn't fall. I managed to get back to solid ground and take a detour around the drop.

Both myself and the other First Lieutenant got to the other side of the course long after everyone else had been picked up and taken back to camp. There was some comfort in the thought that my assignment in Vietnam would probably be at a fire support base and there would be no need to struggle through jungle terrain--one of the advantages of the artillery.

Included in the orientation course was a night operation through some Okinawan farmland. It was dark out, we obviously could not have any lights, and the only way to navigate was with whatever moonlight might be handy. I got into the act and was running through the fields, when all of a sudden, I just was not running anymore. I had fallen into a pit about 5 feet deep and about 6 feet in length and width. Word was that it was a fertilizer pit where various types of animal waste, including that ejected from humans, was stored to be used for fertilizer. Luckily, the pit was empty at that particular time. A kindly Sergeant happened to notice I had abruptly disappeared and came over to help me out of the shithole.

I had put in for five days of leave before shipping out to Vietnam so I could pay a visit to Bangkok. I jumped on an Air Force plane for the trip, flew to U-Tapao Air Base in Thailand and then took a three-hour cab ride to Bangkok. It was a magical place with all kinds of exotic sights. The Thai people were very warm and friendly, but I noticed they were more than happy to relieve you of any excess funds. Several people in the battalion had asked that I buy sapphires for them, so I set about visiting jewelry stores. You would be graciously welcomed, asked to sit, and before you knew it there was a tall beer right at your fingertips. The beer was cool, tasty, fairly strong, and kept being replenished. All of the free beer tended to loosen up your pocket book and impair your ability to bargain. When I got back to Okinawa, the mess Sergeant would not take the gems I got for him, saying they were of poor quality. Oh well, it had been fun.

Shortly after I got to Bangkok, I met a lovely young lady named Somsri, who said to just call her Sam. She was slim, pretty, spirited, and about anything else that you dream about in a woman. (photo #2) Sam's English was quite good and she was proud to say she had visited California and been to Disneyland. We hit it off nicely and spent the rest of my R&R seeing the sights together. Sam also introduced me to real Thai food, including eggs that had been buried in mud or something worse for weeks or months, as well as some the hottest street food I have ever encountered in my life. It made my lips sizzle and no amount of water could cool it down.

As the time approached to get back to Okinawa, Sam told me she had some vacation coming so I invited her to join me on my way back. Since I had not entered the country on a commercial flight with a passport, it was not easy to get clearance to leave but the Thai officials were fairly kind because of my military status and let me go. We got to Hong Kong late and missed our connection to Okinawa, so we spent the night in Kowloon where I encountered my first hotel mini-bar. I don't recall that they charged for the items you consumed. The next day, we flew to Taipai for a short stop and then on to Okinawa. Sam was getting fairly irritated with the Asians along the way because quite a number asked if she was Vietnamese, or Chinese, or Japanese. I don't recall anyone asking if she was Thai.

Captain Zurell and the other folks in the unit were surprised, but pleased, that I had made a friend. They came out to the air strip to bid me a safe journey to Vietnam when I left for that destination on July 19. Sam was to fly back to Bangkok later that day. We agreed to keep in touch. Her favorite song was Sealed with a Kiss, which made it natural to correspond by mail.

After a short layover at Clark Air Force Base in the Philippines, I flew to Tan Son Nhat Air Base in Saigon that same day. When we neared the airport, the plane went into a bit of a dive for a quick landing in order to minimize its exposure to groundfire, which was routine practice. On the way down, it was clear that this was a somewhat hostile environment—the area around the airfield had been defoliated and the ground was pockmarked with craters. I had read in *Stars and Stripes* that heavy fighting had taken place here during the Tet Offensive about four months earlier. However, we landed at the airport without incident. I would leave for home from that same location 407 days later.

3 ● Suspended in purgatory

When I stepped off the plane in Saigon, it felt like stepping into a steam bath. The air was hot and humid. After all, it was the height of the summer season. The temperature was hovering around 100 degrees and the humidity was just shy of 100 percent. It was oppressive. I could feel sweat starting to break out all over my body, even in those places where it does not usually occur. It was not going to be easy to get used to this. Why couldn't we pick wars where there is a decent climate?

The Army was pretty good at getting you directed where you were supposed to go. I first went to Camp Alpha for a day, then to the replacement center at Long Binh. I stayed there a couple of days, waiting to hear what the next step was. Luckily, as in most U.S. military facilities anywhere in the world, there was a nearby officers' club where you could get a beer while killing time. Even better, it was air conditioned.

While waiting around for my assignment, I received several sets of jungle fatigues, a jungle hat, and a pair of jungle boots. The boots had steel plates in the soles to keep them from being punctured by punji stakes, sharpened bamboo stakes that were often dipped in excrement and hidden in pits to injure the unwary, we were told. The sides of the boots were porous so that water could drain out and air could pass through.

My assignment was to the 23rd Artillery Group, a heavy artillery unit that was part of the Second Field Force. The unit had 175mm and 8-inch guns. The 175 has a 34-foot barrel that is 175 millimeters across at the mouth, while the 8-inch has a barrel that is less than half the length of the 175 and 8 inches across at the business end. (photo #3) Both were mounted on tracked vehicles and you could change a 175 into an 8-inch, or vice versa, just by changing barrels.

The 23rd Artillery Group was headquartered northwest of Saigon at Phu Loi. The ride there on a UH-1 helicopter (Huey) was very exciting. The warrant officer pilot flew along just feet above the ground, either pulling up sharply or tilting to the side to get around trees along the line of flight. It was certainly better than any amusement park ride, either before or since. I suspect the pilot thought it was an exciting way to welcome a new arrival to the country.

At Phu Loi, I spoke with Colonel DeArment, the group commander, about my assignment. I asked about being assigned to a firing battery, but that looked like a non-starter right off of the bat. When he saw that I was a lawyer with a two-year commitment and no artillery experience, he said I would be the S-1 for the Second Battalion of the 32nd Artillery Regiment (2/32) in Tay Ninh Province. The S-1 is the administrative officer, a position much like the one I had gladly left behind in Okinawa. Damn! So, I got on a light observation helicopter (LOH, pronounced loach) for Tay Ninh Base Camp, also called Tay Ninh West. The 2/32 was headquartered on the west side of the base camp, which was about three kilometers west of Tay Ninh City. During my stay in Tay Ninh, a brigade of an infantry division was also stationed at Tay Ninh to perform ground operations in the vicinity. When I arrived, it was the 25th Division, later replaced by the First Calvary Division, which was then replaced by a returning 25th Division. The base camp also had a unit of the Philippine Army that preformed civil action work – the Philippine Civic Action Group or PhilCAG.

Years previously, the battalion had been given the name "The Proud Americans" and it was now commanded by Lieutenant Colonel Billy A. McDonald, who was himself a very proud American. LTC McDonald was a back-slapping native of North Carolina, who reminded me of President Lyndon Johnson. Until I learned of his North Carolina roots, I had him pegged as a Texan because he had somehow acquired a Texas twang.

I told the Colonel I would like to be assigned to a firing battery, but he said I would need to stick with the S-1 assignment. He did say that I might be able to take over a battery after about five months on the job. There was no executive officer for the battalion at that time so I was to take on the XO duties until a Major came along to do that work.

During our initial interview, Billy inquired about my previous experience. His eyes widened somewhat when I told him I had worked in a United States Senator's office during the summers of '65 and '66. I believe that information had a bit to do with the relationship the Billy and I had while he was battalion CO. It was not until I started to work full-time in Senator Jordan's office in 1970 that I learned many military officers are deathly afraid of Congressional offices. While I never even hinted that I would attempt to use Congressional influence, it seemed that Billy always treated me carefully.

After getting my assignment, I was given my armament, which turned out to be a classic .45 caliber M1911 pistol, and a nylon flak vest. The vest looked like someone had taken a big wad of nylon thread and stuffed it inside. I was not entirely sure how the rat's nest of nylon was supposed to stop a bullet, but just sort of took it on faith that it might. I was never offered an M-16 or anything more powerful than the .45, but it would not be usual for an artillery type to be involved in close-up combat. I was a pretty good shot with a rifle or shotgun, having grown up on a farm and shot all kinds of pests, but my pistol marksmanship was rather spotty. I hoped I would not have to use my trusty .45 and, as it turned out, I never fired the thing during my entire tour.

The pistol did make a lasting impression, though. When walking along smartly, an officer should let his arms swing back and forth. However, on two occasions I caught my right hand on the hammer, causing a nasty gash and some blood. It became second nature to not allow my right arm to swing. Even to this day, I often find my right arm staying perfectly still as I'm walking along. Years later, I read a newspaper article that said police officers can be identified by doing the same, whether in or out of uniform.

Tay Ninh Province is located northwest of Saigon along the Cambodian border. Cambodia kind of wraps around Tay Ninh Province, bordering it on the north, the west, and a fair amount of the south. The northern part of the Province was triple canopy jungle, while the south was relatively flat farm land. The only high ground in the province is Nui Ba Dinh or the Black Virgin Mountain. (photo #15) It is an extinct volcano that rises 3,268 feet in the air. A U.S. communication facility was located on top, but the National Liberation Front (Viet Cong or VC) and North Vietnamese Army (NVA) owned all of the terrain between the top and the bottom.

Tay Ninh City is located about 55 miles (88 kilometers) northwest of Saigon. The 2/32 had three firing batteries in the vicinity. The first was at Tay Ninh Base Camp, where the battalion headquarters was located. The second was at Fire Support Base (FSB) Barbara (named for St. Barbara, the patron saint of artillery), located in the jungle area due north of Nui Ba Dinh and about 20 kilometers (km or "klicks") northeast of the base camp. The third battery was located at Dau Tieng, about 30 klicks east of the base camp. Dau Tieng is located in Binh Duong Province and sits on the southwest corner of a massive Michelin rubber plantation. The battalion also had a headquarters battery that performed command and control functions, including operation of the tactical operations center (TOC), and a service battery that took care of maintenance and supplies. Both of those support batteries were located at the base camp.

The only safe way to travel from one fire support base to another was by air, although there was an old highway that ran from Tay Ninh to FSB Barbara. The 2/32 used the road to transport ammunition, gun barrels, and other supplies to that fire base. Less than a month into my job as S-1, I processed in a Second Lieutenant, Herbert George Lucas, from Brawley, California. He was assigned to the battery at FSB Barbara. A couple of days later, just 12 days after he arrived in-country, he was on a convoy back to the base camp when it struck a 500-pound bomb, what we would now call an IED or improvised explosive device. The explosion threw the truck a distance of 60 feet. Lieutenant Lucas and three members of our battalion's service battery were killed—Sergeant Donald Edward Horinek, Specialist Fourth Class Edward Lopez, and Private First Class Robert Dennis Murphy. Lucas hardly had a chance to get acquainted before he was being shipped home in a body bag. I often think about the fact that he died among relative strangers.

Just two weeks before that, another Lieutenant and I had gone up that same road to make a solatium (compensation or consolation) payment to the parents of a little girl who had been run over by one of our trucks. It was customary in Vietnam to offer compensation to the family of someone you accidentally killed or injured. We rounded up a driver and an ARVN interpreter and headed up the road with the money and a letter of condolence. After leaving the Tay Ninh City defenses, which did not amount to much, we stopped at an ARVN outpost to get directions to the hamlet where the accident occurred. One of the ARVN soldiers volunteered to go along as a guide. The guide and interpreter found a boy who knew where the hamlet chief lived, so we picked him up and proceeded along. When we got to the hamlet chief's house, he jumped into the Jeep, which was fairly crowded by that time.

When we got to the girl's house, the father brought out some cigarettes and glasses full of ice, which he promptly filled with beer and kept refilling. Instead of being angry, like I probably would have been, he was gracious and hospitable. It was an interesting insight into the Vietnamese culture. I was hoping to learn more about these people, but that did not seem to be possible because Tay Ninh City was off limits to the great majority of U.S. troops.

We did have some limited contact with the people we were supposedly fighting for. Many local nationals (LNs) came onto the base camp on a daily basis to perform maintenance work, hooch cleaning, barbering, and the like. I pitched in with a couple of other officers to hire a hooch girl to clean our rooms. That was common practice on the base. Also, I got haircuts from an LN, who came in every weekday. He cut your hair in a proper military style and then used a tiny bit of shaving cream to trim your neck with a straight razor. I cringed the first few times when he whipped out his razor to sharpen it, but he meant no harm.

Many of the LNs were from Cao Xa, a nearby Catholic village, and were solidly on our side of the war. (photo #5) Most of them had moved south because of religious persecution when Vietnam was partitioned in 1954. Uncle Ho did not like organized religion, particularly the Catholics who were in charge in South Vietnam. Other than seeing the LNs going about their work, most soldiers in support positions had little or no contact with the local population. Of course, the infantry had probably more contact than they wanted out in the field.

Contact with our own people outside of the base camp was not that great because of the telephone system. We had Army field phones that were encased in their heavy canvas covers for protection from the elements. On a good day you could call an office in Saigon directly. There could not have been all that many direct lines because it was usually impossible to make a direct call. So, you had to try to find a route through several exchanges to reach where you wanted to go. Sometimes you could reach Saigon by going through Cu Chi, sometimes through Phu Loi. If those routes were busy, you might try Dau Tieng, to Cu Chi, to Phu Loi, to Saigon. Usually, if you tried enough different routes, you could get the call completed. The more exchanges you went through, the worse the connection. That required you to shout as loud as you could into the receiver so the person on the other end could make out what you were saying. Everyone in our headquarters office could hear your every word, which was not always so great if the CO happened to be listening. Luckily, Billy did not spend an inordinate time at his desk because he was often out in the sun working on his fantastic tan.

As I had feared, the S-1 work was primarily paper shuffling. I did learn important military practices, such as forging signatures on various reports. Apparently, the battalion XO had departed unexpectedly, leaving some unsigned documentation that required his signature. The Sergeant Major counseled that I should practice writing the signature backward so it would look genuine—you overcame your writing tendencies by doing it backwards.

Once again, I was vector control officer, mess officer, and any number of other types of officers. The mess and vector control responsibilities fit nicely together. Each evening an orderly brought the battalion officers' dinners to the officers' club and left them in the back room awaiting chow call. There, the plates regularly collected a blanket of flies, which was impossible to scare off until they were picked up and trotted into the dining room. Nobody but the orderly and mess officer were aware of the infestation, but it did not seem to make anyone ill.

Billy McDonald was dedicated to the proposition that awards and decorations should be liberally handed out and a good part of the work of my clerical staff was to prepare paperwork for decorations. Some were of course deserved, but others were questionable. The service battery commander slipped while running for the bunker when the incoming alarm went off once, suffering a gash on his hand from the wooden walkway. He put in for a Purple Heart and actually got it. In my mind, that just cheapened the award.

One of the tasks that Billy handed me was to put the unit in for a Presidential Unit Citation. I suggested that it might be a bit of a reach but he responded that we might have a chance of getting it so why not try. The more medals, awards and citations accumulated by the unit and its members, the better he looked. Billy must have pursued the quest for the award because, although the battalion did not get that award, it did get a Meritorious Unit Commendation for 1968-1969.

As far as the work went, it was not at all interesting. From time to time I broached the question of another assignment, but that never went anywhere. I offered to work in the fire direction center but Billy said he did not anticipate an opening there. We did have one slot for a forward observer attached to the ARVNs, but he didn't want to make a change there.

The fellow who was assigned as forward observer for the ARVNs really hated the job and would have loved to get back to the base camp. At this point I don't recall what he had done to get Billy riled up with him, but there was no way he was going to be relieved as forward observer. He was with the ARVNs almost continuously and we rarely saw him during his tour. He surfaced about once a month and each time he looked more emaciated. He ate with the ARVNs and, thanks to what we used to call Ho Chi Minh's Revenge, food just ran right though him. Billy apparently had no sympathy because he kept sending the lad back out in the field, despite his declining health. I don't know what happened to him, but he must have survived because he does not show up on the battalion's casualty roster.

As acting XO, I attended the briefings of the 25th Division's brigade commander. There wasn't much of a role for me to play there, but at least I was able to get out of the battalion area. I also went to a commanders' meeting of the 23rd Group in Phu Loi, where I learned that the other artillery units had superior visual reconnaissance (VR) programs because they reported more "significant sightings." When I reported back, Billy determined that we had to label more of our sightings as "significant" so as to improve the rating of our VR program. There was also disapproving mention at the meeting that some battalions were using more than their allocation of ammunition, while others were using less. Apparently, each battalion was expected to use its full allocation, no more, no less, regardless of combat conditions. The big topic of discussion was the up-coming Inspector General (IG) inspection and every battalion was warned to beautify its battery areas, which sounded like it might be more important than the actual combat mission.

While in Phu Loi, I was able to confirm a rumor that had been floating around the battalion. Word was that Colonel DeArment, the Group Commander, had requisitioned funds to build a chapel so that the officers could do some praying, etc. However, when the chapel was completed, it looked an awful lot like an officers' club and was generally used for that purpose. It was actually pretty fancy. I learned that the luxuries of life often make their way pretty far out into the field, at least for officers.

While wandering around the base, I was surprised to see Roy Brixey from Hazelton. I'd known him and his family all my life. Roy graduated from good old Valley High School about three years ahead of me. Roy said he had learned to fly helicopters and his job was to ferry Colonel DeArment around the country in the Group LOH. There were quite a few people from Idaho in Vietnam as it turned out. Several months later, Ron McNevin from Hazelton, who was three years behind me in school, turned up at the Tay Ninh Base Camp. He was flying a LOH gunship for the First Cav. I went to pick him up at his hooch for a tour around Tay Ninh City and found him sitting with his feet in a wash basin full of ice. I'd never thought of that as a way to cool off—doubt that it did much good. Sometime after I saw him, Ron got into a face-to-face duel with a Communist machine gunner and ended up getting shot down. He got medevaced and sent home, with an additional hole in his fanny where the bullet exited.

After about a month, we got in an official XO, Major Myers, so I no longer had those responsibilities. That did not improve things much, because he was a true stickler on paperwork. All paperwork was typed in triplicate on carbon paper. There was no such thing as a correcting typewriter back then. If the clerk made a mistake, he would erase and redo it on the original and all of the carbon copies. But with the advent of our new XO, just one mistake on a document required that it be completely redone.

Even if it was not possible to detect an erasure by careful inspection, Myers would hold the paper up to a bright light to make sure the clerk was not trying to pull a fast one.

Each day the battalion officers would get together for a briefing to report what was going on in their world. It was interesting to hear the intelligence reports about enemy troop movements, contacts that had occurred or were expected to occur, and numbers of casualties on both sides. It did not take long to learn that Billy was most interested in target surveillance—what had been destroyed and how many Commies had been killed, particularly by artillery fire. The Communists killed by artillery were called KBAs, while those killed otherwise were KIAs or killed in action. Billy urged everyone to carefully tally the KBAs, which I took to mean anything that looked close to being a dead body should go into the tally. That was in keeping with the stories that appeared in *Stars and Stripes* regarding battles that occurred around the country. Body count was always mentioned and featured as a measurement of success. I began to think there was a bit of inflation here and there but there was no way of knowing for sure.

I'm not sure why, but I also began suspecting the accuracy of the intelligence being reported at the briefings. It was always presented as factual but it was often like weather reports—it might prove to be correct and it might not. I heard that some of it came from sources that were paid, which raised the question of whether the price might be based to a degree on how exciting the intel was. Again, it was hard to tell.

We were briefed on the status of the guns, whether parts were in adequate supply, what was going on with the ARVNs or Special Forces, how the various batteries were preparing for the IG inspection and a variety of other things. I suppose my report was the least interesting—people coming or leaving, decorations submitted or awarded, papers shuffled or unshuffled, and the like.

After the briefing, the officers all sat down at the tables in the officers' club, which was the signal for the mess orderly to shoo the flies off of the plates and bring them in for service to the hungry officers. After dinner, we would often stay around for a small-stakes poker game.

Getting acclimated to life on the base camp took some time. There were constant explosions in the area, mostly outside of the camp perimeter--artillery fire from the base camp, B-52 strikes in the jungle area, or fire fights between our infantry and the Communist forces out in the field. There was also a fair amount of incoming fire—107mm or 122mm rockets made in Russia or China and 60mm or 82 mm mortars—which usually came in the dark of night. You could not hear the rockets until just before they hit so they were more concerning than the mortars. The Commies manning the mortars were usually close to the perimeter so you could hear the distinctive click when a mortar round was dropped down the tube and hit the firing pin. That provided some warning to duck for cover. Usually, you would hear about 5 clicks in rapid succession, which indicated five rounds were in the air and on their way. If the first round hit at a distance, you need not worry because the rest would hit in that same general vicinity. On the other hand, if the first round hit anywhere near, you dived for cover.

On August 16, there was an artillery incident in Tay Ninh City. It was reported that about 14 artillery rounds somehow landed downtown, killing 18 civilians. There was no report of hostile action, so it is hard to comprehend how that could have happened. It was not an instance of collateral damage. I think the fire came from the 25th Division's artillery. Word was that the Viet Cong were using the incident to stir up the civilians. In addition to the tragic loss of life, it was a big impediment to our mission. We were there to protect the civilians, not to kill them. Sometimes those things happen when there is so much fire going every which way. A day or two later, some of the infantry's outgoing mortar fire fell short and several rounds landed inside the base camp. Luckily, nobody was injured. One round hit in the road near our TOC and laid there a couple of days before the ordinance people finally came around to retrieve it.

With less than a month in country, I got a letter from Sam. She sent a rosary and a Buddha, which covered both primary religious bases in the country. The letter was sealed with a kiss, she said. We continued to keep in touch throughout my tour which made life more pleasant.

The rosary and Buddha came in handy a couple of days later when the Communists launched a rocket and mortar attack on the base camp, prompting a red alert (attack imminent), but not much happened after that. There was a lot of hostile action out in the field, though. Katum, a Special Forces camp up north, got hit hard and some of the bunkers were overrun. The communication facility on top of Nui Ba Dinh was attacked with 6 bunkers being overwhelmed. FSB Buell II, 5 km northeast of the base camp was hit, leaving about 200 attackers dead around the perimeter. It was claimed that 20 of them were Chinese. We watched a Cobra gunship exchanging fire with the attackers on the mountain—a finger of red tracers spewing down from the Cobra's minigun and greenish tracers being returned into the sky by the Commies. It was impressive, but the minigun did not sound like a machine gun in the movies, more like a chainsaw. A couple days later I saw Puff the Magic Dragon in action. Puff was an old AC-47D aircraft fitted with 3 miniguns, and it put on quite a show. It just flew around and around over the conflict area, tipped to the side so that the miniguns fired directly at the target.

The base camp was on red alert for the next few days. My clerks worked during the day and then went out to man the perimeter at night. They were dog tired after a couple of days. It was then that Major Myers caught an almost invisible erasure on a letter after holding it up to a bright light and demanded that it be retyped. I have to admit the incident made me just a tiny bit less sympathetic when he got a piece of mortar shrapnel to the gut while visiting FSB Barbara a month later. He got a Purple Heart and a trip home. I felt much worse about the battery commander, Captain Babb, a West Point graduate and outstanding officer who had both legs cut off at the knees by the mortar round. He was the kind of person you picture in your mind as a true officer and gentleman.

Stars and Stripes reported on August 22 that President Thieu had visited Tay Ninh the previous day to assess the damage from the recent Communist attacks. Apparently, the VC attacked the City also, but had been expelled after heavy fighting. The paper reported that the Communists had suffered 500 casualties as a result of all of the attacks. We had not known about some of this because my personnel had been tied up manning the base camp ramparts and fighting to keep their paperwork free of imperceptible erasures.

I spoke to Billy and the XO again on September 8 about another assignment, any other job, but no soap. Billy said I might be able to have an assistant S-3 job because the guy who had it then was soon going to take over command of the battery at Dau Tieng. That would be an operations position in the fire direction center.

Several days later VC/NVA troops launched another attack on Tay Ninh, taking over a fifty-block residential area of the eastern and southern parts of the City. We heard lots of ordinance going off in that direction, as well as a half dozen B-52 strikes, but had little information as to what was actually happening. Being stuck at base camp while all of that was going on was maddening, to say the least.

Turning back to business as usual at the base camp, some of the shenanigans in the unit were mind boggling as well. The supply lieutenant told me that Billy would sometimes not let him order vital parts because this would show that a gun was down, reflecting poorly on the battalion's readiness. Instead, there were two Conex containers hidden behind the Chaplain's hooch, filled with spare parts. They were purposely concealed from the prying eyes of the higher-ups.

It did not take long to figure out that a lot of things were done for the sole purpose of making Billy and his unit look good. I came to learn that this was fairly commonplace in Vietnam, not something confined just to our unit. Sometimes, problems that needed to be addressed immediately were put off until the CO's one-year tour was over. Then, the problem was handed over to the new guy, who often passed on his own problems to an unsuspecting replacement at the end of his tour. My thought was that longer tours or tours for the duration of the conflict would work better by making people focus on getting the mission done, rather than just completing their year and moving on.

Just three days after I was told there was little hope of getting a better job, things took an unexpected turn. Lieutenant Reape, the artillery liaison officer at Tay Ninh Province Headquarters, also called Sector, was just getting ready to rotate out. His replacement was sent home on emergency leave and would not be returning. That left the position open, so Billy said the position was mine. It was fantastic news, even when I heard the next morning that the place was being mortared. It had to be better than the paper-shuffling purgatory I'd been in for two months.

The evening of that same day, the base camp went on red alert and it just happened that I was officer of the guard for a section of the perimeter, which included several units besides the 2/32. You just visited each bunker along the perimeter to make sure everyone was awake and ready for action. They all seemed to be, but I did come across one bunker that was permeated with a strange aroma, which I assumed was marijuana. Despite being on the cusp of the New Age, or whatever, I had never had any real exposure to the stuff, except for one time when a couple I was visiting insisted that I take just one puff off of a joint—kind of like when you insist that your toddler take just one bite of squash to prove that it is really good. Just to get them off of my back, I did so but did not inhale. This is not to be conflated with a prominent politician who famously and unconvincingly claimed that he had never inhaled the evil weed. Believe it or not, this was my only dalliance with illegal substances in my lifetime (excluding underage possession and consumption of alcoholic beverages).

One other memorable thing happened on the officer-of the-guard tour and it has stayed with me ever since. Just as I reached our firing battery, which was right on the perimeter, one of our 175s fired. I was right under the muzzle and the concussion hit my ears like a ton of bricks, causing them to hurt and ring for several days. They are still ringing to this day, a half century later. It was a memorable last shot before moving on to the new assignment.

4 ● Getting the lay of the land

September 15, 1968, was my first day at Tay Ninh Province Headquarters. Lieutenant Reape picked me up that morning in the ¾ ton truck assigned to the liaison section. He appeared to be extremely happy, which was understandable since I was replacing him. Nobody was more revered in Vietnam than a replacement. Reape said Sector was a great job because neither the CO or XO ever visited to check up on what he was doing. He didn't have to worry about the big brass and had the run of the town, which was off limits to most everyone stationed at the base camp.

The artillery liaison team consisted of four people--an officer, a non-commissioned officer (NCO), and two enlisted radio-telephone operators (RTOs). Reape introduced me to my NCO, Sergeant Haney, who he described as a good fixer of problems and scrounger of goods and services. Haney certainly seemed to be a personable guy and full of confidence.

Province Headquarters consisted of three large French colonial style buildings, which were all heavily sandbagged, and a couple of smaller structures. The main building, which contained the Tactical Operations Center (TOC), would have been attractive except for the stacks of sandbags and general scruffiness. The two other large buildings had apparently been barracks for French troops. One was aligned on a north-south axis and the other on an east-west axis so as to generally enclose a parade ground or assembly area. Those two buildings housed ARVN troops, prisoners, draft dodgers, defectors, and a large array of supplies and equipment. Months later, I learned that one of the buildings contained a gigantic cache of explosive material, including artillery and mortar shells, grenades, light anti-tank weapons (LAWs), and all kinds of ammunition.

The liaison section had a hooch located immediately to the east of the TOC, just big enough for four people. It had a tin roof, sort of a woven bamboo-mat wall extending about three feet up from the floor that wrapped all of the way around it, and screen-door type screening that extended from the top of that mat wall up to the ceiling. My quarters took up the eastern fourth of the hooch and the western three-fourths contained bunks for the enlisted men, as well as our kitchen facilities.

There was a shower just outside of my door, which consisted of four sheets of corrugated metal with a drain at the bottom and a 55-gallon drum full of water on a platform at the top. At that time, we would take the barrel into base camp, get it filled with water, and put it back on top of the platform so that the sun could warm it up for nice warm afternoon or evening shower. Because the drum had no top, a fair amount of water splashed out on the way back from base camp but there was still enough to make it difficult to lift the drum back onto the platform. A couple of months later, Haney was somehow able to tap into a nearby water supply so that all we had to do to fill the drum was to switch on a pump. It made things easier but the water had an ugly brownish-yellow hue and smelled somewhat like rancid sweat socks. I accidentally swallowed some during a shower and it caused a classic case of Ho Chi Minh's Revenge.

My room was walled off from the rest of the team, sort of a BOQ or bachelor officers' quarters. It was big enough for a bunk, two chairs, and metal wall locker. The second chair served as a stand for my fan. The hooch had electricity because Sergeant Haney had worked out a deal to hook into the power supply of the headquarters building. When I first walked into my room, I noticed a somewhat beat-up Coke can sitting on a shelf. Reape told me it was a homemade VC grenade that had been picked up on an operation. Not wanting to risk losing a hand, I just let it be until we moved out of our hooch about six months later. I also noticed about a half-dozen geckos clinging to the screening. I grew to regard them as friends over the coming months.

The bathroom facilities were somewhat rudimentary. There was an old two-seater outhouse just a few steps away but it was literally full of shit. There was half of a 55-gallon drum under each seat hole. The theory was that the drums would be taken out every day, filled with diesel fuel, burned, and replaced empty. It appeared that nobody had gotten the message to burn and empty the drums so they were filled practically to the bottom of the seats, making that outhouse pretty much unusable. Plus, it was infested with rats. Luckily, there was another outhouse a couple of hundred yards away that was tended and cleaned by someone. It came in handy at night, particularly when one had eaten or drunk something during the day that caused severe gastrointestinal difficulties necessitating immediate relief.

The sanitary conditions, or lack thereof, helped to support a thriving population of rats in the Sector compound. One night, shortly after I got there, a rat practically attacked me on the short walk to the TOC. There was first a loud squeal and then I saw a rat reared up on his hind legs just a few feet away. He looked to be about 7 inches tall in that configuration, his teeth were bared and he had a very ugly look on his face. Since he appeared to mean business, I detoured around him, but he did leave a lasting impression. The rat situation did not get any better.

On a couple of occasions, we discovered rat families living in our meager little pantry, which was located on the EM side of our hooch. That was the place where the guys cooked and we ate most of our meals. The idea of rats infesting the dehydrated potatoes and other foodstuffs was unsettling.

The following March, we had to relocate and build a new hooch behind the TOC. The new location bordered on a slough that was a rat haven. Problems with the critters intensified. They were everywhere in the new quarters. I would often hear them skittering around at night when I lay in bed, trying to get to sleep. You could imagine the little varmints waiting until you got to sleep so they could nibble on your toes. More than once it became necessary to throw a boot or rock at the intruders.

A couple of my EMs took the fight a bit too far. I walked into the shower area of our new hooch and found them torturing a couple of rats with electric wires. The rats had been captured in a steel rat trap and the guys were touching both sides of the trap with live wires. A couple of ARVN soldiers were looking on in dismay. I told the guys to knock it off but understood why they had it in for the varmints.

On the south side of our first hooch, there was a long, low building that served as temporary lodging for transient groups of ARVN soldiers or rangers temporarily assigned to the province. When I arrived at Sector, a unit of ARVN rangers, decked out in their distinctive tiger fatigues, was staying there. They were all very friendly, as were the other groups of ARVNs that moved through the area during my stay at Sector. I had the distinct feeling that they regarded us as allies and friends.

During my half year living there, with dozens of ARVNs going back and forth around the Sector compound at all hours, day and night, nothing happened that caused me to believe these guys would harm me or my soldiers. It would have been very easy to toss a grenade or satchel charge under the hooch without being caught, but it didn't happen. The only thing that bothered me was that when each unit came to stay for several days or weeks, they brought their ammunition and explosive ordinance along with them. (photo #6) There would often be stacks of explosive material up to six feet high just a couple of feet from the hooch. I saw mortar shells, LAWs, grenades and scads of ammunition in the stacks. We did get incoming rocket and mortar fire on a somewhat regular basis and it would not have been out of the realm of possibility that a lucky round might hit one of the stacks and that would be all she wrote.

On the north side of our hooch was a one-story building that served as offices for some Military Assistance Command Vietnam (MACV) personnel, as well as the office of the much-fabled Phoenix program. I knew that the Phoenix folks operated the Chu Hoi program, which encouraged communist soldiers to defect, but had not heard until I got back to the States that it was supposedly involved in a variety of nefarious activities. From what I have read since, I think the program was unfairly tarnished. It was designed to take out the VC infrastructure, but why wouldn't it be? We were engaged in a war and our adversaries were not particularly gentle persons. I never heard any screaming coming from the Phoenix office.

The operations center for the ARVNs was located in the TOC. The main job of the liaison section was to obtain clearances for U.S. artillery fire and airstrikes in all of Tay Ninh Province. When a request came in from U.S. forces to shoot or bomb a particular area, my people would check with the ARVNs to make sure there were no ARVN forces or civilians in the area and try to get approval for the strike. That also entailed knowing where U.S. forces were, as well as any operations under control of the U.S. Special Forces.

The ARVNs also checked with us to make sure that their forces were not going to be shooting their artillery into an area where U.S. forces might be operating. With explosive ordinance being slung around or dropped by a variety of units, we needed to carefully coordinate so that there were no casualties from "friendly fire" and that there was no "collateral damage" to civilians. Those terms were odd euphemisms that are still being used by the military. Friendly fire is anything but friendly, since it means your people are being killed or injured by your own bombing or shooting. However, it does happen. Collateral damage is a convenient term to soften the fact that you're killing or maiming civilians, which also sometimes happens during a war.

Lieutenant Reape hastily acquainted me with all of this information, introduced me to the ARVNs I would be working with, and then suggested that we take a tour around town. The largest part of Tay Ninh City was located to the east of Sector, spread over a wide area. The Tay Ninh Canal ran in a north-south direction just to the west of Sector. When one crossed the canal bridge, driving toward base camp, there was a fresh food marketplace immediately on the left and a commercial section along the street that included a hardware store, a bakery, a trophy shop, several restaurants, and a variety of other businesses.

Reape first took me to a place across the river that he said was a good place to get a beer. I believe the name of it was the Green Door. It looked a bit sketchy but the people running it seemed to be friendly. He gave me his first piece of advice – insist that your beer bottle be opened in your presence because, otherwise, it may contain the collected dregs left by previous beer-drinking customers. The beer of choice at the Green Door was Tiger Beer. The beer came out warm but was served with a large irregular-shaped chunk of ice. Reape said there were no particular sanitary standards for the ice but it was generally okay. He was not aware that any of the ice ever included tiny shards of glass, which is something that we had been warned about at various times. That is, the VC were said to freeze little pieces of glass into the ice with hopes that GIs would ingest it and suffer grievous injury. Reape said it was more likely that we would be drinking someone else's stale beer.

We then proceeded to what I took was another of his haunts right on the main street. Reape led me, Haney and an interpreter into the first floor of a two-story building where several women were squatting near a cook stove. We watched as they cooked some sort of dish and then started wrapping it in something that looked like waxed paper. I assumed they were spring rolls of some sort but wondered why the filling would be wrapped in paper. When I asked what the paper was, I was told it was rice paper and that it was edible. The rolls were passed around and were actually pretty good. Reape had not said what kind of establishment this was but after finishing the rolls he informed me that it was what one might call a house of ill fame or bordello. I knew he was trying to give me the lay of the land, but I thought this might be taking it a bit too far.

When we left the establishment, the first thing we saw was a dozen or so ARVN soldiers arrayed in a semi-circle around the entrance. They were all armed and none of them looked any too happy. I asked the interpreter to find out what the problem was and he reported back that they were angry because American troops had been welcomed into the business premises while they had been turned away. The ARVNs did not seem to be so angry at us as they were with the working ladies. I thought, what a great way to start my liaison work. We left without further incident. I went back to the Green Door a couple of times but steered clear of the other place.

We then visited B-32, a U.S. Special Forces B Camp that I would be working with. Contrary to the Sector compound, B-32 was fairly well fortified. It was surrounded by a wall with firing bunkers every so often. The wall was surrounded fairly closely by barbwire fencing. You had to go through a checkpoint to enter the compound. Even then, it was located near residential dwellings and did not have wide-open fields of fire. (photo #4)

My liaison duties would encompass the Special Forces (SF) units located within Tay Ninh Province, which were administered through B-32. There were two A camps located north of us in very hostile territory just south of the Cambodian border--Katum and Thien Ngon—and one southwest of us--Duc Hue, which was just over one klick from Cambodia on the north and a bit more than three on the west. The Special Forces operated a training camp at Trang Sup, located about 6 km northwest of Sector, where Civilian Irregular Defense Group (CIDG) soldiers were trained. At times the SF folks called the CIDGs Cambodians or Khmer Serei, which meant free Cambodians. They were anti-communists who did not like the pro-communist stance of the Cambodian leader, King Sihanouk. They had joined the CIDG but I got the idea that many of them were planning on overthrowing the King when the time was right.

At B-32 headquarters I was introduced to the officers I would be working with and then taken to the B-32 club. Army bases around the world have clubs where alcohol beverages are served, but they are usually divided into officer's clubs, NCO clubs, and clubs for enlisted men. All ranks were welcome at the B-32 club. There was a wide array of uniforms and head gear at the club – tiger fatigues, regular jungle fatigues, camouflage fatigues, berets, jungle hats, and whatever else. Many years later when I saw the first episode of Star Wars, the bar on Tatooine, with its wide variety of creatures and dress, reminded me of the B-32 club scene. Although I did not visit the place all that often, it was my go-to bar during my service at Sector. There were always interesting people on hand to drink and converse with.

Reape told me that his relationship with Billy had been somewhat rocky and he was irritated that Billy had given him what was probably an honest rating on his officer efficiency report. When an officer rotated out of the unit, the commander wrote up such a rating. The problem was that the ratings were routinely better than the officer was entitled to receive. It was like grading on a curve. Since almost everyone else was graded above his actual performance, an officer who got the rating he actually deserved looked like a dud. So, most commanders rated higher than the officer actually deserved. Billy didn't and I heard all about it from Reape.

After dutifully showing me all the sights, Lieutenant Reape gladly headed off for base camp, where he would catch a Huey to Saigon for the trip home on a Freedom Bird, which many GIs called the World Airways planes that flew them back to the U.S. It had been a great day for me, also. Just getting away from my paper-shuffling job at the battalion gave me a new lease on life. After getting a bit more acquainted with my team members, I tried to get comfortable in my Army-issue bunk and go to sleep. Since our hooch was accessible to anyone who could get into the Sector compound, I loaded and cocked my government-issue .45 pistol and stuck it under my bunk—a ritual that I repeated every night during my stay there.

I spent the next several days getting acquainted with our Vietnamese counterparts. Most of them spoke enough English that we could communicate fairly well. In one respect that was unfortunate because I was not forced to learn more Vietnamese. Junior Lieutenants (Thieu uy) Dinh and Tanh were the officers we generally worked with on the ARVN side. There were several enlisted men, whose names I do not recall, including a Sergeant we all called VC. I learned that my rank was Trung uy, which is what the ARVNs called me.

The two Lieutenants seemed fairly old for the rank they held. I thought they were both in their mid-30s. Both Dinh and Tanh had about ten years of service in their rank. A comparable Second Lieutenant in the U.S. Army at that time would generally have been promoted to First Lieutenant within a year of service. Several months later, I asked an ARVN friend, Captain (Dai uy) Vinh, why officers didn't seem to get promoted. He said they did not care if they got promoted because it meant they had to do more work for little additional pay. He said the pay increase from First Lieutenant to Second Lieutenant was 300-400 piasters, while the increase from First Lieutenant to Captain and Captain to Major were both about 500. I was told that a dollar was about equal to 125 piasters. That certainly gave people very little incentive to rise in the ranks.

Dinh was friendly and rather outgoing. We formed a good personal friendship. Tanh was friendly but fairly reserved, pretty much like me. (photo #7) We had a good friendship but there was not a lot of chatter. They were both genuinely good people.

Both of the Lieutenants were from Cao Xa, a Catholic village located about two klicks west of the base camp. Dinh told me that he and the other villagers were originally from Cao Xa Village in North Vietnam but they had pulled up stakes and moved south after the country was partitioned in 1954. Dinh recounted how the Catholics in the north had been persecuted by the Communist government to the point that they felt compelled to move south for their safety. He said a cousin of his had been gunned down on the street for no apparent reason, other than being a Catholic. The village priest, Father Dzu, had moved his flock south and set up their own village west of Tay Ninh City, taking the village name along with them.

During my time as S-1, the battalion Sergeant Major had filled me in about Cao Xa and Father Dzu. It always seemed like there was a lot of action at night in the direction of Cao Xa and I do think there were frequent hostilities between the Catholics and the Communists. The Sergeant Major thought some of it was for show and that Father Dzu was making a little excess noise to gain favors with the big brass in charge of the base camp. He regarded Father Dzu as a cagy character who was always trying to get his hands on U.S. supplies. After getting to know the Sergeant Major a bit, I thought the two might be fairly equally matched.

Many years later, I checked online to see if there was any information about Father Dzu. The search turned up a fascinating story written by Hal Drake in the March 15, 1970, issue of the Chicago Tribune. The story spoke of the hostilities between the villagers and their Communist tormentors, starting in the early nineteen-fifties and continuing into the nineteen-seventies. It tells how the Communists made repeated attempts to conquer the village, only to be repeatedly beaten back. Drake relates that Father Dzu and his flock used a "makeshift, crazy-quilt arsenal of American and communist weapons." And, somewhat echoing the Sergeant Major, he then says: "Anything that can be begged, borrowed, or seized is put in the arsenal. Many of the weapons are American, obtained by a gifted scrounger—Father Dzu. American commanders tolerantly look the other way as Dzu wanders around their base and asks for 'sympathetic understanding' from those who might be able to furnish ammunition and other supplies." The all-knowing internet has no further word of Father Dzu or the fate of his village and its people.

It ran through my head that the TOC would be a pretty good place for a sleeper agent, since most of the coordinates for artillery and air strikes would be known to our ARVN counterparts ahead of time. It did give me some comfort that most of the ARVNs we worked with were Catholic, who had a lot to lose if the Communists were to prevail. They didn't have much incentive to help the other side.

Some of the other ARVNs were members of the Cao Dai Church, whose headquarters were located in Tay Ninh City. The Cao Dais had had their own army until 1956, when private armies were disbanded by President Diem. I was told that the Cao Dais had tried to remain fairly neutral from that time forward, not wanting to incur the wrath either of the South Vietnamese Government or of the National Liberation Front. While there did not appear to be outright hostility between the Communists and Cao Dais, it was well known that the Commies took a dim view of religion in general. I did not think there was much chance that they would be subversive.

The ARVNs were usually pretty good about responding to our fire requests. There were times when requests were denied for no apparent reason or where the request seemed to be slow- walked, but those were generally the exception. We did not necessarily need to get clearance for strikes in War Zone C, the free-fire zone, but would often check for the presence of civilians in the southern fringes of those zones near inhabited areas. There was a hamlet we referred to as the Woodchoppers' Village, located northwest of the base camp, whose people would sometimes go into areas they were warned away from in order to get timber or firewood. We generally checked for clearance in those areas. B-52 strikes were preplanned and rarely occurred outside of the free-fire zones. We usually kept those under our hat. We had the exact coordinates where the B-52s would drop their bomb loads and this was information that didn't need to be shared with anyone. We generally knew when there were ARVN troops in those areas, which was not a common occurrence. The ARVNs conducted almost all of their operations in the southern part of Tay Ninh Province.

The U.S. rules of engagement also factored into the clearance process. It only made sense that we needed to be more careful about shooting and dropping munitions near populated areas. It is hard to win the hearts and minds of the people you are purportedly trying to protect if you jeopardize their safety. It is interesting that we are still grappling with the propriety of loose rules of engagement in Iraq, Afghanistan, and Syria. I suppose I was a bit more for the loose side of the rules of engagement issue during the first part of my tour in Vietnam but, having seen the tragic and counter-productive effects of loose rules, I came to believe they need to be fairly strict when you are fighting a counterinsurgency.

Another thing that struck me was that it took special clearance from higher up the chain of command to fire within one klick of the Cambodian border. If you fired over the border, you better have a darn good explanation for it. It became readily apparent to me that the VC and NVA were well aware of these restrictions and took great advantage of them. All they had to do was zip across the border into Cambodia and it was a definite King's X. I'll have more to say about that later in the book.

My daily routine was to join my people for breakfast, which one of them would cook for all of us. We were all on separate rations, which meant that we got paid extra to buy our food on the local economy. Actually, it didn't really work that way. Sergeant Haney was an excellent scrounger and was generally able to get all of the food supplies we needed from the quartermaster folks at the base camp. If there was a problem, we would all just chip in a little cash to buy food on the local market but that did not happen too often. The section generally had lunch together also. Dinner was often on your own. Since I went to participate in the battalion briefing at base camp, I occasionally had dinner there.

Shortly after I got to Sector, I found that Haney had a thriving business of selling beer and soda to any and all persons who had either Vietnamese piasters or U.S. military payment certificates (MPCs), the official currency for American personnel. All of his beverages were nicely chilled at the point of purchase, as he had a refrigerator, which was a bit rare at Sector. He sold a lot of beverages and I'm not sure how the quartermaster people at base camp accounted for the significant volume he was able to get from them. However he got his supply, he was always well stocked.

He also had a fairly brisk trading business, which included weapons that had been confiscated from dead or surrendering Communists. I'm not sure how he acquired the weapons. Whenever we needed some type of equipment, he was usually able to get his hands on it. I don't think there was anything that Haney was not capable of acquiring one way or another. He was kind of a poor man's Milo Minderbinder, the master trader in Joseph Heller's *Catch 22*.

I also learned that he had a house in town that he used as a hangout at night. Apparently, he was renting the place from a local landlord. This was almost certainly against Army regulations, besides being a rather dangerous thing to do. I can't imagine that the neighbors would not know the place was frequented by American GIs and there was little security in this spread-out town. I probably should have done something about that but I have to admit that I hung out there also from time to time.

The attack that injured Major Myers and Captain Babb took place on September 20. Babb was evacuated to a hospital in Japan, while Myers stayed a few days at the MASH unit at the base camp. I visited him there and saw a number of GIs with an assortment of bandages and medical devices. I had to hand it to the doctors and medical staff who worked there. It would be hard to take. They soldiered on through it all and saved many lives. The only place I visited at base camp that was measurably worse was the graves registration unit that took care of the remains of our troops who died. I had gone there as S-1 to take care of paper work for one of our guys. It was rather strange, but while waiting around there, I noticed the water cooler and the fact that there was a layer of what looked like rusty sediment about an inch thick on the bottom. And, people were drinking that stuff every day.

Shortly after Major Myers was sent back to the States, he was replaced by Major Keith Painter from Logan, Utah. Logan was just a couple hundred miles from my hometown and it was not uncommon for kids from southern Idaho, including my brother-in-law, to go to school there to study agriculture at Utah State University. Painter was a definite improvement over Myers, particularly since he would probably save my skin about 6 months later.

The Vietnamese people I met, both military and civilian, were darn good people. The only exception was a particular beggar who was a regular fixture in the commercial strip just across the bridge. (photo #8) He had lost part of one leg and got around with a fairly rugged stick that he used as a crutch. He sometimes wielded it threateningly when asking for money. The fellow moved fairly fast so you had to be on your toes. His hard-sell approach did not seem to work very well.

It was a surprise to find a trophy shop in the commercial section. In looking around the store, it appeared that the business was primarily geared toward the U.S. military. There were a lot of plaques with the insignia of units located at the base camp, as well as Sector. There were some with the Proud Americans insignia, as well as Special Forces. Apparently, the various units came down to the trophy shop to get plaques for their service members who were headed home.

The baker along the same strip produced the best bread you could imagine. Some of the loaves were shaped like the homemade bread that my Mom used to make but about 50% taller. There were also loaves that looked like French baguettes, which you might expect based upon the long French occupation. They were all delicious. I brought some loaves into the base camp to let some of the folks at battalion have a taste. Captain Agostinelli, who we called Gus, the commander of the firing battery at base camp, loved the bread. The bread contained what looked like sesame seeds and they added nicely to the texture. Several times when I was at the bakery to get bread, I noticed the open sacks of flour. It became apparent that what looked like sesame seeds in the baked bread were actually weevils that you could see prancing around in the flour sacks. That didn't bother me too much but it didn't seem to sit too well with Gus. I would not have said anything to him but after several months of raving about how great the bread was and how much he liked those little seeds, he asked me what they were. Out of shear honesty I had to tell him. He got a disgusted look on his face and never asked for another loaf, ever.

The food marketplace just across Tay Ninh Canal contained just about everything. There were live chickens in cages, dead chickens with their feet sticking up in the air, crayfish, assorted other kinds of fish, stuff that looked like guts, all sorts of fruits and vegetables, dried stuff that looked like roots of something, and about anything else you could imagine. Each stall was shaded from the sun by a piece of corrugated metal and tended by a small woman squatting to the point that it looked like it would break a person's knees. Nobody spoke English but the ladies were always very accommodating in helping these tall Americans with big noses get what they needed from the market. Of course, the price was always inflated two or three times what the locals paid, even if you bargained until you were blue in the face.

The hardware store had a collection of almost anything you could possibly need. It was kind of like a miniature Walmart with hundreds of items all jammed together in a fairly confined place. What struck me is how clever these people were in recycling things. One time I was looking for some paint and found a can of just the right color. It was in an old C-Rations can that had been cleaned, filled with paint, and resealed. There were sheets of aluminum for sale that must have been discarded by American beer manufactures. The aluminum had been printed for beer can labels and must have contained defects. There were several sheets of Coors can metal. There were also smaller pieces of the beer-can sheets that were used as fasteners on the corners of trunks, chests and other types of wooden containers.

There were several shops that sold finely crafted brass items— candle sticks, vases, and the like. On closer inspection, I found that they were fashioned from 105mm howitzer canisters. A 105 round is like a very large bullet. When it is fired, all that is left is the brass canister, which was often discarded. The artisans also used brass from the dusters, which were 40mm anti-aircraft cannons that were used as anti-personnel weapons on the base camp perimeter. The items were crafted using hammers and flame.

There was always a lot of traffic across the bridge during the day—people moving stuff to and from the marketplace and the businesses along the street, military traffic, and so on. The civilian traffic included ox carts, donkey carts, motor scooters, bicycles and what we called cyclos (pronounced sickle-o). In Tay Ninh, a cyclo was a motor scooter with a two-wheeled cart hooked on behind. They were used both as taxis and for carting all sorts of goods. A person could hail a cyclo with other passengers already on board and be transported to his or her own destination. Often, you would see a cyclo with upwards of six people crammed into the cart. Sometimes the cyclos had amazingly large loads of goods stacked on the carts, like a half dozen 100-pound bags of rice. It was uncommon to see a civilian car and then it was probably a government official. There was virtually no civilian traffic at night, as I think there was a curfew when the sun went down. There was a fair amount of military traffic during the day and some during the night, which included Military Police (MP) from the base camp checking for the presence of unauthorized personnel in town.

The restaurants along the commercial strip often had whole dead pigs out front early in the morning in various stages of being butchered. They looked like they had been scalded and partially cooked, often with hairy bristles sticking out all over. I have to admit it didn't do much for my appetite.

There was a restaurant right along the canal near Sector that we visited from time to time. The name of the place was Yen Lan, which I ran through Google Translate when writing this book. Yen Lan was helpfully translated to mean Yen Lan. So much for that. Our favorite meal was water buffalo, which was cooked nicely pink with many cloves of garlic. The steaks were served with French fries and salad. Another dish that was pretty good was a curried chicken. Several times we had frog legs at Yen Lan but the problem was that we were always served the whole cooked frog. The legs were tasty but it was difficult to figure out what to do with the rest of the frog.

We met a lot of good people at the restaurant. One time we bought a beer for an ARVN Major, whereupon he invited us over to share his fish dinner. Along with a couple of small plates of fish and a large bowl of rice, he had a sizable cooked fish swimming in a large bowl with tomatoes, peppers and onions. He urged me to take a piece of the fish, which I did, and it was pretty good but extremely boney. It had bones where you wouldn't image a fish would have bones. I suspect it was carp, kind of like the trash fish we found in our irrigation canals at home and which I would not have eaten on a bet. I do have to say it was rather tasty but about 3:00 the next morning I had to make an emergency run to the latrine with a classic case of Ho Chi Minh's Revenge. It could have been the fish or it may have been the ice that was served with the Export 33 beer. This was the only time I experienced gastrointestinal problems from eating at Yen Lan. It was a fairly common occurrence when I dined with my ARVN friends elsewhere. The effect was much like I imagine a person would get nowadays from a high colonic cleansing, clean as a whistle but at a much lesser cost.

Another time while at the Yen Lan, we bought a beer for an ARVN Sergeant. He told us he had a restaurant in another area of town and invited us for lunch. Every table had a small glass just larger than a shot glass, with sprigs of some kind of herb. I was told it was for chewing on after the meal to help settle your food. It had quite a unique taste, something I had never had before. It wasn't until many years later that I identified it as cilantro. In any event, the food kept coming at the Sergeant's place, including some small round steaks with a bone right in the middle. It was some of the toughest meat I have ever encountered and not particularly tasty. I asked the Sergeant what it was and he pointed to a dog that was roaming around the floor scarfing up scrapes. Argh. We were also served boiled chicken legs and chicken wings fried in batter. The wings had been chopped into 3 or 4 parts, which was the way chicken was often served. I never quite understood why it was done that way because you ended up with a mouth full of bone fragments. It may not have been the dog, more likely the Tiger beer served over a chunk of ice, but about 3:00 the next morning I made the ritual run to the latrine.

These were hospitable people. If you were invited to have a meal with them at a restaurant, it was considered an insult if you offered to pay. They were willing to use meager resources to entertain a guest in style. They were very gracious, always offering the best portions to a guest. This was not always so delightful because the most desirable portion might consist of eyeballs, feet, or various organs that Americans would not generally relish.

One of the people I really grew to like was a MACV interpreter who we all called Tom. Unfortunately, I did not write down his real name and after these 50 years it just does not come to mind. Tom was short, even for Vietnamese standards, but had fairly thick features. Although his position was apparently funded through MACV, he was generally available when we needed him to go on trips around town or wherever. His language skills were very good and he provided valuable insights into local customs and attitudes.

The liaison unit was available to help MACV with its artillery needs, but they generally liked to keep to themselves. The ARVNs did not have a great deal in the way of artillery assets, but I think their attitude was to make do with what they had. According to Sergeant Haney, they had sometimes complained that when they called for U.S. artillery support, it took too long to get clearance. Most of the ARVN operations were in the southern part of the province and when they called for U.S. firepower it was generally near the Cambodian border or in what we considered restricted-fire zones close to villages, both of which required the personal clearance of the base camp commander. That often took some time. One would think that caution would be a good idea when putting fire near inhabited areas. On the other hand, they were more familiar with conditions on the ground and may have felt they knew where they could shoot and where they could not. In any event, we did not have a particularly close working relationship with the MACV folks. Despite that, I did strike up a friendship with Dai uy Thanh, an ARVN Captain who commanded a 105mm artillery battery. He was a genuinely good person and an exemplary officer. He was about 30 and he and his wife had two kids. If the ARVN officer corps had been composed of people like Thanh, they would have been invincible. (photo #9)

I did get along very well with the Special Forces (SF) people at B-32. Going in, I had trepidations that they would be a little snooty, but they were not. They welcomed me as a member of the team, which I appreciated. I attended their briefings and gave input with regard to artillery issues. When I started work at Sector, the commander of B-32 was a Major, who was just filling in while awaiting a Lieutenant Colonel. Around the first of October, a new commander, Lieutenant Colonel Harry Hilling, took over as CO. He was a great guy. He looked pretty much like Eddie Albert and you could not help but like him. We had a good working relationship.

About ten days after I got to Sector, another SF unit blew into town. It was another B team, B-36, which was called a Mobile Strike Force or Mike Force. I was told that it consisted of Special Forces advisors and Cambodian irregulars who may or may not have been mercenaries. The B-36 commander told me that they were planning to conduct an operation with two battalions, starting from Trang Sup and running along the Cambodian border to the A camp at Thien Ngon, way up north in War Zone C. It sounded fairly dangerous to me. He asked me to fix up a fire plan for the operation. I had never done a fire plan but got busy putting one together. In essence, I made a determination of strategic points along the way and designated certain defensive areas where they could count upon pre-planned artillery fire, or defensive concentrations (DEFCONS), if they encountered enemy forces. They seemed to be happy with it and I gave a copy to our fire direction center. For the biggest part of the operation, there were only four guns that could provide them support – two 175s at Tay

Ninh and two at FSB Barbara. With the slow rate of fire of the 175s, one round per minute, that did not provide a great deal of support. They would have the benefit of 8-inch fire for the southern part of the operation and then they would be within reach of the two 105s at Thien Ngon for the northern part. I enjoyed doing the work because it now felt as if I was contributing. Nobody ever said how the operation turned out.

I did get a chance to go to the A camp at Thien Ngon a couple of days later, as well as the A camp at Katum. Our battalion supported the artillery at both camps logistically, in addition to providing fire support. My mission was to make sure we were doing everything they needed, but I did not introduce myself by saying, "Hello, I'm Jim, I'll be your artillery server."

The Huey stopped first at Katum, which was pockmarked with craters of various sizes. All of the foliage had been cleared for about a half a klick all around the star-shaped compound. Further out, the landscape had been sprayed with a generous dose of Agent Orange so the trees and bushes had been largely stripped of foliage. The camp was surrounded by several lethal-looking wire fences. The Huey came in pretty fast and landed near the command bunker. There was an air strip on the camp, which was about its only source of supply. I was told that supply aircraft came in sharply to land, that they kicked out their supplies, turned around and got the heck out of there pretty quick. I noticed some metal debris off to the side of the air strip that looked like damaged portions of aircraft. There were about a dozen Special Forces personnel at the camp and many more CIDG troops. A lot of them had their families at the camp along with them. It didn't seem to be an ideal situation.

As we were taking off, a number of the CIDGs tried to pile into the Huey, but the Special Forces guys threw them off. I guess I can understand why they wanted to get out of there because Katum was isolated, near the Cambodian border, and the subject of frequent mortar, rocket and ground attack. In fact, it had withstood a major attack on August 19, just over a month earlier, leaving about 59 Communist bodies in and around the camp's wire.

We then flew to Thien Ngon, which was pretty similarly situated. The one difference is that the CIDGs did not try to get into the chopper as we were leaving. Thien Ngon had been attacked by about two enemy battalions just three days before my visit. The attack was repulsed with about 130 Communist casualties and 4 CIDG dead. Four SF advisors had been injured. It was genuine hostile territory.

On the way back to base camp, the pilot took us on a thrill ride at about 110-120 knots right across the tree tops. Again, that was to keep from making an easy target for anyone down in the foliage but it was still a thrilling ride.

During my first month at Sector, two events occurred that demonstrated how things can go very wrong in a combat situation. One was a friendly fire incident involving the CIDG forces at Trang Sup and the other was a fire mission that may have targeted civilians. The night of October 26, the AN-TPS-25 "Tipsy 25" ground surveillance radar at base camp picked up some movement around the perimeter. We had not been advised of any operations in that area so we granted clearance for artillery fire. The 25th Division put two batteries of 105s and one battery of 155s on the job. After the first volley, a check fire order was given, which brought the barrage to a halt. It turned out that a CIDG operation launched from Trang Sup had mistakenly gone outside of its area of operation and that is what set off the radar. The artillery killed two of the CIDGs and wounded 14 others. We were told that about 120 CIDG troops were involved in the operation. It is a good thing that the check fire went into effect so quickly because another 36 rounds of 105 and 155 fire had been programmed for the mission, along with several 8-inch from our battery. But for the quick check fire, a lot more of them would have been killed.

When I went to B-32 the next day, the S-3, who was twice my size and all muscle, became very belligerent about the incident, to the point of threatening physical violence. I wasn't about to put up with a bunch of crap from him because we were in the right. It is likely that as operations officer he may have played a part in the snafu. I told him that the job of artillery was to kill people and when unidentified people are seen sneaking around the perimeter of an American base camp at night without disclosing their presence, they can expect to be killed. About that time, Colonel Hilling happened along and got the S-3 calmed down a bit. It was a very unfortunate event but it demonstrated the absolute necessity of close coordination.

The other event occurred in mid-October. The first I heard of it was at a battalion briefing where Billy was absolutely ecstatic with a fire mission that had taken place just northwest of Nui Ba Dinh. Our battalion S-2 (intelligence officer) Captain Roth, who we all called the Eagle, was doing visual recon in a Bird Dog when he reported seeing about 45 people and a truck out in the open. He assumed them to be Vietcong so he called in a fire mission. He was granted all necessary clearances and the 8-inch guns at FSB Barbara when to work on them. He reported 22 KBAs. Billy was just beside himself with that body count. However, we soon got word that the people may have been civilians from Suoi Day hamlet, which was in fairly dangerous territory, either in or near War Zone C. I was assigned the job of investigating.

The fire mission had taken place at 1400 hours (2:00 p.m.) on October 17, during broad daylight. Billy arranged for a LOH to take me to Suoi Day two days later to find out what had happened. I have to admit that it did not seem to be the best idea at the time. Our guns had reportedly just killed up to 22 people a couple of days earlier, either family members of the villagers or VC or some of each, and it was not a particularly friendly area in any event. On our side, there was just the pilot, me and my pitiful .45 and nobody to interpret. But, Billy knew best, so off we went.

There was an ARVN outpost near the hamlet and we dropped down there to see what we could learn about the incident. The outpost was manned by a couple of ARVN regulars, neither of whom could speak English, which was not a surprise. I'd heard some concern among our troops that the soldiers in charge of the little outposts located in hostile territory might have non-aggression arrangements with the Communist forces. After all, the outposts were obviously exposed, under-manned, and would be easy pickings. The thought did cross my mind that these guys could possibly get the drop on the pilot and me and then hand us over to the VC. The idea of spending the duration of the war in a tiger cage, or worse, was not very appealing. By that time in my tour, I'd had little contact with the ARVNs and did not know what kind of behavior to expect from them. These two guys seemed to be friendly and anxious to help, so we just got down to business.

The pilot and I conversed as best we could with the guys at the outpost, using our hands and whatever slang we could think up, and the ARVNs reciprocated. As best we could determine, three civilian women from Suoi Day had been killed by artillery fire on the 17th and a truck had been destroyed. I'm sure it would have helped to have an interpreter on hand. After getting back to Sector, I had the ARVNs there radio the hamlet chief, who said that three women had been killed and a tractor destroyed. Troops from the 25th Division searched the area and found a man's body but no women.

Billy and our group commander, Colonel DeArment, were both genuinely concerned about the incident. I personally brief Colonel DeArment about my findings. I did not hear anything further about the incident and I don't know that Captain Roth did, either.

The incident demonstrated that really bad things can happen in a combat situation. I was not flying fire missions at the time and I'm not sure what I would have done if I had come upon the scene that presented itself to Captain Roth. The people were in an area where they should not have been. It was a free fire zone and we were told that frequent warnings were given to people living in the vicinity to stay out. When he called in the fire mission, the ARVNs gave their clearance. On the other hand, it is unlikely that the Communists would have been out in the open during the middle of the day. Even if they were, when the spotter plane appeared overhead they would most likely have dashed for cover. Later, when I started doing observer missions, I would have thought long and hard about shooting a target where people were operating a truck or a tractor in that area in broad daylight. That was not something the Communists typically did.

Another thing the incident illustrated is that body count figures can be hard to determine from the air. People lying on the ground can be killed or injured, or they can just be clinging to the ground for dear life. Since commanders loved to chalk up body count, there may have been a general tendency to err on the high side, rather than the low, when there was a question.

One further thought has to do with who should get appointed as investigating officer in situations like this. I have seen reports out of the wars in Iraq and Afghanistan, questioning the practice of appointing an investigator from the same unit that was suspected of causing civilian casualties. It presents a classic conflict of interest, even if the investigator does his level best to act objectively. It was an awkward situation for me to be investigating the propriety of Roth's decision to call in the artillery fire. Although he was a friend, I like to think that my investigation of the matter was even-handed.

As the 1968 presidential election approached, there were concerns among the troops about talk of a U.S. bombing halt. *Stars and Stripes* reported in early October that Hubert Humphrey, the Democrat candidate, was speaking of halting bombing in North Vietnam. It was not entirely clear, but it sounded like he was focusing just on the B-52 strikes in the north, conducted in what was called Operation Rolling Thunder. Rolling Thunder was an appropriate name because when a B-52 strike took place anywhere near the base camp or Sector it would sound like nearby thunder, in addition to rattling your teeth. I was not too keen about a bombing halt up north because it seemed this would only give the Communists an opportunity to safely send more troops and arms south. Since War Zone C was a main terminus of the Ho Chi Minh Trail, that would not be a particularly good thing for Tay Ninh Province. I gathered that it would not apply to the Arc Light missions or B-52 strikes in the south, which we really loved, whether or not they were effective.

President Johnson did call a halt to bombing in the north on Halloween Day, to begin on November 1. By that time, around 30,000 American troops had died in the war. Little did any of us know at the time that there had been some good progress made in settlement negotiations with the Communists or that Richard Nixon had pretty much sabotaged the chances of settlement in order to improve his chances of winning the presidential election on November 5. It is not clear that the sabotaged negotiations would have produced a settlement but it is clear that America suffered another 28,000 fatalities from that point to the end of its involvement in the war.

October produced a few other interesting items. The Special Forces people gave me a rocket propelled grenade (RPG) launcher for Billy, which he really appreciated. He did not pat me on the head but I could tell he thought I was doing a fine job. I had not asked SF for the gift, but I guess they were happy with the support we gave them.

October 21 brought a great surprise to South Vietnamese who traded in Military Payment Certificates. They were not supposed to have MPCs, but often traded in and with them. MPCs were the currency of the U.S, forces, but also of the black market. Periodically, the U.S. Military sprung a surprise "C-Day" where old MPCs were traded for a new design. As of 1800 hours on the 21st, the old design became worthless, except for souvenir purposes. It had to be disappointing for those who did not get surreptitiously warned ahead of time. We turned in our MPCs before the deadline and were issued new ones the next day.

Sergeant Haney demonstrated his trading prowess by scrounging an SKS rifle with Chinese markings for me. I had not asked for it but appreciated it nevertheless. The SKS is a semi-automatic rifle of Soviet design. Many of the VC had them but, with all of the more advanced arms coming from the north, more of them were being armed with the fully automatic AK-47. The rifle was well worn and had obviously seen plenty of use. Haney also said that the province chief had put us both in for a Vietnamese Cross of Gallantry. I couldn't think of anything that would have merited the medal, but I was not about to object.

Major Painter surprised me a couple of days later when he asked if I knew anything about Haney trading on the black market. At the time, I obviously knew that Haney had a thriving beverage business, that he did lots of trading and scrounging, and that he had a house in the city, but I was not aware of any black-market dealings.

I did ask Haney about some of his dealings from time to time but did not think he was engaged in criminal activity. I told the Major that I had not to that point observed any black marketeering on Haney's part. He asked that I keep my eyes open and let him know if something of the sort was going on.

When I got back to Sector, I told Haney that he was suspected of being involved in black marketing and that the battalion brass were going to be keeping an eye on him. I told him the time had come to close his beverage business as that had likely caused some suspicion.

As time went on, I came to believe that Haney was the primary source of his problems. He liked to brag about his free-wheeling Sector life to the people at base camp.

Word about his exaggerated exploits would ripple through the battalion until they reached the CO and XO. This was not the last I would hear of it.

5 ● Adopting an orphanage

It was easy to make the transition to life at Sector and to the routine of the work there. It finally felt like I was actually doing something useful. The freedom to come and go as I pleased and to get to know so many different people—MACV, ARVN, Special Forces, local nationals—was really liberating and uplifting. There was a lot of hostile activity throughout the province and that kept the liaison section busy with artillery and air strike clearances. Intel reports continually predicted that there would be a major attack on the Sector compound, but other than sporadic mortar and rocket fire nothing of note happened for the first couple of months.

What was rather interesting is that the day after the bombing halt went into effect in North Vietnam, Arc Light (B-52) strikes in Tay Ninh Province substantially increased. The liaison section cleared all of those strikes so we knew exactly when and where they would occur. The B-52s flew so high that you could not hear the sound of the aircraft until the bombs actually started ripping into the jungle. The majority of the strikes took place north of Nui Ba Dinh in War Zone C, but there were also a number southwest of Tay Ninh on vacated farmland around Duc Hue SF camp. That camp was nestled under the Angel's Wing, a piece of Cambodia that jutted into Vietnam, shaped like (you guessed it) the wing of an angel. The bottom of the Angel's Wing was 20 klicks north of the tip of the Parrot's Beak, a piece of Cambodia that was often described as pointing like a dagger at Saigon.

Unless there was some type of emergency, we could not give clearance for fire from the 175 guns when a B-52 strike was scheduled. When a 175 is shooting at its maximum range of about 32 klicks, the round has to go very high in the air to get that far. I don't think that a 175 round, even under those circumstances, would reach so high as to be able to hit a B-52, but we were not allowed to give a clearance in any event.

The bombing halt in the north may have accounted for the increased number of Arc Light strikes in the south. The Air Force would not want the B-52s and their crews to just be sitting around with nothing to do. On the other hand, it may be that General Westmoreland was determined to wipe out COSVN, the Committee on South Vietnam, which was reputed to be the overall command center for the NVA in South Vietnam. It was rumored that General Westmoreland believed COSVN to be located somewhere in War Zone C and it was kind of his white whale. He launched one of the largest operations of the war there in February of 1967. Operation Junction City, which involved 22 U.S. and 4 ARVN battalions, was designed to destroy COSVN. It produced a body count of 2728 Communists, but it did not turn up any large NVA command and control center. The General seemed bound and determined to blow it to smithereens with the B-52s.

In any event, I had pretty much settled into my routine at Sector by the first of October. There were things to do each day but it became apparent that I was going to have some time on my hands. There was a good stash of books available at battalion headquarters so I took advantage of that during the day when nothing much was happening. I sat on one of my chairs, reading a book, while my trusty electric fan, which sat on the other chair, blew continuously at full blast. Sometimes I would get a beer from Sergeant Haney's beverage stand to help replenish the bodily fluids that got sweated out every time I moved. To be quite honest, it was a little boring at times.

About that time, I ran into a fellow who worked with the Agency for International Development (AID), Tom Vida, who told me about an orphanage in Tay Ninh that was operated by the

Cao Dai Church. He said the orphanage needed some help and offered to take me there to check out the situation. The orphanage was located about four klicks east of Sector. Vida, Sergeant Haney, Tom the interpreter, and I went for a visit on November 8. The orphanage was in a building that looked rather shabby on the outside, but which was relatively clean on the inside. We were told that there were 73 kids, ranging from two-and-a-half months to 17 years old. One room contained a number of cribs for the youngest kids, some of whom looked undernourished and a bit sickly. Some had skin conditions that begged for medical attention. There was a staff of about a half-dozen women, who were all dressed in white ao dais. An ao dai is a traditional Vietnamese dress for women, consisting of a tight-fitting top that is slit on each side from the waist down and worn over loose-fitting pajama-like trousers.

Vida told me there were not a lot of orphanages around the country, even though a lot of parents were casualties of the war. He thought there was only one orphanage in Tay Ninh Province. He said that relatives or friends usually took in the kids when parents were killed in the war or died otherwise. The orphanage kids had nobody willing or able to take them in.

I told Vida that my section would take on the project of getting supplies for the orphanage. It looked like they needed new clothes, soap, blankets, towels, and firewood, among other things. And, I figured the kids could always use some toys. I also wanted to get our battalion surgeon out to the orphanage to see what he could do about the skin disease and some of the kids' other medical problems. Tom inquired of the staff as to the food situation and was told the kids got two meals a day, one of which was rice soup. The soup was fairly weak but there wasn't enough rice to serve it steamed style so they had to thin it out with liquid to make it stretch. I thought we could do something about that.

The supply officer at B-32, Lieutenant Leapack, was able to give me a 100 lb. bag of rice and said he would start requisitioning two bags per week for the orphanage. Bless his heart. Haney, Tom and I went back to the orphanage a few days later, bringing the rice, some towels, candy, toothbrushes, and soap. This time we met the matron of the orphanage, a small white-haired lady who looked to be in her seventies. She was very gracious, inviting us to sit down and watch some of the girls perform traditional dances. (photo #10) She served tea that looked fairly weak but which had a rather unique flavor. Tom said it was peanut tea. It was okay but would not have convinced me to become a teetotaler.

I reported back to the battalion about the orphanage and Billy agreed to make it a battalion project. We put a notice in the daily bulletin that went out to the troops, asking for kids' clothes, money for laundry soap, and the like. We were off and running. The orphanage had a regular need for firewood so we set about scrounging up a load a week for them.

As I mentioned, the orphanage was run by women from the Cao Dai Church. I had never heard of the church until I got to Vietnam, but it seemed to have a large presence in Tay Ninh Province. The church folk claimed the church had about three million members in Vietnam and the adjacent countries. I had actually toured the main temple before I knew that the orphanage existed.

The church was founded in 1926 as a universalist religion. As I understand it, Cao Dai means "Supreme Being." Members of the church believe the Supreme Being sent a spirit message on April 24, 1926, saying all great religions of the world were encompassed within this new religion. According to a publication I got directly from the Pope of the church, the message said:

Formerly, the peoples did not know one another and lacked means of transport; I then founded at different epochs, five branches of the Great Way: Confucianism, the Worship of Genii, Catholicism, Taoism, Buddhism, each based on the customs of the race called particularly to apply them.

Nowadays, all parts of the world are explored: people knowing each other better, aspire to a real peace. But because of the very multiplicity of those religions, men do not live always in harmony one with another. That is why I decided to unite all those religions in one to bring them to the primordial unity.

Moreover, the Holy doctrine of those religions has been, through centuries, more and more denatured by those who have been charged to spread, up to such a point that I have firmly resolved to come Myself, to show you the Way.

The faith has a pantheon with five levels, Buddha being at the top, followed by Great Immortals such as Confucius, then by a number of Saints, then by venerated spirits or ancestors, with humanity at the bottom. Included within the Saints are French poet Victor Hugo, Chinese revolutionary Sun Yat-Sen, Nguyen Binh Khiem, a Vietnamese poet and educator, Shakespeare, Jesus, Mohammad, Moses, Lenin, Thomas Jefferson and Joan of Arc. Some of those individuals were contacted and enlisted through spirit mediums.

The main church, the Great Divine Temple, is located in the Cao Dai Holy See. The architecture of the building reflects the universalist theme of the church, incorporating elements of Catholic churches, Buddhist pagodas and Islamic mosques. The interior of the Temple is colorful, ornate and quite unique to the Cao Dais. Some people have called it phantasmagorical. At the rear of the Temple are statues of Nguyen Binh Khiem, Victor Hugo and Sun Yat-Sen. There are two rows of dragon-wrapped pillars leading up to the alter, where there is a star-studded globe with a giant eye. (photo #11) The eye represents the left eye of the Supreme Being who sees and knows the entire universe.

The Holy See was about a square kilometer in area. It had an impressive entry gate and was surrounded with a decorative fence. The compound contained administrative buildings, guest quarters, gardens, the Pope's office and residence, a medical facility, and a variety of other buildings. The Temple was the main attraction for visitors to Tay Ninh at that time, and still is. The church members tending the Temple were always happy to show visitors around, provided they left their shoes at the entry.

The first part of December, we began planning a Christmas party for the kids. Since the Cao Dais regarded Christians as being encompassed within their religion, it didn't seem that we would be treading on their religious sensibilities. Nevertheless, we decided to keep the program secular. I wrote the newspapers back home – the *First Segregation News* in Hazelton (segregation related to the segregation of irrigation water, not social, ethnic or racial issues), the *Northside News* in Jerome, and the *Times News* in Twin Falls – to request money, clothing, and toys for the party. I got a fairly good response. Boxes of clothing came in from my family and a number from other folks back in the States. The fund-raising effort produced over two hundred dollars, which went a long way on the open market in Vietnam, especially if locals were doing the buying.

We were able to line up treats for the party from the base camp – cake, ice cream, cookies, Kool-Aid, fruit, fruitcake (sorry about that), and candy. On December 16, we took seven boxes of clothes, four boxes of cookies, 200 lbs. of rice, and five boxes of soap out to the orphanage. Later in the week, I made two trips to the Long Hoa market, which catered almost exclusively to locals, to get gifts for the party. Tom and our hooch girl went along to do the bargaining. I know how an NBA player must feel, towering over everyone around them. There were over 100 locals walking around in the marketplace and I was about a foot taller than all of them—something a 5'11" guy does not often experience.

We bought enough material so that all of the kids could have new clothes. The ladies at the orphanage had said they would sew the cloth into school uniforms for the school-age kids and also make some sports clothing for all of the kids. In addition to the material, we got balls, badminton sets, bows and arrows, crayons, pencils, notebooks, marbles, balloons, and a variety of other things for the kids. Not to forget the women who worked in the orphanage, we got an umbrella for each of them. We also got some plastic water hose that the orphanage needed rather desperately.

The party at the orphanage took place on December 22, and what a party it was. The kids had never encountered ice cream before and they loved it. It was not exactly what Americans would have expected from a taste standpoint, but it was still pretty good. All of the milk products provided to U.S. troops were from reconstituted milk, which many GIs did not like very much. Anyway, the kids did not know or care about that. It was really great to see them enjoying themselves so much. The girls put on a dance performance for us, but mostly the kids ate their fill and then played until they were worn out. I think the staff had a good time and I know my people did also. The ladies were particularly pleased with the umbrellas, as I would find out 50 years later.

On Christmas day, I took Captain Gus for a visit to the orphanage and a tour the Temple. We brought out a couple hundred pounds of rice and other supplies. In a bit of a surprise, the matron presented me with a certificate of appreciation from the church for helping the orphanage. Tom claimed it was a "rare" recognition. Whatever it was, I did appreciate it, even though it did not seem as if we had done all that much.

While preparations were underway for the party, the VC were stoking up some hostile activity. Early in the morning on December 6, they shot about 40 rounds of 82mm mortar at Sector and four days later shot another 28 rounds of the same, which landed about 800 meters from the TOC. As far as I know, there were no friendly casualties. They were not the best shots, but it looked as if they were getting somewhat closer to the target each time. On both occasions, I grabbed my pants and headed into the TOC because it was a sturdy building with thick walls that were fortified with sandbags, but also because the visiting ARVN troops had a small ammunition dump just a couple of feet from our hooch.

At the beginning of 1969, I started a new journal, which got burned up about three months later. That has made it a bit difficult to reconstruct events for January through March. During that period, the liaison unit visited the orphanage and brought supplies at least once a week. We had a couple of ice cream socials for the kids that were not nearly as elaborate as the Christmas party. One was a Tet party that took place eight days before the actual Lunar New Year. Each of the kids got a pair of new sandals and we served ice cream, cake, cookies, candy and nuts. They did not get fruitcake this time and I expect they were quite thankful for that.

Sometime in February, we received word that our hooch was going to be torn down because the ARVNs were planning to build a new TOC bunker on that location. The section got busy building a new hooch just south of the TOC, which we completed about the first of March. It would turn out to be a blessing in disguise. Actually, I kind of liked the old location but it did cause me concern that the visiting ARVN troops always stacked big piles of ammunition and explosives right next to us. The new location would give us more cover from the north, which is where the rocket and mortar fire usually came from.

During the first three months of 1969, there were a number of instances where Sector was targeted for fire, but nothing actually hit inside the compound. There was substantial fighting in Tay Ninh Province during that time so my section kept pretty busy with artillery and air strike clearances. Nevertheless, we were able to keep up our work with the orphanage.

The battalion was now fully behind the orphanage project and really did a lot of good. People in the service battery put together a whole set of playground equipment, painted it very nicely, and transported it out to the orphanage. After much wheedling and cajoling, we were able to get a gas-powered water pump for the orphanage from the 25th Division. It was one of our most important projects. The water supply had previously been hand pumped by an ancient long-handled water pump. Now, they just had to flip a switch to start the pump and there was a steady flow of water. We got a television set so the kids could watch educational programming on government television. We discovered an electric converter was required since the electric supply was direct current, while the TV was AC. I bought one at the hardware store but didn't get a chance to bring it to the orphanage.

Ever since I first saw the orphanage, I had wanted to try to get the place painted. It really did look dull and dingy. In February, the battalion came up with enough paint to get the job done and troops from the service battery took obvious pleasure in slapping it on. It looked 100% better.

Several years after I got home, there was quite a bit of information in the media about lead-based paint. The thought had not even occurred to me during my tour of duty in Vietnam. I read that the Army used a lot of paint containing lead and that caused me a lot of heartburn. I wondered whether the paint that had been scrounged up by the battalion might have contained lead that might start flaking after a number of years. That was a periodic thought for many years. However, 49 years later I learned that the Communists had closed down the orphanage when they took over South Vietnam in 1975.

The afternoon of April 11, I received a call from Major Painter, who suggested that I spend the night at the battalion. He did not give a reason for the invitation and it was rather unusual. During the past seven months, I had only stayed overnight at the battalion twice, once for my promotion party in November and once for Christmas. I told him I needed to get back to Sector before nightfall because there had been a fair amount of enemy activity of late and I thought I might be needed there. We agreed to talk about it when I came to the evening briefing.

The briefing took place, as usual, at 5:00 p.m. and then the officers sat down for dinner. After dinner, Billy asked me to step forward. He proceeded to read a citation for an Army Commendation Medal. I was receiving the ARCOM for my civic action work, particularly the work with the orphanage. It was quite touching. He pinned the medal on and then suggested that I stay overnight at the battalion, have some drinks with the other officers, and perhaps engage in a little poker.

I did have a beer with the guys and then said I really needed to be getting back to Sector. Major Painter insisted that I stay overnight at the battalion and play poker with the other officers. I thought it was a little unusual for Painter to suggest that I engage in gambling because he was a member of the Church of Jesus Christ of Latter-day Saints, which opposes gaming. In any event, I did relent, played some poker, and stayed the night.

Early in the morning, I heard a lot of explosions coming from the direction of town. As I was shaking off my slumbers, an enlisted man asked me if I had heard what was happening at Sector. I said, what? He said that Sector had been attacked. It was thought that a rocket had hit an ammunition cache in one of the Sector buildings and that everything had blown sky high. I could hear many loud explosions from that vicinity as we spoke. I jumped in my Jeep and drove to Sector as fast as the vehicle would go. When I got there, smoke was pouring out of every part of the compound and rounds were cooking off left and right. I had to park a block away and walk to the compound along the entry road. Off to one side I saw what looked like three elongated marshmallows that had cooked to a puffy black in the fire. They were the charred bodies of three people. Each was about three feet long and slightly curved into a fetal position. I was able to make out the head of one of the bodies because teeth were visible. The flesh had burned away from the teeth, leaving them exposed.

I proceeded into the compound. The building across the courtyard or parade ground that lay on an east-west axis was pretty much leveled. (photo #12) That was where the ammunition and explosives had apparently been stored. I went around the south side of the TOC, away from the courtyard, where our new hooch had been built and it was burned to the ground. Everything was destroyed. I walked around the building and headed toward the parade ground area and noticed that the low building that had been just to the north of our old hooch had largely been destroyed. The roof was still on, but the force of the blast had essentially emptied out the rooms, including the Phoenix office. In fact, there was a Jeep sitting almost on top of a desk in the Phoenix office. It had been blown through the front of the building.

The trees in the parade ground were all blasted apart, with gnarly branches hanging here and there. There were mounds of rubble with destroyed vehicles interspersed between and among them. I saw a big of hunk of what looked like somebody's shoulder and several other body parts scattered here and there. Just as I was surveying the situation, another large explosion occurred. Rounds were still cooking off in the rubble so I got out of the way. (photo #13) The front of the TOC was severely damaged, the blast having bashed a large hole into the interior. The back of the building was still standing.

I found my section members about a block away at the Province Chief's Headquarters. Sergeant Ingram, who was then my NCO, told me that one of our guys was in the TOC when the rocket hit, but he had been able to get out the back before the secondary explosions. Ingram and our other man were shielded from the explosion because their part of our hooch was behind the TOC. Had we not moved from our old location, both of them would have been toast. He said that he had rescued the Province Chief, who was in the TOC at the time, an action for which he received a Bronze Star with V (for valor). Ingram was that kind of guy. He would keep his head, take charge, and do what needed to be done.

What had happened is that the VC had shot a few rockets at the Sector compound and gotten lucky. One of the rockets hit the ammunition dump and that set off about 240 tons of mortar and artillery rounds, other explosives, and ammunition of all sorts. The explosion killed about 80 ARVNs, 50 assorted VC suspects and draft dodgers, and 10 civilians. Ingram said it was extremely lucky that I had spent the night at the base camp, because my room was the only one that was not protected from the blast by the TOC. My room took the full force of the blast. Perhaps the good Lord was saying thanks for helping the orphans.

The reason my journal did not record the first three months of 1969 is that it burned up with everything else in the hooch. There was a small building about a block from the TOC, right next to the Province Chief's Headquarters, where we relocated. It was some sort of administrative office or perhaps servants' quarters. The

TOC operation was moved to the Province Chief's Headquarters. Everything was up and running within a matter of hours.

It was interesting to read what *Stars and Stripes* had to say about the attack. The April 13 edition reported that several Communist rounds hit an ammo dump "near the joint U.S. – Vietnamese headquarters" in Tay Ninh, killing two ARVN soldiers and wounding 76. It said that nine civilians were wounded and 80 persons were reported missing. Next day's edition reported 12 persons killed, 100 injured and 80 missing. The paper said that estimates of the missing ranged as high as 150, about half of whom were thought to be "prisoners who may have been Vietcong guerillas or unfortunate peasants without papers." The report said that "courageous little South Vietnamese soldiers probed for bodies in the rubble." I don't know why it was necessary to call the ARVNs "little." That seemed condescending to me. The report said that most of the bodies dug from the ruins were identified "as militia men, wearing bits and pieces of military uniforms." The paper reported that the ammo dump contained about 14,000 artillery shells and 10,000 rounds of small arms ammunition. It said that a smaller ammunition dump nearby, with mainly small arms rounds for South Vietnamese rangers, was also blown up. That would be one of the stacks of ammunition and explosives that had periodically occupied the space next to our old hooch. A tiny article on April 15 said that 80 ARVNs and 5 civilians had died and that up to 150 persons were missing and presumed dead. As a general practice, the Armed Forces papers did not dwell upon losses sustained by our side, particularly ARVN losses, but played up body count on the Communist side. I suppose that it was designed to bolster moral on our side, but sometimes it gave a misleading picture of what was happening.

My hometown weekly newspaper, the *First Segregation News*, which many of us referred to as the "weekly wipe" back in those days of outdoor toilets, had a brief story on the award of the ARCOM and the blow-up at Sector. According to the paper its story was based on a report "receivd from Jones by his pants." I suspect the readership of the *News* was surprised that the paper staff had a direct line of communication with my pants. Or, perhaps the report came from my parents.

Just three weeks after the attack on Sector, the liaison section terminated its operations there and we all moved back to the base camp. I'm not sure why, but Billy decided we could handle clearances through the battalion's fire direction center. We were still able to carry on our work with the orphanage, although it was a bit more difficult to pick up Tom the interpreter and to make arrangements to get supplies from B-32.

The following months saw a substantial uptick in combat in and around Tay Ninh. Of particular concern was an attack by several companies of Viet Cong that focused on an area about two klicks west of the orphanage. There was fairly heavy fighting in the city for a couple of days. I went out the orphanage about a week later and everything seemed to be in good order. It was a big relief. Sergeant Dunn, who had served as my NCO at Sector right after Haney, went along with me and we brought five gallons of bug spray, 110 lbs. of canned fish, four bags of cement (to repair a large water storage barrel), and a bunch of clothes and blankets.

We began planning for a summer party to take place at the base camp. The folks at battalion got their hands on some parachutes and used them to set up a colorful party venue that would also provide some shade. The kids were all decked out in the clothes that the orphanage ladies had sewn together with the material we gave them at Christmas. They all looked really sharp. (photo #14) We fed them hotdogs, Coke, potato salad, and all the other stuff you might expect at a stateside cook-out. It was all new to them, but they seemed to love it. The battalion troops probably had as good a time as the kids. *Stars and Stripes* did a story about the party with a neat picture of some of the kids.

On the 31st of July, we scored a bonanza. Ever since taking on the project, we had been trying to get a reliable source of electricity for the orphanage. It was promised that they would be hooked up to the city power supply, but the hook-up date kept getting put back. We were able to scrounge a gas-powered generator for them to use until they could get hooked up. Also, we brought them 1,000 lbs. of sugar, several cases of powder milk, powdered eggs, and dehydrated potatoes. I was headed home soon and wanted to make sure that they had some backup supplies.

I had been trying to find someone to take over the project, but none of the battalion officers seemed to be interested. There were several Sergeants that expressed an interest so it looked like there would be someone to carry on.

My last visit to the orphanage was August 17. When Tom and I arrived, we found that the ladies had set up a party for us with Vietnamese snacks and cookies. It was really nice. After the party, we were invited to an audience with the Pope at his office in the Cao Dai Holy See. He was a real delight. He was a slight man who looked to be in his eighties. He had white hair and a wispy white beard that was about 5 inches long, curled upward right at the tip. He started out by saying how peaceful it was in the church compound. He thanked me for my work with the orphanage and wished me a good trip home. He gave me a number of photographs of the disbanded Cao Dai Army and of Cao Dai ceremonies and activities, as well as a couple of publications about the Cao Dai religion and another certificate of appreciation. I felt a little discomfort when I realized I was packing my sidearm, but he didn't seem to be bothered by it. He was a thoughtful, serene, and genuinely gracious person.

I don't think anyone ever told me his name, but I saw it in a newspaper report when I was working in Washington, D.C., in 1971. It spoke of how Cao Hoai Sang, the Cao Dai Pope, had died on April 26, 1971, and how his funeral had been attended by all of the major South Vietnamese political figures. They were campaigning for an election and went to the funeral to curry favor with Cao Dai voters. I checked the certificate of appreciation I had gotten during my papal visit and it had been signed by him. He was one of the three persons who had established the church in the 1920s.

6 ● Jim Jones for the defense

Even though I chose to serve my time in the artillery branch, rather than being an Army lawyer, I ended up doing quite a bit of lawyering throughout my tour of duty in Vietnam. That is, I represented defendants in about a dozen special courts martial.

A special court martial is not particularly special, if you are a defendant. It is not for serious crimes, which are handled in a general court martial. Someone charged with a lesser offense in our battalion would either be subject to an Article 15 proceeding where the unit commander would impose a certain penalty, or a special court martial, where a person could be subjected to greater penalties, including incarceration.

In a special court martial, neither the prosecutor nor the defense counsel had to be a lawyer in Vietnam. In our battalion, Billy would appoint one of the officers as prosecutor and then the defendant could choose any other officer as defense counsel. The prosecutor could not be a lawyer if the defendant was not represented by a lawyer. On the other hand, a defendant could have a lawyer as defense counsel, regardless of whether the prosecutor was a lawyer.

Billy made the decision as to whether or not someone would be brought up on charges in a special court martial. He would appoint a three-member court martial board, which would consist of battalion officers. I believe the defendant could ask that one of the members be an NCO.

When word got around that I was a lawyer, I became the go-to guy for those charged with misconduct. My first two courts martial came up during my time as battalion S-1.

The first defendant was charged with three offenses, including insubordination and purposely injuring himself. I can't remember the technical name of the latter charge, but what the fellow did is light his Zippo lighter, partially closed the top so that it got heated up with the flame, and then essentially branded himself on the arm with the hot lighter lid. I don't think he was trying to render himself unfit for duty, but just to show how tough he was. It didn't seem that any of the offenses deserved a special court martial but that's what he was faced with.

I have to admit it was not a very memorable case but I did get a not guilty finding on the self-injury and other charge, but he was found guilty on insubordination.

The second fellow was charged with fraternizing with a civilian, or something like that. Fraternizing is defined as forming a friendship with someone, "especially when one is not supposed to." I think I would have chosen another word to describe what he did. However, he emphatically told me that he "did not have sex with any woman."

The fellow was stationed at FSB Barbara, which was located in a fairly dangerous area. Soldiers were prohibited from going outside of the wire for personal purposes, such as consorting with local women. It was alleged that my client had done just that. He told me during our interview that he had not been outside the wire and had not consorted with anyone. I learned a lesson that I'd heard about in law school but which hadn't really had a chance to sink in yet. Don't always believe a client charged with a criminal offense.

When my client saw the court martial board, he told me that one of the members had it in for him. Apparently, he had previously been in the headquarters battery and its battery commander, who sat on the board, had caused him to get transferred to the firing battery out in the weeds. In recognition of his concern, I respectfully asked the headquarters battery commander to recuse himself. He stated in response that he could be fair and declined to recuse.

Everything was going well until my client's Sergeant got on the stand. He was a man of unimpeachable honor, with a solid reputation for truthfulness. He proceeded to testify as to how he had been gazing outside the wire of FSB Barbara when he saw the defendant stand up from behind a bush, pulling up his pants. He then noticed a young lady getting up, putting on her dress. I leaned over to my client and asked him if there was something he had failed to tell me about. Well, it is not a surprise that he was quickly convicted.

Several weeks later, I was fairly astounded to learn that the conviction had been overturned by the Judge Advocate folks in Saigon. Apparently, the records of all special courts martial were sent to Saigon for review. That was done without any input from either the prosecution or defense. If an error was discovered, the case was overturned. The reviewer in this case concluded that the headquarters battery commander should have recused himself and, therefore, the conviction could not stand. I was rather surprised, but very pleased at the same time.

After I went to Sector, I was still defense counsel of choice for the miscreants in the battalion. Most of the cases were prosecutions of individuals who, when on ammunition runs to Saigon, ended up getting entrapped in the delights of that city. The first case I had at Sector involved a fellow who had gotten drunk and done some regrettable things. He was charged with: (1) misappropriating a Jeep, (2) having an unregistered weapon (a Chicom or Chinese Communist pistol) in his possession, (3) resisting arrest, (4) having a loaded weapon (a shotgun), and (5) misappropriating an M-88 (a tank recovery vehicle).

My successor as battalion S-1, Captain Dumas, was appointed prosecutor. Things moved fairly quickly because the matter came up for hearing four days after the charges were filed. I had looked at the regulations defining the offenses and noticed a number of ambiguities. I decided an argument on the law would be more effective than one on the facts. Things looked a little grim during the presentation of the prosecution, as well as the defense, but closing argument saved the day. I explained to the board that the regulations my client was charged with violating were confusing and could not have adequately warned a person of what conduct was prohibited. The defendant was convicted on two charges – misappropriating the Jeep and resisting arrest – but got off on the other three. He got a fairly light sentence – reduction from E-5 to E-4 and loss of half of his pay for four months. I felt pretty good about it.

About a week later I got word that Billy was rather upset with the outcome. He thought his court martial board should have thrown the book at the guy. That would be a continuing theme in most all of the subsequent prosecutions. On several occasions, Billy called the board members in and gave them a bad time for not convicting on all charges. He never gave me a rough time about it, although we did have several discussions. A couple of times, I told him he could solve the problem by appointing me as prosecutor. However, he understood that this would not work because then he would have to find a lawyer to act as defense counsel.

In October, I defended a fellow who was accused of stealing 480 cases of beer in Saigon. The case against him was not all that strong, partly because he did a pretty good job of covering his tracks. In any event, we tried to poke holes in every weak point of the prosecution's case and he was found not guilty. I never did learn where he got all of the beer or what happened to it. That was a lot of beer.

Several weeks later I had three more young lads who requested me as their court martial counsel. The three were on an ammunition resupply convoy to our battery at Dao Tieng when they decided to skip out at Cu Chi and head to Saigon for a bit of fun and frolic. It didn't look good for any of them.

The first fellow came up for his court martial on Pearl Harbor Day, which was not very auspicious. I was ready with a defense but just before the trial started he said he had decided to plead guilty. That was his choice and it wasn't the best one. He got four months' confinement and forfeiture of two-thirds pay for four months. I thought he was the least responsible of the three and that the sentence was much too stiff.

The second fellow had his court martial three days later and was found not guilty on all charges, which was quite surprising. The more serious charge – violating a general order by going to Saigon on other than official business--was exactly the same charge to which the first fellow had pleaded guilty three days earlier. The second guy was found not guilty on two additional charges – reckless driving and leaving the scene of an accident. I don't recall for sure, as I did not make a note of it, but I think the charges against the third lad were dropped as a result on the not guilty finding with respect to the second defendant.

I had another defendant who was charged with being absent without leave (AWOL). The guy went home on extension leave (leave that you can get when you extend your duty tour) and stayed 39 extra days to work on Senator George McGovern's presidential campaign. The same day, I had a young fellow who needed legal advice regarding a divorce. My legal business was going quite well. The only problem was that it was all pro bono work.

There were about a half-dozen cases between January and August of 1969 that I didn't make notes about and can't really recall that well. One that I do remember involved a real miscarriage of justice. Two young fellows went down to Saigon on an ammo run and got caught up in houses of ill fame, drinking, and a little of thievery. One guy was a fairly innocent, gullible type from the Midwest who just went along. The other guy was a crafty operator, who should have spent some time in the stockade. I got the crafty operator as my client.

We went through the court martial and I was able to get some of the prosecution witnesses tripped up and then confounded the court martial board with some differing interpretations of the regulations at issue. The board found my client not guilty. Billy called the board in afterwards and read them the riot act for letting the guy off. Although the guy was not convicted, that was not the miscarriage of justice.

The innocent, gullible kid from the Midwest for some reason ended up with Captain Dumas, the S-1, as his defense counsel. I think Dumas was afraid of Billy and talked the kid into entering a guilty plea. He got sentenced to six months of confinement in the Long Binh Jail or LBJ, as we affectionately called it in honor of the President. I thought Dumas was a dumbass for pleading him, especially after the mastermind got off.

There was another case where a Sergeant and an enlisted man took a detour into a whorehouse in Saigon, got drunk, and had a certain amount of fun. Both came up on charges. The battery commander handled the Sergeant personally with an Article 15 proceeding. The guy got slapped on the wrist. My client, the enlisted man, was set up for a court martial. He was guilty and probably should have been convicted. However, I did something that was not proper – injecting into the proceeding the fact that the Sergeant only got an Article 15. The prosecution called the Sergeant as a witness to outline all of the evil deeds performed by my client. I just asked him what punishment he had gotten and, of course, he related that he had received an Article 15. In keeping with Army custom, the guy in charge should always be the one who suffers most for the misconduct. The court martial board couldn't bring itself to convict my guy, which sent Billy into orbit. He told the board members in no uncertain terms that they could not and should not have taken into account the punishment received by the Sergeant.

My last case was a fragging incident. Fragging was where somebody throws a grenade under a superior's bunk, or something similar. This fellow was stationed at FSB Barbara and apparently did not like something the First Sergeant had done. He threw a grenade under the First Sergeant's bunk but, luckily, the First Sergeant was elsewhere. I agreed to defend the fellow, but it was right at the end of my tour and for some reason the case did not get set for hearing before I left.

I have to admit that I got into just a little bit of legal trouble during my tour. When I arrived at Sector, we had a truck that we used for transportation between the base camp and Sector every day. There were only four of us in my unit and I thought it was stupid to follow the usual protocol of having an enlisted man drive me around. There just weren't enough people. Somebody had to be working through the night, so at least one EM was usually sleeping during the day. The battalion Sergeant Major mentioned on occasion that I probably ought to have somebody drive me but I always told him it was not a very good use of resources. Besides, I had been driving since I was 14 years old – about 12 years. So, I drove the ¾ ton truck back and forth every day, unless somebody happened to be going with me.

I had been pestering the headquarters battery commander to get me a Jeep and he finally did on December 20, just in time for Christmas. So, I drove that while the other members of the unit used the ¾ ton truck. We outfitted it with red seat covers and a red cover for the spare tire on the rear. It certainly stood out.

After Major Painter raised the issue of Sergeant Haney potentially being involved in the black market, I did as the Major asked and kept an eye on him. Two or three times after that, Billy also raised the issue with me. He was growing more suspicious of Haney as rumors of unseemly behavior continued to circulate around the battalion. I spoke up for Haney on each occasion because I didn't think he was misappropriating property, although I guess there is a fine line between misappropriating and routine scrounging. Haney was a first-class scrounger, which was not generally regarded as improper. He also engaged in what was called midnight requisitioning, which was kind of on the borderline of theft, unless it was for a really worthy purpose.

Each time the issue was raised by HQ, I told Haney that he needed to be careful about what he told people at the battalion regarding his exploits. After the meeting with Painter, I told Haney to shut down his beverage business. When Billy got involved, I told him he needed to vacate the house in town. That didn't help, however, because Billy finally had it and said he was going to bring Haney back to the battalion. That took place toward the end of February. When I broke the news to Haney, he was very distraught and lashed out because he thought that I had not protected him. I told him that there was nothing that I could do and that I had actually been a strong advocate for him. He didn't seem to buy it.

I knew that Haney was close with the military police (MPs) who monitored traffic in and out of the base camp. It was a surprise, however, when I got pulled over on my way to battalion headquarters in early March. This was not long after Haney was yanked back to base camp. To get to the battalion, you had to drive past the air strip and were required to stop at the edge of the air strip before proceeding, unless you were following a convoy. I was following a convoy and did not stop. At that point there were some MPs handy and they pulled me over, wanting to see my driver's license, which Haney knew I did not have. It was easy to pick out my Jeep with its red accoutrements. The MPs arrested me for driving without a driver's license and hauled me to their headquarters. I got my free call to the Sergeant Major and told him I had been arrested. Within about 20 minutes, the Sergeant Major appeared with two driver's licenses. One was from the headquarters battery and the other from the service battery. Both indicated I'd gotten good grades on my driver's exams. The MPs had no choice but to release me. They had no grounds to stop me in the first place and everybody seemed to agree with my conclusion that Haney had set it up.

Based on my experience with it, I have to say that the military justice system worked okay. There was certainly a problem with command influence, which should not have happened. I don't suspect that Billy was the only commander who tried to influence the outcome of courts martial. However, the members of the court martial boards did demonstrate some independence and dedication to properly carrying out their responsibility. It didn't always happen, but it happened more than one might have expected. The board members were not trained in the law and I think any success I had with them was due to the fact that they exercised common sense and fair play once they were informed that the prosecution had the job of proving every part of the offense that was charged against the defendant.

What was interesting, also, is that all of the cases went to Saigon for review and, as I have said, there were a number of cases where convictions were actually reversed. I think that happened in about a third of my cases. I did have a chance to find out who was doing the reviewing.

After the big explosion at Sector, I submitted a claim to be compensated for my lost property. That included the electricity converter that I bought for the orphanage. I got a call from the JAG folks in Saigon, saying that my claim was in order, except for the electricity converter. They wondered why I had one in my possession and said that I would need to come down to Saigon to discuss the matter. I was able to catch a ride to Saigon, walked into the JAG office, and got a big surprise. The person who I met with, Captain Steve Berry, had been a year ahead of me at Northwestern Law School. Steve had made a big impression when my roommate, Alby Anderson, and I were living in the old Navy barracks building near Navy Pier. It had been converted into a dormitory for law students. The rooms were small so we often left our hallway door open. On more than one occasion, we would hear a loud yell down the hall, getting closer as it approached our doorway, and when we looked up we saw the heinie of Steve Berry flashing by.

Mooning was a big thing at that time. The moon issue did arise during our conversation in Saigon, which helped to break the ice. We enjoyed discussing good old NU Law. When he got the facts about the converter, Steve agreed that it was a compensable item.

He was kind enough to offer a travel tip, suggesting I get what he called a blow bath and steam job at a local massage emporium before returning to Tay Ninh. When he explained what it was, I thought perhaps it would not be the best idea. Apparently, they lived a different life down in Saigon. His explanation gave me a better picture of why some of my clients jumped off of the truck on ammo runs to Saigon.

It was not until I went to Jerome in 1973 to set up my law practice that I met another attorney, Bill Hart, who had started a law practice in Jerome about eight months earlier. During our visit we found we had been serving in Vietnam at the same time. Bill said he had served as a JAG officer in Saigon. I asked if he knew a guy named Steve Berry, and he said Steve was a good friend and that the two had worked together in that office for most of their respective tours. I related how the convictions in a number of my cases had been overturned in Saigon and he said that that was not an unusual thing. The JAG guys who reviewed court-martial convictions were aware of the fact that some commanders exercised undue command influence so they tried to level the playing field from time to time. I thanked him for his charitable attitude and then reflected on how small the world can be at times.

7 ● Bird dogging in the jungle

On November 9, I went with Colonel Hilling to watch a CIDG heliborne operation near Thien Ngon. I had told the people at our fire direction center that I would be going with the SF and might be asked to call in some fire for them. They gave me a radio and sent me on my way. When we boarded Colonel Hilling's Huey, I thought everything was in good order.

We flew quite a way into War Zone C to a clearing in the jungle, which was going to be the landing zone for the CIDG troops out of Thien Ngon. A chopper first flew around the edges of the clearing, spewing smoke to give the troops some cover. Colonel Hilling asked me to put some artillery fire into the jungle along the west edge of the operation but it didn't work out so well. I radioed in to the battalion TOC only to discover that the command channel was not used for fire direction purposes. Nobody had mentioned that there was a specific fire direction frequency that was changed each day, as per a classified communications sheet. It had not occurred to anyone that I would need the sheet for that day. I tried everything I could think of to get them to give me the frequency over the radio, such as disguising it in a sports score, a measurement, and several other types of number associations. Nothing worked. Needless to say, it was rather embarrassing. I wasn't able to get any artillery on or around the landing area. They did have a couple of Air Force jets come in to soften things up, but that didn't help my attitude.

Luckily, there was no enemy engagement at the landing zone. We went on back to the air strip at Tay Ninh East, which was located just north of Sector and west of the B-32 compound. Later that afternoon, the VC sprung an ambush on the CIDG, killing 14 and wounding about 40. I was told the operation ended up in rather total confusion.

I got up in the air again on December 21, this time with Allen 10, the Air Force forward air controller (FAC) assigned to MACV. His plane was an old grey Bird Dog. We flew around doing visual reconnaissance for about two hours in the afternoon and then another hour in the evening. We had planned to adjust DEFCONs for Phuoc Tan, an ARVN base just two klicks from the Cambodian border, but our battery at the base camp was tied up shooting counter- mortar fire for FSB Barbara.

The Bird Dog is a two-seater aircraft, with the pilot up front and the observer in the back. You could open the Plexiglas windows on either side of the back seat and latch them on to the underside of the wings and enjoy the cool air passing through. It felt kind of like heaven. I took my flak vest along for the express purpose of using it for a seat. It may just be a male thing, but the idea of losing the ability to procreate and related stuff was the foremost thing in my mind.

We went up again the next day and were able to shoot and adjust the DEFCONs, after waiting 45 minutes while more counter-mortar fire went up to FSB Barbara. They were apparently getting lots of incoming mortar fire.

Come February, I got the additional title of Assistant S-2, which meant that I was the assistant intelligence officer. The S-2 was Captain Roth, who you may recall was called the Eagle because of his visual reconnaissance work. Now, I would also be doing VR missions. The officers in the battalion started calling me the Hawk because I was flying, not because of my stance on the war. The new job was great. I loved it.

We got our olive drab Bird Dogs from the 74th Recon Aviation Company (RAC) in Phu Loi. They would fly up to the base camp, pick us up, and we would generally fly over War Zone C, looking for targets of opportunity or shooting targets identified by various intelligence sources.

There was a broad range of intelligence sources: intelligence gathered in infantry operations, paid or unpaid informers, clandestine operations, and the like. The Army had sniffer planes, which flew over the jungle with equipment that could detect smells associated with the NVA or VC. Quite frankly, I don't know what smells they were trying to pick up. It may have been the smell of cooking fires or fish sauce or whatever. There were planes with SLAR, side-looking airborne radar, that could pick up personnel moving through the jungle, supposedly. There were planes equipped with infrared sensors that could pick up cooking fires, body heat, or any other heat-emitting source. There was what we called the Black Bullet, which was a seismic device placed along trails to pick up movement of equipment or personnel. And then there were the Eagle and me, who flew over the terrain at about 800 feet, looking for anything that might be suspicious or out of place.

On my first mission in early February, we were flying near the north edge of War Zone C, about two klicks south of the Cambodian border when I saw three people on bicycles. Well, they weren't on the bicycles they were walking and pushing the bicycles. That was a favored method for transportation of goods, although it didn't look as if there were any goods on these bicycles. They were headed north toward the Cambodian border so they must have dropped off whatever they were hauling and were on their way back. A main branch of the Ho Chi Minh Trail emptied south into War Zone C from Cambodia, so it was likely that these fellows had delivered supplies and ammunition directly from Uncle Ho.

The only guns that could reach the target area were the two 175s at FSB Barbara. I called in a fire mission just as the bikers were headed into some thick foliage. A large part of the northern area of War Zone C had been defoliated by Agent Orange, but the Ranch Hands, the fellows who sprayed the defoliant from their C-

130 aircraft, must have cut off the spray operation as they approached the Cambodian border. In any event, I lost sight of the individuals, but knew the general direction they were traveling. The battery got a couple of rounds off and they landed somewhere in the vicinity. The 175s could only shoot about one round per minute per gun so by the time they were ready to shoot again the subjects were within a kilometer of the Cambodian border. We could not shoot into that strip, unless we had been taking ground fire, which we weren't. I couldn't see them anymore so I guess it didn't make much difference. That was the only time I saw people on bicycles out in an open area.

Getting up in the air above Tay Ninh Province was a real revelation. I'll take you on a tour of the province's border with Cambodia, starting with the northeast corner of the province. At that corner, which is the bottom of what was called the Fish Hook, the border between Vietnam and Cambodia heads almost due west, serving as the northern boundary of the province. (Map # 1) The same corner is the beginning of the boundary line between Tay Ninh Province and Binh Long Province, which is located on Tay Ninh's east side. From the northeast corner, the Vietnam-Cambodia border meanders west about 27 klicks to a place just on the north side of the border that was reputed by intelligence to have been an NVA rest and recreation (R&R) center. The Katum SF Camp is located about seven klicks south of that center.

The border meanders in a northwesterly direction for another 25 klicks and then turns sharply south. As it goes south, the border intersects with Highway 22, which crosses into Cambodia at a point about eight klicks north of the Thien Ngon SF Camp. About ten klicks west of that is a feature of the border called the Elephant's Ear, which unsurprisingly resembles the ear of an elephant, pushing into Cambodia. The western edge of the Elephant's Ear contained a reputed NVA camp in a 12 square km slice of disputed property between Cambodia and Vietnam. The Elephant's Ear constituted the northwest corner of Tay Ninh Province. There were various branches of the Ho Chi Minh Trail that lead into Vietnam along the width of the northern border.

Moving out of the Elephant's Ear, the border between Vietnam and Cambodia heads in a general southerly direction about seven klicks to a reputed NVA hospital and then continues south another six klicks to a bulge into Vietnam which contained a reputed NVA camp just on the west side of the border.

The border continues south, taking a turn to the east and then south again to a wooded area on the Vietnam side. The triple canopy jungle in the wooded area had a four km straight north-south border, earning it the name Straight Edge Woods. The border then headed in a general southeasterly direction into the feature I have previously described as the Angel's Wing. The Angel's Wing is west of the cities of Trang Bang and Cu Chi. The Duc Hue SF Camp was at the bottom of the Angel's Wing. The border between Cambodia and Vietnam heads almost due south from the Angel's Wing. The Army maps of that area, which were current and reliable, showed the part of Cambodia immediately southwest of Duc Hue to have just a scattering of buildings. However, flying over the bordering areas of Vietnam around Duc Hue, one could see a great number of buildings in Cambodia that did not show up on the map. It was fairly obvious to me that this was a major NVA base camp just over the border in Cambodia. We could not touch it. And, again, we were not supposed to fly within one klick of the border, according to the information that filtered down to me. That didn't seem to make a lot of sense. Further, it took approval from higher headquarters to shoot artillery into that one km strip.

The common border between Cambodia and Tay Ninh Province reached its southern limit at the southern tip of the Angel's Wing. From that point, the province boundary headed in an easterly direction, while the Cambodia-Vietnam border headed south and then southeasterly to the very tip of the Parrot's Beak.

The battalion intelligence Sergeant prepared an ingenious map for me that encompassed the entire province and then some. It was 8 inches by 15 inches and about an inch thick. It contained all of the current military maps of Tay Ninh Province at a scale of one inch per km. The maps were good enough that a person with reasonably good map-reading skills could pinpoint a location on the ground to within five or ten meters. I could usually get my first round from one our 8-inch guns right on target, while it generally took several rounds to get a 175 on or at least near the target.

The maps divided the terrain into square kilometers. To determine the location for an artillery strike, one would use terrain features on the ground and find where they coincided with features depicted on the map—roads, water courses, villages, buildings, and so on. The maps were good enough that it was not difficult to figure out where a feature on the ground was located on the map. Then, you determined an eight-digit coordinate for the ground location. The first four digits were for the east-west point and the second four were for the north-south point. Take my word for it that you could pinpoint a location on the ground and provide the fire direction center an accurate coordinate for the location.

The protocol for adjusting artillery fire is generally to bracket the target. If the first round lands short of the target, you call for the next round to go beyond the target and then split the difference with the third round. If the first round went long, you just did the reverse. There wasn't much point in doing that with an 8-inch gun because it was so accurate. If you had the correct coordinates, you could drop the first round directly into a pickle barrel, if you could have found one handy. The 175 was a different story. Sometimes your first round landed somewhere near where you hoped it would, but not all that often. The deflection—the right or left factor-- was usually correct but the range was usually short or long.

The problem with the 175 was its long barrel and high velocity. There was a lot of internal wear and tear on the barrels because of the gun's high velocity. At the time I was shooting them, barrels wore out and had to be replaced after firing 300 rounds. The barrels manufactured later were harder and lasted longer. The more rounds you put through a barrel, the more it would erode internally, which caused air to leak around the projectile. As a barrel got closer to the 300 round maximum, it would not shoot a projectile as far. That is, the more barrel wear, the shorter distance the round would go. Also, when the barrel of the gun heated up, it would droop slightly, causing a round to go a shorter distance. If several rounds were fired in succession, the barrel would get hot and the gun would not shoot as far.

Getting exactly the right range with a 175 was sometimes frustrating. On one fire mission in the center of War Zone C, I called for fire and was told a round had been shot. I looked all around the vicinity of the target but could not see where the round landed, so I called for another round. There was no sign of the second round but the person at the fire direction center insisted that both rounds had been fired. I happened to look toward the firing battery and could see two smoke plumes about 5 klicks short of the target. That was a bit unsettling. On another fire mission toward the end of my tour, a round targeted for about 2 klicks short of the Cambodian border actually landed about half a klick inside of Cambodia. I doubt that it hit anything worthwhile but it made me feel good since there were plenty of NVA in that particular area.

There was a variety of ammunition available for use on fire missions. The most obvious one was the high explosive, which was the mainstay of our work. The 8-inch rounds weighed 200 lbs. and those of the 175s were about 146 lbs. An 8-inch shell exploding in the air was very lethal for the length of a football field. The main force of the blast went out perpendicular to the length of the shell.

We could also call for white phosphorus (WP or Willie Peter), which was particularly nasty. White phosphorus burns at about 1,700 degrees Fahrenheit and can cause horrific burns. Jumping into water will not help a victim, because it burns underwater. Air Force FACs used WP rockets as marking rounds for air strikes. It was also useful as a smoke screen to restrict visibility on a battle field. The Army Bird Dogs usually carried two WP rockets.

I called for a few Willie Peter artillery rounds just to see what the effect was but didn't think it was too useful for my purposes. A high explosive round was much better for most purposes. A Willie Peter round could engulf a target with an incendiary fireball, but a high explosive round encompassed a wider area with lethal force.

It never would have occurred to me to use Willie Peter in an urban area. The only reasons I could think of for doing so would be to create terror amongst those in the target area or to burn down buildings – not exactly an ideal way to win the hearts and minds of the afflicted populace. I was flabbergasted many years later when I saw TV news video footage showing the Israeli military using Willie Peter rounds in populated areas during the 2014 Gaza war. Not only were they using WP rounds, but the rounds were set to burst in the air, which resulted in dozens of burning white phosphorus wedges being spread over an area with a radius of up to 125 meters from the point of the blast. To do this in a populated area is unconscionable.

I later saw footage of the same tactic being used by U.S.-led forces in Mosul, Iraq, and Raqqa, Syria, in 2017. This, too, was unconscionable. Our forces were apparently given the green light to use Willie Peter in these urban combat situations by virtue of a loosening of the rules of engagement in 2017. The looser rules, including the use of Willie Peter munitions, is likely the reason for an almost tripling of civilian deaths in the U.S.-led campaign against the Islamic State terrorists during that year.

Another pernicious munition that became available to our battalion in the late spring of 1969 was the firecracker round. This is what is called a cluster munition. It contains a number of small bomblets or grenade-sized explosive devices that are spread over the target area when the shell bursts a few hundred feet above the ground. When the battalion first had them, I called a couple of firecracker rounds while I was flying over the base camp at night. There were dozens of small explosions that were spread over a fairly wide area. It didn't much impress me. You didn't have the accuracy or explosive power of a regular high explosive round.

Plus, I was told that many of the small explosive devices would not detonate, creating a hazard for anyone who might later be walking around the area. It just didn't seem like a good idea. Some of those little bomblets still populate the terrain in Vietnam to this day, causing war-related casualties, particularly among curious children.

After the liaison section was brought back to the base camp, I served for a period of time in the battalion fire direction center. One night, a 25th Division fire base, FSB Crook, was attacked and we were called on to shoot up the Commies. The artillery guy from the 25th Division, a Captain Kramer, wanted firecracker rounds. I told him that high explosive was the better choice to decimating the enemy ranks and that we could put those rounds closer to the perimeter of the fire support base. Firecracker rounds weren't right for the job so I refused his request. The attack was repelled and everything worked out fine. However, the brigade commander from the 25th Division apparently called Billy to complain that we should have used firecracker rounds. I'm sure that with the firecracker being new to the battle field, they wanted to get in on the novelty so Billy said we ought to try to keep them happy. That night, Captain Kramer called to ask for some firecracker around the fire base and I told him we would be happy to oblige. I then launched on a fire mission of my own against beloved Captain Kramer, using every profanity in my vocabulary, including some that I had never used before. The enlisted men in the TOC were absolutely astounded but spell-bound by my performance, it seemed. Several had their mouths gaping open, apparently thinking that this mild-mannered Captain must not be the choirboy they had thought. In any event, Captain Kramer got what he wanted and I had happily been able to purge whatever evil thoughts I had been harboring about him. We both felt better.

The other type of round we had available was the illumination round, which could practically turn night into day. Our use of these around the base camp or the scattered fire support bases was fairly common. An illumination round from a big gun like ours could really light up the night. The round would go off high in the air, unleashing an incandescent unit that slowly floated to the ground with a parachute. The parachute would often rock back and forth, causing a surreal sensation on the ground. They were fairly effective in discouraging attacks or exposing the attackers. It provided a certain measure of comfort to those on the ground who were operating in the dark.

There was also an array of fuses that we could use. The regular fuse caused an artillery shell to explode when it hit the ground or something else fairly solid. They were not ideal when you were firing into triple canopy jungle because the shell would often explode when it hit the upper branches. The shrapnel did not often make its way down to the ground. In heavy jungle, or if you wanted to have a round penetrate the earth and blow up underground, you used a delay fuse. That would cause the round to go off a tiny bit after it hit. Then, there was a time fuse that caused the round to explode a selected number of seconds after it was fired. Sometimes you might use that type of fuse if you wanted an air burst. However, the best way to get an air burst was to use a variable time (VT or Victor Tango) fuse. A VT fuse was triggered by elevation and it was the perfect way to get an air burst. They generally went off about 20 feet above the ground, which directed shrapnel straight into fox holes and uncovered bunkers. Victor Tango was the belle of the artillery ball.

One of the more troubling things about the VR program was our good old Bird Dog aircraft. They were more old than good. The problem first came to my attention on my first night mission. The pilot and I were doing mortar watch, which consisted of flying over and around the base camp at night to look for mortar flashes or rockets being fired. We were flying about 15 klicks west of the base camp, which was a little far afield for mortar watch, when the pilot said something like "oh shit." That is something you would prefer not to hear from the pilot's mouth. He said the oil pressure had dropped nearly to zero, which I took was a bad thing based of his tone of voice. In case you're wondering how we communicated, our helmets were wired for sound and connected together through the airplane's sound system. In any event, we headed back to base camp and landed safely. The pilot explained that the engine could freeze up or fail if no oil was being pumped through it. This was not the last time for oil problems.

There were four other similar events. On July 6, I was out on mortar watch again. The pilot and I were standing by to adjust artillery at a small contact west of base camp when the plane all but conked out. The following morning the pilot told me we were lucky to get back to the air strip. When I related the incident to the Eagle, he told me that he had just had a similar experience. An oil seal had busted on his plane and he, too, was told by the pilot that they were lucky to get back.

These planes were built as observer aircraft, starting in 1949. A number of them had been in service for a couple of decades by 1969. They were certainly old dogs but that did not necessarily mean they were dangerous. The Eagle and I suspected that poor maintenance was a big contributor to the problem.

During my last month in Vietnam, I had two additional close calls. On August 4, we were shooting up a suspected base camp northwest of FSB Barbara when the pilot said our oil pressure was getting low and that we should head back to base camp. I put in two more rounds and then we headed back. Just as we got to the near edge of the air field, the oil pressure dropped to zero.

On August 20, just ten days before heading home, I was flying near Duc Hue SF camp with one our regular pilots, Captain Schooley. We had registered a 105mm howitzer for the troops at a 25th Division fire base, FSB Elaine, and then done some VR work afterwards. We started back to the base camp when Schooley noticed the oil pressure gauge was in the danger zone. We forced a landing at the nearest air strip, Duc Hoa (not to be confused with Duc Hue) and filled up with oil. The little plane took seven quarts. That was a lot of oil. The Eagle and I had taken to calling the 74th RAC "Death Trap Airlines."

Being curious about the safety record of these little puddle-jumpers, I checked online recently and found part of the answer.

During the course of the war, a total of 469 Bird Dogs were lost from all causes—mechanical problems, accidents and hostile action. The Army, ARVNs, and covert operators lost 284, the Air Force 178 and the Marines 7. There does not seem to be a breakdown of the maintenance losses.

While the planes and their upkeep might be called into question, the pilots were great. Captain Schooley was a great pilot who slightly resembled William Shatner, but with blondish hair. He seemed to be the one who generally got the crappy airplanes, but he always got us back safely.

Captain Spoor probably flew me around more than anyone else. (photo #16) He was an interesting character, always looking for some adventure. Some of the pilots carried Willie Peter rockets, but rarely if ever used them. Spoor preferred high explosive rockets and loved to shoot them. I can't tell you how he aimed the things but he was a remarkable shot. One day when we were flying along the west edge of War Zone C, we spotted a guy just on the Cambodian side of the border. When the fellow saw us, he jumped behind a tree. Spoor shot off one of his rockets and I was amazed to see it explode on the very front of that tree, about 3 feet above the ground. If the guy had remained standing where he had been when we first saw him, the rocket would have impaled him.

Spoor and I experienced a maintenance problem when I needed to stop and pay a visit to our fire support base at Dau Tieng. When we started to take off from the air strip, Spoor said that we had a problem. He said the plane was ground looping. I didn't know what that meant but he said the brake on one side was not working, which sort of caused the plane to veer to one side as we were going down the strip for takeoff. I think it had something to do with the fact that the plane was a tail dragger. That is, there were two wheels right under the fuselage and one small one at the tail. Most modern aircraft have three wheels – one in front and two right under the fuselage. In any event, he said that we could not take off because of the ground looping.

He radioed to his headquarters and they said they would send a Beaver aircraft to pick us up and take me to Tay Ninh. It is a larger aircraft with a neat-looking radial engine in front. The Beaver landed at Dau Tieng after the sun was down and we started back. The interior of the Beaver was quite a bit bigger than the Bird Dog. The pilot and Spoor were sitting side by side up front and I was in the back of the aircraft. They wanted to converse and kept shouting and motioning for me to plug in my helmet. I looked high and low but could not find an audio plug anywhere. There had to be a place to plug into the plane's audio system but it was too dark to see anything. I thought they were pointing to a funnel type thing as an alternate means of communication. I picked it up and yelled into it a couple of times but got no response. Then I heard the pilot yell in a very loud voice, "You're yelling into the piss tube." It apparently did not work so well as a communication device, although the NVA down in the jungle may have wondered where all of the sound was coming from.

One of the things Spoor liked to do was fly over the part of Cambodia at the bottom of the Angel's Wing. The Vietnam side of that whole area lay fallow, even thought it was farm land. I believe that the farmers and other civilians had all been moved east of the Vam Co Dong River as part of the counter insurgency program. I guess nobody ever told me that, but there were no people living in the area and if you saw someone rooting around down there it was probably VC or NVA. As a matter of fact, there was the large NVA encampment just on the west side of the border several klicks below the Angel's Wing. In any event, there were rice paddies on the Cambodian side of the border and Spoor enjoyed flying over that area to observe the farmers working. I don't know why it didn't occur to either of us that they might be something other than peaceful Cambodians. Our last trip over the area was on August 18, about 12 days before I headed home and about two weeks before Spoor was set to go home. We were about a mile inside of Cambodia, watching a few farmers, when they opened up on us with AK-47s. It sounded like a popcorn popper.

Spore went into a steep dive to pick up some speed and was able to get out range before we took any hits.

We spent the next 10 or 15 minutes trying to figure out whether we dared to call in artillery. We had taken ground fire, but we should not have been anywhere near the place. Had we been on the Vietnam side of the border and taken ground fire, we probably could have justified a fire mission on the people on the ground. But, even then, we were not supposed to be flying within one klick of the border. After debating the issue back and forth, we decided it would not be a good idea to alert U.S. artillery of what had happened. So, Spoor picked up a bit of altitude and flew back over the would-be farmers, spraying a couple of clips of M-16 fire. I don't think he hit anything, but you could see geysers of water flying up in the paddies and about a half dozen people and 3 water buffalo scattering every which way for cover.

There were some pilots, not many, who were a problem. I can't remember the name of the jerk, but when he was assigned to take me out on a VR mission the Eagle said something like "good luck." And he was that kind of guy. He knew everything and apparently regarded himself as having to deal with a world of idiots. The guy liked to talk and as we were flying around he chattered incessantly.

I gave him the coordinates of an intelligence target that I wanted to shoot. When we reached a location on the Saigon River about five klicks from the target, he announced that we were there. I told him the target area was about five klicks south. We got into a discussion that became somewhat heated. I told him matter-of-factly that "I'm going to come up there and kick your ass." Which prompted him to yell, "trouble in the plane, trouble in the plane." I was wondering whether he thought it was a case of mutiny. In any event, he relented and flew me to the place I wanted to go. I called my first round of 8-inch on the coordinates that we had been arguing about and the first round fell just where I told him it would. He kept his trap shut after that.

Another pilot who I only had once was probably even worse. He scared the living daylights out of me. We were up north in War Zone C to register the 105 mm howitzers at the Thien Ngon SF Camp. Registering is essentially adjusting the guns—sort of like adjusting the sight on a rifle. The guns were shooting toward the north and south edges of Katum SF Camp and we wanted to ensure that they were hitting where the fire needed to be in case of an attack.

The pilot apparently did not understand the concept of the gun-target line. That is, a round travels from the gun to the target along a straight line. It goes quite a way up into the air and then back to earth. When you are in a Bird Dog, you try to stay out of the gun-target line when the gun is firing. Usually, it is best to be right above the target so that you can see exactly where the round lands. This pilot took a wide swing around the target and always seemed to be exactly between the gun and the target when the gun fired.

I was tracking the trajectory of each round in my mind every time the gun fired and it just seemed to me that we were smack dab in the way. I could almost feel each of about four rounds going right through the little airplane. I was hoping that it would hit him instead of me. It probably would not have made much difference, because the round would have exploded when it hit the plane.

I tried to tell the fellow in a pleasant way that we needed to be out of the gun-target line when the gun went off, but it didn't seem to sink in. He just kept doing it. Luckily, we did not get hit.

When flying mortar watch during the night, we would get either Army pilots or Air Force FACs who may have been stationed at the base camp. They were all pretty good pilots. We would meet at the infantry brigade's officers' club and take off an hour or so after sundown. There was one interesting thing that I noticed about the pilots. The Army guys generally would not have any alcoholic beverage to drink before we lifted off, while it was not unusual for the Air Force guys to take a nip or two. I don't know that it affected their flying, but the Army guys seemed to be a little more uptight.

I also flew missions with Allen 10, the FAC attached to MACV at Sector. He was a good guy. We would go up and Allen 10 would have F-4s come in with their 20mm cannons blazing away at a target he would identify with Willie Peter marking rounds. The F-4s would also shoot rockets, drop bombs, and occasionally drop napalm. When the napalm hit it would first flash red and then that would be enveloped in an angry-looking billowing black cloud. You could feel the heat all of the way up into the Bird Dog – a sudden blast of hot air on your face. It was scary and captivating at the same time. I would then put in a few rounds of artillery, just in case anything was left over to shoot.

The battalion's VR program had significantly improved from the time I attended the Artillery Group commanders' meeting in Phu Loi during my acting XO days early in my tour. The Proud Americans now had more "significant" sightings and more fire missions than any of the other heavy artillery battalions. The Eagle and I had taken Billy's suggestion seriously-- that we label more of our sightings as "significant"-- thereby reaching the ranks of VR stardom.

It was clear to both of us that what Billy really wanted was body count. I can't say the Eagle manufactured body count that did not exist, even though his estimate of body count at the Suoi Day incident was pretty darn high. I was not much inclined to manufacture false body count because it was both dishonest and an unreliable metric as to how the war was going. During battalion briefings, Billy often suggested that it would be desirable to tally up more KBAs, so I tried to accommodate by getting fairly inventive with other types of target surveillance.

First, though, I should tell you about one of the contributing factors to the battalion's number of fire missions. It was the ammunition supply rate (ASR). Billy told me early on in my VR work that we had to be mindful of the ASR. He explained that you got so many rounds per month, based on what you had fired during the previous month. If you did not use all of your allocation of ammunition during the current month, you would likely be cut back during the succeeding months. Therefore, you always used up all of your supply of ammunition and asked for more the next time. If you asked for just what you needed, it would be assumed by the higher-ups that your request was inflated and you would likely get cut back. That's how the ASR worked. Regardless of whether we had targets, we needed to shoot up all of our allocation of ammo so as to keep a steady supply coming. That concept would come in handy during my government service years later.

Now, granted, there were usually lots of things to shoot at. Our intel targets included suspected base camps, bunkers, supply caches, troop concentrations, and you name it. I once shot up what was reported to be a suspected NVA radio station. If there was a radio station at the coordinates we were provided, it went off the air. The thing is, you could never find out what the actual target surveillance was when you were dropping rounds into triple canopy jungle. When there was nothing really to shoot up, you looked for suspicious things and shot at them.

Just like any other type of hunting, you had to keep your eyes peeled for the slightest movement or anything that appeared out of place. It was not always easy to concentrate with the plane jostling and bumping around in the air currents. Early in 1969, we were provided with a set of image stabilizing binoculars. They did stabilize the images on the ground, if you could find the area you were hoping to surveil. The image was magnified to the extend it was often hard to get the binos focused on the right area. Also, they had a battery pack that was not particularly easy to get positioned in the confined back seat of a Bird Dog. Overall, I did not find them to be very helpful.

Targets of opportunity were sometimes hard to find. First, there was heavy foliage everywhere in War Zone C, which made it pretty tough to see anything or anyone that might be there. Second, when anyone down below heard an airplane or chopper overhead, they weren't about to make themselves known. When you did see someone, you had to use some judgment as to whether or not to call for artillery. I would not shoot at people on the fringes of the free fire zone unless it was clear they were up to no good. On one occasion, Captain Spoor and I spotted a fellow with an oxcart about 2 klicks inside of War Zone C. He was not far from the Woodchoppers' Village and we figured he was going out to get a load of wood. Spoor just fired a rocket in front of him and he made a quick about face. It never occurred to either of us to go after him.

Artillery observers and FACs were in a difficult position because they had to make life or death decisions with very little information to go on. Unless there was someone on the ground calling for and directing fire, they had to make their own determination of whether a person on the ground might be a hostile. Essentially, you were the judge, jury and potential executioner. It was not something to be taken lightly.

Absent suspicious circumstances, I would not fire at people tending or working with water buffalo because they were more than likely farmers or woodchoppers. Nor would I have shot at untended water buffalo because they were used by the civilians for transport, plowing and other heavy-duty work. Killing one would have been pure vandalism and worked a hardship on the owner. We did see a big cat once, probably an Indochinese leopard, and just let it be. The wildlife had all they could handle with the war, Agent Orange, and everything else. The only time anyone saw a motor vehicle (other than a U.S. military vehicle) in the free fire zone was the incident at Suoi Day. I like to think I would not have shot in that instance because the Communists did not tend to conduct their business out in the open. They did have trucks on the other side of the Cambodian border and probably used them to transport supplies into Vietnam at night. During the day, the vehicle of choice was the bicycle. If you ever saw a bicycle in that area during daytime hours, it would definitely be a target.

Even if there were no targets, we still had to expend our full allocation of ammunition. And, of course, Billy expected significant target surveillance—stuff destroyed—so a person had to be fairly creative to deliver the goods for Billy. I had seen an intelligence report where the place where a trail intersected the Saigon River was called a sampan loading point. After that, if I shot up a similar area, I reported a sampan loading point having been destroyed. On one occasion, I saw a pile of logs near the river and reported the destruction of some sampan building materials. I also destroyed several suspected punji pits, which I grant you would be very hard to identify from 800 feet in the air. But, you needed to send in sightings of significance. I may have overdone on a couple of targets when I reported trail junctions having been destroyed. Actually, they were just two trails that crossed. Group headquarters kicked those back, saying they didn't count. I think they also kicked back a sampan building materials report. We were simply asked to redo the reports to describe the destruction of something more acceptable to Group. Nevertheless, our battalion still kept the title of best VR program.

A lot of times, it was difficult to know what actually had happened on the ground. On one occasion, I was flying mortar watch with a 25th Division pilot. He spotted something right along the east side of the Vam Co Dong River about eight klicks west of the base camp that he thought was a rocket-launching chute. I saw it but it didn't necessarily look like something you would use to launch rockets toward the base camp. In any event, he was going to call for fire from the 25th Division peashooters, so I called for some 8-inch fire with Victor Tango fuse. My first round landed exactly on top of whatever it was. That was that. I didn't report any body count but did report that a suspected rocket launching facility was destroyed. The next day, I took off for Cu Chi for my one and only mission as a forward observer for an ARVN operation in that vicinity. I didn't get back to the battalion until May 10, three days later. Billy was just ecstatic, telling me that the commander of the 25th Division's brigade at the base camp had taken some troops out to search the suspected rocket launcher site and found four VC bodies, as well as several blood trails leading out of the area. Maybe the brigade commander was just trying to claim some body count for his artillery because the brigade's 105mm howitzers had put a few rounds out there also. Or, maybe he was telling the truth. You just couldn't know in the body-count atmosphere that existed in Vietnam.

On another occasion, I was doing some VR work near Duc Hue SF camp, when we got a call from the battalion that the SF camp was taking 122mm mortar fire. (photo #17) I got hooked into the communications with Duc Hue and asked them to describe the impression that the rounds made on the ground. Although I had heard that some of the larger military facilities in Vietnam had counter-battery radar that could determine the source of artillery or mortar fire, it was not generally available, particularly to a small SF camp. But, there were ways to determine where an artillery or mortar round came from. When the round explodes, it leaves a "V" on the ground since the main force of the explosion goes out perpendicular to the length of the shell. It is easier to tell the source of an artillery shell because it comes in at a flatter angle. A mortar shell goes high in the air and comes in from a higher trajectory making a broader V. The open top of the V would point back to the direction from whence the round came. What you do is dissect the V in the middle and follow that line back to the origin. You can get an idea of the distance by how wide or narrow the V is.

When the SF guys on the ground told me the direction from which the round came and the width of the V, I looked for features on the ground that might act as cover for a mortar crew in the general vicinity from where the fire had to come. There was a recess in the ground next to an abandoned farm house just smack dab in that general area so I called artillery on it. The only guns with the range to hit the target were the 175s at our base camp battery. The first round was almost a miracle because it hit exactly where it was supposed to hit. Generally, it would have taken several rounds to get one within 20 meters of the target but this one hit right on the money. The 122mm mortar is a large one and probably had a four-man crew. I didn't report any body count but did report that a suspected mortar emplacement had been destroyed. I never heard whether the SF camp checked out the target area or whether they took any more 122mm mortar fire.

Our mission over Duc Hue had lasted much longer than expected, which brought up a problem with the little Bird Dog aircraft. The planes had no restrooms facilities, not even a pee tube. One ironclad rule was to seek relief before going up in the air. However, we had to drink lots of water to keep from getting dehydrated. As we headed back to base camp after our extended mission at Duc Hue, I was about to burst. Then, I noticed the stick on the floor. It could be hooked into the tail controls so that the backseat passenger could control the plane in an emergency. The stick was hollow with a cap on the top. Problem solved. I filled it up a couple of times and emptied it out the window. Some poor NVA guy was probably on the ground underneath, wondering where the droplets had come from.

The Duc Hue situation just points out the problem of determining what you might or might not be accomplishing if you are not actually on the ground. For the shooting we did in the triple canopy jungle, which was most of the time, there is no way you could really give a truthful count of bodies. There was just a lot of fudging going on and it didn't really provide an accurate picture of how the war was going. What would be more telling would be how many villages we were able to keep safe, both during the day and during the night.

I never really worried about taking ground fire because most of my flying was over heavy jungle. We could not see down through it and people on the ground could generally not see the Bird Dog through the foliage. A fair amount of War Zone C had been defoliated by Agent Orange, but there were still lots of tangled tree branches that kept people on the ground and in the air from seeing each other. The only time I had any concern was when we were flying around Nui Ba Dinh because for the most part it was just a pile of rocks without much foliage. Somebody could hide behind a rock and shoot at you without giving away their position. I thought somebody on the mountain could get a better bead on you where you were about straight out from them instead of being up above them. Also, it seemed like we were closer to the unfriendlies when we were flying around the mountain. We didn't fly around Nui Ba Dinh that much, but when we did I could imagine a bullet coming through the plane from just about any place on the mountainside. Then, I would consider what part of my body the round might tear through. It was more comforting to be sitting on my flack vest while we were flying over the top of the jungle, instead of having nothing between me and any shooter, other than the flimsy side of the Bird Dog.

I did shoot artillery at the side of the mountain several times. One time the battery commander at FSB Barbara wanted some direct fire at a target area his people had identified as a mortar emplacement. I think they had been taking mortar fire from that general vicinity and were getting fed up with it. The target area about straight out from the fire base, just a hundred or so feet up the mountain. It only took a split second for the round to hit. There was no lobbing the shell up in the air – it went just straight into the mountain. They said we got several rounds right on their target but it was difficult to know if we really hit anything. They seemed to be pretty happy, though.

One of my most interesting missions took place while I was on mortar watch one night. I was told that there was a target area they wanted to have saturated with fire. It was located northwest of the base camp, about five klicks from Cambodia. I was told I had all of the 25th Division's artillery, as well as our guns at the base camp and FSB Barbara. As I understood it, that was about eighteen 105mm howitzers, six 155mm howitzers, four 8-inch guns and four 175s.

When I got out to the target area, I called upon all of them to fire and then adjusted all of the various batteries to cover all parts of the targeted area. I felt somewhat like a conductor of an orchestra – calling for the 25th Division's guns to add a couple hundred meters and deflect to the right several degrees, for the guns at FSB Barbara to swing one way or the other, and for the guns at the base camp to do something else. I don't know how many rounds were expended but it had to be several hundred. I think they called it a mad minute, although it lasted longer than a minute. Nobody ever told me if there was any target surveillance by the infantry afterwards.

With all of the artillery and air strikes going into Tay Ninh Province, the terrain was pock marked with craters. (photo #18) The lion's share of the those were created by many dozens of B-52 strikes. The big birds carried 500 lb. and 750 lb. bombs, which left very large holes in the ground. Flying over Tay Ninh Province, some areas resembled Swiss cheese. I never saw one of the craters up close on the ground at the time, but 50 years later I did see one that had been preserved by the Communists at a location they claimed to have been the COSVN headquarters. It was about 25 feet across and 5 feet deep. It would have made a nice group foxhole or back yard swimming pool.

When the monsoon season came, all of those craters filled up with water. One could have called it the land of several thousand ponds—not quite as catchy as Minnesota's Land of 10,000 Lakes slogan. One of my ARVN friends told me that it did not take long for fish to populate the various craters. He claimed there was a variety of fish that could scoot a short distance over land from one body of water to the other so that most of the bomb craters were fishable. I don't know that I particularly believed it, but he fervently claimed it was true.

I had a good advantage in being able to anticipate the B-52 strikes, because we knew exactly where and when they would occur. On a couple of occasions, I was up in the air on a VR mission when a strike was scheduled. On those occasions, I got as close as I could to where the strikes were to go in so I could watch the bombs fall and take some pictures. It was absolutely breathtaking. (photo #19) Again, you could not hear the planes until the bombs started hitting. They dropped two by two so there were two rows of bombs going off in a line that extended for about two kilometers. When each pair of bombs hit, they sent a geyser of smoke, flame, dirt, and plant matter flinging into the air. You could see the concussion of the bombs going off in a rapid expanding sphere around each explosion.

I often thought about the poor guy on the ground who sees the first bombs going off a distance from him but then watches the progression of the two lines of bombs headed straight for him. The only hope would be that the bombs were all expended before they got to you. In reading reports about the effects on people who were near an explosion, but not injured by the blast or shrapnel, the concussion itself was enough to cause serious injury – bleeding from every possible bodily orifice.

All that being said, I suspect that quite a number of the bombing runs, perhaps even the majority, blew up nothing but uninhabited jungle. That was probably the case with a lot of our artillery missions and air strikes by fighter aircraft. It all pretty much hinged on the accuracy of the targeting intelligence.

On my last VR mission, I did something that had tempted me for quite some time. There was a concrete bridge over the Saigon River where the old Highway 13 crossed the river. That was on the border between Tay Ninh and Binh Long Provinces. It was 16 klicks north of our battery at Dau Tieng. The bridge was not passable because the supports on the southwest end had been destroyed, causing that end to fall into the river. However, the concrete span was still intact. I always thought it would be fun to put a round right in the middle of the span to see if I could buckle it. So, on my last VR mission I did just that. I called in the coordinates (49156355) and asked for fire on a suspected NVA bridge structure. The first round landed smack dab in the middle of the span, which caused the bridge to buckle. Mission accomplished. It did not contribute much to the war effort but it was satisfying to actually see the results of a mission.

8 ● Living it up at Sector

On November 28, a year to the day after I reported to Fort Sill in 1967 to begin artillery training, I got promoted to Captain. I was now Dai uy (die we) Jones. Billy asked me to come forward at the evening briefing that day and presented me with my Captain patch. He was going to pin it on but, when he couldn't find a pin, he just licked the back and acted like he was putting a stamp on my lapel. I had to hand it to him. He did have a good sense of humor at times. We had a few drinks and then I headed back to Sector for the night. I don't know that I would call it much of a promotion party.

The Special Forces folks were not going to let me get off that easy. The next night, I went to the B-32 club and, in keeping with their tradition, bought a $25 chit book and told everyone the drinks were on me. There were a lot of people drinking and, looking back, I don't know how $25 could have covered the cost. I may have added more later in the evening but have absolutely no recollection of doing so.

After eight Canadian Club and waters, I figured I had held up the honor of the artillery and started to get up. Just then, Sergeant Mills brought out a bottle of champagne and Colonel Hilling started a chant of "drink chug-a-lug." It was not my choosing but, again, to uphold the dignity of the artillery I downed the bottle. Mills then brought out another bottle, which I also finished off. I was told afterwards that a total of 13 bottles were shared amongst the group and that I had finished two or three of them. I have no memory of what happened from that time until I woke up the next morning in the bunk of one of the SF enlisted guys. Needless to say, my head was throbbing with pain. The fellow whose bunk I was in said that he had heard his door slam open in the middle of the night and that I essentially dived into his bunk just as he jumped out. He was kind enough to let me stay there for the night.

As I walked out into the morning daylight, all of the hooch girls looked at me as if I was the creature from the black lagoon. I have to admit there was somebody's puke all up and down my fatigues. It gave them quite a kick. That was what the SF guys expected a promotion party to look like.

I was told that six in-coming rockets had impacted just a short distance from the compound during the night. It would not have been an ideal time for a ground attack. There was a beehive of activity because B-36, the Mike Force, had arrived that morning for an operation to try to rescue a couple of our POWs that the intelligence people thought were being held in War Zone C.

A couple of Darvon helped to get my head back in order. I went to our headquarters at the base camp with two SF Majors to make sure the artillery was coordinated for the operation. B-36 had set up a command post at the B-32 compound and they were laying out plans for an assault on the suspected POW location. One of the Majors who I had taken to the base camp was sitting hunched over a radio with his shirt off and it looked like he had suffered major shrapnel wounds in the past because there were massive scars all over his back. He looked like a real no-nonsense guy. I was told the operation would kick off the next day or two, December 1 or 2, and that they wanted me to go up in the command and control chopper.

I received a visitor from the 25th Division's artillery on December 1, a Lieutenant Murphy. He told me that his commander had been asked by the brigade S-3 to send someone over to coordinate. When he asked his commander what he was supposed to coordinate, he was told, "I don't know, just go over and coordinate." It didn't make much sense but it was par for the course in my dealings with the brigade artillery folks.

I understood that the Mike Force operation did not materialize because the intelligence did not seem to pan out. During the confusion of that operation and my promotion party, I had somehow lost my Colt .45 sidearm. I looked everywhere but could not find it. I don't know that it was all that essential, as I would only need it if a Bird Dog went down and then it wouldn't do all that much good. I had fired a friend's .45 out in the desert near Eden during my college days and have to admit I couldn't really hit the broad side of a barn with it. I was pretty good with a rifle or shotgun, but pistols were not my forte. I did find it after several days. Apparently, either I or somebody trying to be helpful had checked it at the B-32 club and I was able to retrieve it there.

Billy paid a visit to Sector on December 17. It was his first. I think he was accompanied by the commander of the infantry brigade that was currently stationed at the base camp. They met with the province chief and then toured the TOC. For some reason, I was outside when the shot was fired. As soon as we heard it, I saw Billy crouch down and slap his right hand on his good old Colt .45 pistol.

The shot had come from inside the TOC so we all went to investigate. There was Hong, the province chief's son, writhing in pain on the floor. He was regarded as a bit of a screw-off by both the ARVN and U.S. troops. Anyway, Hong had been cleaning his M-1 carbine, which was a good thing, but it was unfortunate that he had overlooked the round in the chamber. The bullet hit him in the shoulder but it was not a life-threatening wound. Ingram went right to work performing first aid and got the situation under control in short order. Hong recovered nicely. I appreciated Hong's work because Billy high-tailed it right back to base camp and never paid us another visit.

The New Year started in the best possible way. I landed in Bangkok on January 2 for a five-day rest and recreation (R&R)

visit. Sam was at Tommie's Tourist Center, the R&R agency, to meet me. We had been corresponding so we had arranged our get-together ahead of time. It was really great to see her again.

I had also been in touch with Larry Crumrine, who graduated in the class ahead of me at dear old Valley High School, the home of the Vikings. Larry was a Captain in the Air Force and he was flying bombing missions out of Udorn Air Base in Thailand. Sam and I met up with Larry and she introduced him to one of her friends. Our happy foursome saw all of the Bangkok sights—the floating market, the Royal Barge, the Reclining Buddha, the Jade Buddha, Jim Thompson's Thai Silk Shop, and everything else. We rode a small elephant, at least long enough to get the obligatory photograph, and watched an inebriated bear in a cage chug-a-lug as many beers as people would give him. I don't think he was doing it to celebrate any type of promotion but I had to sympathize, knowing how his head would likely feel the next day.

Larry and I had lived in different worlds during high school. He was into sports, while I was inclined to be a borderline juvenile delinquent. We got along fine but were by no means close. Larry spent a couple of years in Nigeria as a Peace Corps volunteer. He joined the Air Force in 1966 and retired 27 years later as a full Colonel. He amassed 845 combat hours flying an F-4d fighter on missions, which he described as mostly "into NVN with about 1/3 going somewhere else (Big secret huh?)." He received 29 Air Medals and 2 Distinguished Flying Crosses, among other decorations. Besides all of that, he had such a magnetic personality that people were quickly drawn to him.

It may be that we formed a bond in Bangkok because we were both engaged in the business that some irreverently described as "killing Commies for Christ," but I definitely think we felt a mutual brotherhood. Over the years since then, I made a couple of efforts to get in contact with him but had no luck. Larry died on August 15, 2014. I was told that when he was informed his condition was terminal, he had a drink, smoked a cigar and then departed on his last flight into the great beyond. I have kicked myself since then for not making a more concerted effort to get back in touch with him. He only had a 3-day leave so Sam and I had two days together after he went back to Udorn.

Between my two Bangkok trips, Sam and I had written back and forth on a weekly basis and I was growing quite fond of her. She was smart, good-hearted, and not reluctant to speak her mind. I was interested in shopping for Asian antiques and she did not hesitate to criticize my bargaining skills or, better stated, lack of the same. During one of our shopping ventures, I found an ancient wooden carving of the head of what looked to be a Mongol warlord, festooned with a couple of dragons. Try as I might, I could not get the merchant to reduce the price to a reasonable level. Sam mentioned several times that I did not know what I was doing. Several weeks after I got back to my unit, a package arrived and it contained the warlord's head. She informed me she'd gotten it for about half of my last offer.

I learned more about Sam on this trip. She said she had grown up in the country and had the misfortune of having gone through an arranged marriage to a local big wheel in her teen years. Having gotten to know her strong independent streak, I was not surprised that she dumped him and fled to Bangkok to make her way in that world. I admired her gumption.

I had bought a new journal in Bangkok and started recording my 1969 ventures when I got back from R&R. The new journal burned up, along with all of my other belongings, in the attack on Sector on April 11. As a result, I have no written notes of what occurred during that three-month period. But, I still have a number of memories of that time.

One thing that sticks out in my mind is the nighttime temperature. Although it never got cold in the southern part of Vietnam, January was probably the coolest month. The daytime temperature was generally in the high eighties and, of course, there was always the humidity. A few times in December or January, the night-time temperature would get down close to 70 degrees. Most of the time I slept with just a sheet but when the temperature got down near 70 a sheet did not do the trick. That required one or two Army blankets. For those whose bodies had acclimated to the hot climate, 70 degrees was teeth-chattering weather. It seems strange that you would have to bundle up at that temperature. During the warmer weather, I would generally have a shot of brandy or schnapps at bedtime because the heat made it hard to get to sleep. In the wintertime, that was not necessary but I did it anyway.

Another thing I recall was the fact that so many older women had deep red or black teeth. I was told it was because they chewed betel nuts. I never tried them, but I understood they had a stimulating effect. The nut is the fruit of the areca palm and is widely used in South and Southeast Asia. Men also chewed betel nuts but it didn't seem to be quite so noticeable.

One time when I was driving in Tay Ninh, an ARVN solider flagged me down to show me his teeth. He opened his mouth and pointed to his two top front teeth. One was bright red and the other was robin egg blue. Both had upside down gold hearts implanted in them. I assumed that the red and blue parts were enamel. He must has just gotten the teeth fixed and was very proud of them. I nodded my admiration and have to admit I have never seen anything like it. They were certainly more attractive than teeth stained by betel nut.

Having grown up in farm country, it was unusual to see crops growing in the wintertime but it was just business as usual in the hot South Vietnam climate. I was told that rice farmers could produce three crops per year and they really worked hard at it.

Before planting, they would plow the fields to turn over the stubble from the last crop. I suppose that in some places they used tractors for plowing, but in Tay Ninh Province the farmers did their plowing behind a water buffalo. (photo #20) After the field was leveled a bit, they would go out to plant rice seedlings in a muddy rice paddy. They would poke a small stick into the ground and stuff a seedling into the hole. It had to be exhausting and uncomfortable work. When the rice was ready to harvest, they would go out with a hand scythe to cut it down. The severed stocks would be gathered into small bundles to dry. When they had dried sufficiently, the bundles would be thrashed into a basket with woven reeds on three sides to keep rice kernels from flying out onto the ground. They would whack the sheaves into the catch basket at the bottom until the kernels came off. Then they would take the basket of kernels to be processed by removing the husks.

I would often hear servicemen at the base camp speaking about how the Vietnamese were lazy but they had never seen these people working in the field. Quite frankly, I don't know how they did it, especially in the heat.

It was interesting to observe the customs with respect to special occasions. Once I was driving through Tay Ninh City with Tom, the MACV interpreter, when we encountered what I took to be a funeral procession. There was a very ornate horse-drawn wagon that resembled a brightly-decorated stagecoach. Tom said it was a funeral hearse that contained the body of a deceased. There were quite a number of people in attendance and I remarked that it must have been a prominent person. Tom said that some of the people were paid mourners. The more money a person had, the more mourners he could hire for his funeral. I'm sure there were people in attendance who weren't paid, but that was the first time I had ever heard of paid funeral attendees.

Weddings were obviously more cheerful events and nobody had to be paid to attend. My friend, Thieu uy Dinh, invited me to attend his sister's wedding at Cao Xa Village. He said it would be a seven-day celebration and that I was invited to attend the whole thing. I figured two visits to the event was about all I could do.

I went to the first day, which was on February 1. I arrived at Cao Xa after the marriage ceremony but just in time for a party at the bride's family home. There were a number of older gentlemen, including the bride's father, sitting on either side of a long, narrow table in the family home. They were all wearing black formal-looking gowns. We started out drinking rice brandy and smoking loosely-packed cigarettes. I had quit smoking several months earlier but figured I would join in as part of the festivities. We were fed royally with all kinds of dishes, accompanied with rice wine and beer. Some of the food was pretty good but some was sort of hard to get down. There were bone fragments in the chicken, as usual, and some of the pork still had the skin attached. Everyone was so cordial and friendly that it was not too difficult to overlook the imperfections in the food. It is all in what you were used to eating.

The next day, Sergeant Haney and I accompanied the bride and her family on a ritual march to the groom's house where a large party was underway. (photo #22) There must have been 400 guests at the party. There was a large open-air gathering place filled with tables, all of which had large pots of food on them. I was doing fine until I came across a big chunk of fat, hairy meat, which I kept shoving down to the bottom of my bowl. Eventually, I sneaked it off to the side when nobody was looking.

There was a band with typical Vietnamese instruments – several stringed instruments that kind of resembled guitars or banjos. All of the younger people had access to American rock and roll and I think they just assumed that I knew all of the songs by the Beach Boys and anyone else that was popular at the time. Quite frankly, I was a nineteen-fifties person – Elvis Presley, Bill Haley and Comets, and some of the folk types like Peter, Paul and Mary. The younger people kept pestering and imploring me to sing an American song. The only lyrics I could come up with on the spot were several verses of Tom Dooley. I know it wasn't exactly the right song for a wedding but luckily there were not many people who recognized the words anyway. I did a fractured rendition of what I could remember and people seemed to be somewhat satisfied. Several of the younger people suggested an encore, perhaps hoping for something better. Thankfully, nobody pushed very hard for more. The only other song that came to mind was "Here we have Idaho," which would not have been much better for the occasion. Even though my singing was pitiful, everyone was very kind and friendly. I felt a real kinship with these folks. (photo #21)

When I think about the Communists taking over Cao Xa Village six years later, it still causes me great pain. Those in this little Catholic village who had fought so hard against the Communists for so many years to preserve their freedom and religion were likely either killed outright or sent to wretched reeducation camps, if they were not lucky enough to escape to Cambodia, which was just a few miles to the west.

There was a lot of concern that this year's Tet, which came on February 17, would bring another attack like the Tet Offensive of 1968. However, that did not materialize. On the evening before Tet, we had a party with a group of ARVN airborne troops who were then occupying the transient quarters next door. That afternoon I had seen ducks and chickens being slaughtered and their blood being drained into bowls. I knew that the fellows did not let anything go to waste – feet, eyeballs, heads, and everything else – and decided I would hole up in my room. Sergeant Haney was aware of my plans but decided to upset them. While everybody was gathering next door, he yelled for me to come, which pretty much gave away the fact that I was there. So, I joined the celebration. There were many delicacies, most of which involved every conceivable part of a duck and chicken having been crushed up and soaked in duck and chicken blood. If it were not for the gracious attitude of our hosts, I might have bailed out but that would not have been right. (photo #23)

During my days at Sector, all of the Vietnamese folks I dealt with on official business were men, primarily ARVN soldiers. I also had the opportunity to get acquainted with a few Vietnamese women. All of the people who worked at the orphanage were women and I worked primarily with the matron, who was elderly, and her second in command, who was probably around 40 years old. Both were really nice people.

Shortly after I started working with the orphanage, I became acquainted with a lady who I believe was a government social worker. Her name was Mai and she was probably in her mid-30s. She invited me to visit a school whose student body was comprised of mentally and physically handicapped kids. I have to admit I was a little surprised that such a school existed, but it looked like the kids were well cared for and they were sure nice youngsters. I still have a folder with pictures that they drew especially for me. We had a party at the school and, except for my inability to speak the language, it would have been just like a party back in the states for a similarly-situated student body.

During future years, I often had occasion to be with social workers who were dedicated to helping people and Mai would have been indistinguishable with that group in her actions. She did speak some English so we could converse without the need for an interpreter.

When we had parties for the kids, I did not have to invite Mai because she usually got word and was there pitching in along with my team members and the ladies at the orphanage. Our relationship was strictly professional, although I somehow got the idea that she might be interested in me. Maybe it is just an inflated male ego.

I did make the acquaintance of a lady named Snow, who was reputed to be the wife of an ARVN Major. She was a Chinese national, who spoke fairly good English. I would see her around town for time-to-time and always enjoyed conversing with her. There were a quite a few women who worked in the Cao Dai Holy See but I did not have an opportunity to get acquainted with them during my tour of duty. It was interesting to me that during religious gatherings in the main temple, the men would be on the right side of the long hallway leading up to the altar, while the women would be over on the left side. All in all, it was a male dominant society, pretty much like ours at that time.

Another thing I remember clearly was the proliferation of ARVN outposts. These were just little two or three men posts that seemed to be scattered all around the area. There had been one north of town when we went to pay solatium to the parents of the child who had been run over by an ammo truck, another when I went to investigate the artillery incident at Suoi Day, and I passed one every day on my way to and from base camp. They looked like a large water well with sand-bagged sides and a peaked hat on top. They sat on top of a raised mound of earth and I believe they had a fortified bunker down below. Every time I drove past the one on the way to base camp, there would be a couple of ARVN soldiers inside of the well, either taking it easy in hammocks or playing some kind of instrument. It didn't look like they could withstand much of an attack. However, on one trip into base camp early in the morning, I saw two ARVN soldiers about 100 feet from that outpost looking down at three dead bodies neatly stacked in a pyramid configuration. I assume that they must have had a fire fight during the night so maybe the outposts were not as toothless as they appeared.

Even though the country was at war, the civilians did seem to have pastimes to keep them occupied. One thing that I remember is a motorcycle race that went from Saigon to Tay Ninh and back. I was out driving with Tom on the main road, still within the city limits, when a parade of motorcycles started coming into town from the direction of Saigon. I asked Tom if he knew what it was all about and he said it was a motorcycle race.

While there weren't many civilian cars on the road, there were quite a few motorcycles. There were a few young guys on motorcycles that hung around the commercial section of Tay Ninh, looking like hoods or juvenile delinquents. They must have been acquainted with James Dean and his movie motorcycle buddies because they had that look about them. I don't know that they got into criminal mischief, but they certainly seemed to want to give that appearance.

One of the problems for our ARVN friends was government corruption. It was not unusual for policemen and government officials to expect payment under the table for performing certain official acts that citizens would have a right to expect for free. It was common knowledge amongst the populace that this was just a fact of life. I asked Lieutenant Dinh how people put up with it. He said that there wasn't much you could do about it. He said that people did not really get upset about it unless an official got greedy. There was a generally-acceptable level of corruption that everybody expected, primarily because the pay for government officials, soldiers, and the like was unrealistically low. The only people that were regarded as crooks were those that exceeded the acceptable level.

I think one of the things that eventually lead to the downfall of the government was the fact that so many people were too concerned about feathering their individual nests. When corruption goes to an extreme, it is very difficult for the afflicted populace to support the government – something that the U.S. seemed to ignore in Vietnam.

Although it was not outright corruption, Billy sort of treaded around the periphery in his quest for military decorations. One of the things he tasked me with was to get him metals from just about any possible source – the Air Force, MACV, the Philippian Civic Action Group, and the Vietnamese government. Let's start with the Vietnamese government. Not long after I went to Sector, Billy asked that I get some sort of military decoration for him from the Province Chief. I turned that job over to Sergeant Haney, who had a knack for getting just about anything from just about anyone. It didn't take long for Haney to report back that the Province Chief would be happy to confer a Vietnamese Cross of Gallantry with bronze star upon Colonel McDonald. However, Billy had gotten wind of a Vietnamese award called the Medal of Honor. He asked that he be awarded that metal, instead of the gallantry cross. When I reported back that the Medal of Honor was a lesser decoration, that didn't seem to make much difference. Apparently, the wording of the lesser medal conveyed a more heroic message. Eventually, Billy settled for a Cross of Gallantry with bronze star, which he received shortly before the end of his tour.

Billy knew that I worked with Allen 10 (I can't remember his name, just his call sign), the Air Force FAC assigned to MACV, and he asked me to propose that the Air Force award him some kind of decoration. The next time I went out on a fire mission with Allen 10, I reluctantly raised the subject with him from the back seat. I prefaced my remarks by saying I thought it was inappropriate but the Colonel had requested that I ask that he be put in for an award. He said he would check but I don't believe he ever got back to me on it. I merely told the Colonel that the request had been made and was under consideration.

Billy also asked about getting an award from PhilCAG. I didn't have any contacts with them, other than seeing some their people at the orphanage once. Nevertheless, I asked Sergeant Haney to see what he could do but I don't think anything ever panned out with that. Billy was also interested in an award from MACV and we gave that a try but I don't think Billy ever got a medal from them.

Around the end of February, Sergeant Haney was brought back to the base camp and replaced by Sergeant Dunn, an Army lifer who had volunteered for Vietnam duty so as to enhance his chances of promotion down the line. That was not an uncommon strategy for those who wanted to make a career of the service. Combat experience was essential for the career guys.

Dunn was not a wheeler dealer like Haney, but he did a decent job of scrounging for our little group. He settled in fairly quickly, getting into the details of the work, as well as getting acquainted with some of the local nationals, particularly a young lady he introduced as Dolly Tan. Having been confined to the base camp for the first part of his tour, Dunn took advantage of his new-found freedom to get himself a steady girlfriend. I didn't have any particular heartburn about it so long as it did not interfere with his work. Haney had had any number of lady friends, but no steady girl. We had a couple of parties for the kids during Dunn's tenure and he brought Dolly to both to help out. The ladies at the orphanage did not seem to mind and Dolly certainly did her part.

Some of the ARVNs took an interest in Sergeant Dunn, particularly when he would take his hat off in the TOC. I noticed a time or two that several of the ARVNs would titter a bit when he removed his hat. I asked Lieutenant Dinh what the deal was once and was told the giggling was because Dunn was pretty much bald on top. Apparently, they believed that baldness resulted from too much self-pleasuring. After I related this tidbit to Dunn, I noticed he seemed to keep his hat on more of the time.

Dunn did something that caused me great displeasure after he had been at Sector for about a month. One night, I heard some shooting that sounded like it was fairly close. It was not particularly out of the ordinary and I wrote it off as a little dust-up or nervous trigger finger. Come to find out the next morning, Dunn and one of my RTOs had been whooping it up around town and squeezed off a number of shots into the air for some unknown reason. I told Dunn that there would be a visit to the stockade if anything like it ever happened again. Although it was not related to this incident, he was brought back to the battalion soon afterward to help out on a firing battery. He was replaced by Ingram, who had come to the liaison section as a Specialist First Class several months earlier and just been promoted to Sergeant. He was the best.

One thing that greatly saddened me during this period of time was an occasion that I went to the Tay Ninh East air strip to go out on a VR mission with Allen 10. His plane was based at the air strip, which was located just west of B-32 and north of Sector. I was climbing into the Air Force Bird Dog when I noticed a stack of body bags at the end of the air strip. There had recently been some heavy contact at a couple of infantry fire support bases in the province. I would estimate that there were somewhere around 15 body bags stacked on the air strip and they looked larger than those that would have accommodated ARVN troops. It occurred to that they had been hauled over to the Tay Ninh East air strip to await air transport to Saigon so that they would not be obvious to the troops near the air strip at the base camp.

It was also during this period that a horrendous collision occurred between two Cobra gunships at the base camp. Apparently, they were located side-by-side in their revetments. Both gunships took off at the same time and it appeared that they had gotten their signals crossed on which way each was going to go. Instead of going in opposite directions, they flew toward each other, colliding into a gigantic fireball. I didn't witness it but I came on the scene not too long afterwards. It was one of those things that just broke your heart.

Just like everyone else in Vietnam, I kept a close track of how many days I had left on my tour. I was scheduled to serve a year in-country, which would have been up on July 17 or 18. However, if I went home then, I would still have about four and a half months to serve until I was released at the end of November. One of the other officers in the battalion said that they would probably send me to someplace like Fort Carson, Colorado, to march in military parades until my time was up. That did not appeal to me in any fashion.

I started looking at the Army regulations and found that a person could extend his tour any number of days up to a year. If your Vietnam tour ended with 90 days or less left to serve, a person would be released from active duty upon return to the US. Now, that seemed to be a much better alternative.

I put in my paperwork to extend my tour by 45 days so that I would land at Travis Air Force Base in California with 89 days left to serve. A request for an extension was pretty much a no-brainer for the big brass because they were strapped for personnel. People at home were burning their draft cards, traveling to Canada, signing up for National Guard units and doing just about anything else to keep from taking an all-expense-paid trip to the Republic of Vietnam. With the approval of my extension request, I was now scheduled to jump on the Freedom Bird at the end of August.

Then came April 11 when all of my earthly possessions were blow up at Sector. The various explosions and consequent fire destroyed my SKS rifle, my beloved flight helmet, my flak vest, my uniforms, my passport and other papers, and just about every other meager piece of property I owned in Vietnam. Luckily, I had sent my carved Mongol head home before that happened and it still hangs on the wall in my home. I put in a claim for the destroyed property, including the electricity converter that prompted my trip to Saigon, and the Army kindly paid it.

However, I was planning to take a seven-day leave in Singapore in the next several months so I had to go back to Saigon to get a new passport. This time, I had to actually go into town for a short period of time and I really marveled at the sights. It was a real city, as opposed to Tay Ninh, which was somewhat of a backwater. I thought it would be nice to actually have some time to go to some of the tourist places, but there was not enough time for that on this trip. There was air conditioning all over the place, which felt great until you stepped outside.

On May 1, the same day I went to get my new passport, the liaison section terminated its operations at Sector and moved back to the base camp. While we had been able to effectively move our liaison work to the Province Chief's compound, it was not ideal. The only memorable thing about our quarters there was that they were infested by gigantic flying beetles. These things were about 3 inches long and hard as a rock. When they hit a metal light shade, it sounded just like a bullet striking. It took a while to find out what was making the noise. The beetles would see the light, they would fly towards it, they would hit the light shade, and everybody would duck.

The monsoons started just about when I got back to base camp. About 3:00 pm every afternoon, the skies would open up and pour out more water than you would imagine a cloud could hold. It was amazing how it rained so regularly and so much. A person got soaked through by just standing in the rain for a minute or two. It had a wonderful effect on the roads in the base camp. The soil was red volcanic ash and, when it got soaked, it turned into the clingiest mud you could imagine. If you took a step, almost an inch of it would cling to the bottom of your boot. Another step would cause another layer to attach. After several steps, you had about 4-5 inches of the stuff on the bottom of your boots, which caused great instability. It was practically impossible to get it off. By late morning the next day, the mud would be dried out and you would be choking on clouds of red dust stirred up by vehicle traffic. It was hard to decide which was worse—the clingy mud or the choking dust.

On May 8, I got word that Ingram and I were to go out on a field operation with the 15th ARVN Armored Cavalry Squadron. The operation was to take place somewhere between Cu Chi and Trang Bang. As Ingram and I were getting ready to head to Cu Chi, we were approached by the ARVNs, who said they would need fuel for their vehicles. I'm not sure why that job fell to us but I told them we would try to take care of it for them.

Ingram made arrangements for the ARVNs to get their trucks through the base camp perimeter to load up at the fuel farm, or whatever they called it. There were three long tanker trucks and all three started slurping up fuel from the storage tanks. It dawned on the folks at the base camp that their supply was going to be seriously depleted and they got busy trying to cut off the supply. The ARVNs resisted so it took a while to break them loose from their hoses. It seemed like the ARVNs were taking advantage and they did end up getting lots of fuel before the base camp folks brought the fuel heist to a halt.

That evening at the Cu Chi Base Camp, we were speaking with some of the people stationed there. They described an odd phenomenon that occurred some nights when everything was quiet. They said at times they could hear people speaking in Vietnamese late at night, which was really odd because all of the local nationals left the base camp before sundown. They said it was hard to explain. About 30 years later I read The Tunnels of Cu Chi, which provided the explanation. It is very likely that the Vietcong had tunnels right under the base camp at that time. Weird!

We went out on the field operation the next day. I got paired up with an old Army Major, who was a MACV advisor assigned to the ARVN unit. He reminded me of Major Jones in The Comedians. The fellow had been in the Army for 30 years but he was still just a Major. He was rattled at times and he talked practically non-stop, but he was decent sort.

His Jeep had cans of Pabst Blue Ribbon Beer shoved into every nook and cranny. As he drove along, he would reach for a beer for himself and offer me one. I guess it had never occurred to me to drink hot beer, but it wasn't all that bad. As he was veering back and forth, he mentioned that there were mines and booby traps all over the area, which turned out to be close to the truth because the ARVNs lost a tank on a mine that same day.

I didn't have occasion to call for any artillery until the middle of the night. The ARVNs were a bit nervous in the dark and requested that we call in some illumination rounds. I did so and learned what it sounded like to be close to an incoming giant projectile. You could hear the round coming and it sounded like an approaching freight train. The rounds went off high in the air, providing a bright, eerie light for what seemed like a couple of minutes. I was surprised that the rounds came in just where I had hoped they would because it was not particularly easy to call in fire where you want it from a position on the ground, especially at night.

It only took one day of tramping around in the field for some sort of fungus to form on my feet. The infantry folks were happy to lend some foot powder and that helped. It made a person appreciate what the ground pounders had to put up with on a daily basis.

The next day, the First of the Fifth U.S. Cavalry, which was operating along with the ARVNs, also lost a tank. I had been out for two days and not seen much action, except for trying to keep the Pabst Blue Ribbon cans from exploding when I opened them for the Major and myself. Later in the day, Lieutenant McQuestion from our battalion was flown out to the field to relieve me. I was scheduled to begin my seven-day leave in Singapore on May 12.

It was that evening that Billy told me how pleased he was with the body count on the rocket launcher mission. It was great to see him so happy. I spent that night at the battalion and was awarded my first Air Medal. It was a bit of a surprise, because I did not realize that anyone at the battalion was keeping track of my flying time. Apparently, every time I went up with the 74th RAC, somebody tallied up the time. They didn't do it when I went out on mortar watch or with Allen 10. I calculated that I had a total of about 300 hours in the air. It was by far the best time in my tour of duty.

I arrived in Singapore on May 12 and Sam was there to meet me at the Airport. She was very pretty in a lavender dress. When we got into the taxi on our way to the hotel, I had an interesting experience. The driver asked us what our names were. When I told him I was Jim Jones, he practically laughed his head off. Apparently, that was an unusual name, or perhaps a funny one, in Singapore.

We stayed at the storied Raffles Hotel that evening. The hotel had a large lounge with big overstuffed chairs. As I recall, there were large fans attached to a series of shafts hooked to the ceiling. These were not rotating fans, but a row of fans shaped like gigantic catalpa leaves that were affixed to each shaft. The shafts with their attached fans were moved back and forth in tandem by a motor. I think they had been operated by hand in British colonial years.

My 27th birthday was on May 13. Sam and I had champagne and enjoyed the celebration. It was so great to be staying in the lap of luxury with a charming woman. I put Vietnam completely out of my mind for the seven days.

Singapore was a very clean city. We saw signs indicating that you would be in big trouble if you threw chewing gum on the sidewalk. We saw all of the sights – the Tiger Balm Gardens, established by the maker of that all-purpose salve, snake charmers on the waterfront, and whatever else. There were plenty of obnoxious people wanting to sell you something, show you something, or get you enmeshed in some kind of scheme to take your money. As long as the head of this little country was going after the gum chewers, he could have also taken action against the obnoxious hucksters.

One afternoon, Sam and I went to a restaurant that served dim sum. I thought it was some kind of food, but it turned out to be waitresses walking around offering you any number of different dishes that you would select and then pay for. It was my first encounter with dim sum and I thought it was great idea. One night we went to a Russian restaurant and I have to say it was nothing to write home about.

I had taken an interest in antique figurines of Asian ladies carved out of various types of minerals. I bought a lady carved from jade, one carved in gold stone, and another out of tiger eye. They were exquisite. I got all three of them at a lapidary shop and offered my American Express card. The shop owner declined, saying that he would be charged 7% by American Express and I would have to pay more than the agreed price. However, he said he would take a check. That just about floored me. Somebody in Singapore was willing to take a check from somebody who lived in the United States that he didn't even know? He said he figured I was good for it. He would not place the check for collection in Singapore but would endorse it payable to a lapidary shop located west of Chicago to pay for items he got from that shop. This was an interesting lesson in international commerce.

After a couple more days, Sam and I had seen all of the sights of Singapore and heard that the nearby city of Johor Bahru, Malaysia, had an interesting mosque and palace so we decided to pay a visit. We hired a taxi to take us to see the sights and had a good time. What I did not realize is that Thai citizens do not have the same ability to travel freely from one country to another like Americans do. At the border crossing back into Singapore, Sam was initially denied entry because she did not have the proper visa. Apparently, her visa from Thailand was only a one-entry permit, or something like that. After spending about a half an hour going back and forth with the immigration people, they took pity and allowed us back into Singapore.

On May 19, I reluctantly said goodbye to Sam at the airport. We talked about perhaps getting together after my tour of duty was over. And, we continued to communicate back and forth on a weekly basis.

When I got back to the base camp the next day, I was informed that I would be the night duty officer in the battalion fire direction center until a replacement arrived. I thought that would be an interesting change of scenery because the action generally happened at night. On the other hand, many nights turned out to be very boring. One benefit was that the TOC was the only air-conditioned building in the battalion. It had to be kept cool for the FADAC computer.

After several boring days, the Communists kept us busy the night of June 5. They hit just about every unit in the vicinity with rocket and mortar fire. We were answering calls for fire practically all night. They shot about 87 mortar rounds and 25 rockets into the base camp. The next night they hit FSB Crook with a ground attack. It was located out in the jungle generally northwest of the base camp. The infantry reported a count of more than 400 NVA bodies the following morning.

A week later, the new officer arrived to take over the assistant S-3 job on a permanent basis. At that point, I became the assistant intelligence officer, which put me back up in the air. As we were filling the plane up with fuel that same afternoon, a couple of rockets landed on the air strip – one of them landed just about 100 meters from us—a tiny bit more elevation would not have been good. That was an exciting way to get back into VR work.

The night of June 20, I spent about 5 hours in the air on mortar watch because there was a lot of fighting going on in the southern part of the city. There was not much we could do about it because we had no contact with friendly forces on the ground. But, while we were over the base camp, we noticed flares were being fired over in Cambodia and, every once in a while, we could see a shell exploding. It looked as if some fairly serious fighting was going on over the border but I never learned whether U.S. forces were involved or whether it was between the Communists and Cambodians.

On June 27, I had a strange experience while out on mortar watch west of the base camp. I noticed lots of new lights just across the border in Cambodia. Every time we flew near them, all the lights went out. When we left the immediate area, they all went on again. The intelligence people had reported that the 88th NVA Regiment was supposedly in that area. The next day, I went out on a VR mission in that same area. The place where all the lights were the previous night was now occupied by two large herds of water buffalo. There were lots of recent truck and foot trails, showing heavy traffic. It was all in King's X land so there was nothing we could do about it.

The infantry brigade commander at the base camp implemented a new counter-mortar program on July 8 that left people scratching their heads. Gen. Ewell decided that there was not enough counter-mortar firing going on so he set a standard of 200 rounds for one of his batteries and 200 rounds for others. So, each time the base camp got some incoming mortar fire, a minimum of 400 rounds had to be fired back, if you could even figure out where back was. After the policy was implemented, two rounds of incoming impacted outside of the berm. A total of 1,300 rounds were fired in accordance with the counter-mortar program. The problem was that the grid where the mortar fire was suspected of having come from could not be cleared by the Vietnamese. So, all of the counter-mortar fire had to be shot at other places. Weird.

On July 9, Billy bid farewell to the unit and headed home. We got a new Lieutenant Colonel as commander of the battalion. He was not impressive enough to merit a note in my journal, but I can tell you he was a bit of a zero. He may have been the guy in charge of the battalion when it took part in the Cambodian incursion the following year. If so, he got some good people killed in that operation by sheer stupidity.

On August 15, I went back to Sector so that the Province Chief could pin a Vietnamese Cross of Gallantry with bronze star on my lapel. Sergeant Haney had told me eight months earlier that the Province Chief was putting me in for the medal. I still didn't know what the decoration was all about. The following year, when I was working in the U.S. Senate, I sent the citation to the Congressional Research Service for interpretation. It said:

As an outstanding officer with combat experience and great determination to exterminate the Communists, Captain Jones always accomplished his assignments successfully.

He ranked first in coordinating the counter offensive operation in Ninh Thanh Village, Phu Khuong District, Tay Ninh Province on June 7, 1969. Despite strong enemy forces and vigorous resistance, the above-mentioned officer concentrated his firepower accurately and efficiently so that the operating unit prevailed and routed the enemy from the defensive zone. His great contribution to the victory amounted to the defeat of 83 Communists and the capture of weapons of all types – 04 B.40 – 04 K.54 – 02 Carbine – 18 AK guns and related ammunition and important documents.

Parenthetically, a B-40 is an RPG and a K-40 is an NVA pistol. The certificate was signed by Lieutenant Colonel Le-Van-Thien. I was kind of at a loss to figure out what it was all about. It could be that he was talking about the busy nights we had on June 5 and 6, or it could be something that was essentially made up. I don't know. It didn't make a whole lot of difference because they got my service number wrong anyway, mistaking a 7 for 2 since the 7 did not have an additional line through it. I didn't figure it was worth the effort to try to correct the mistake so that the medal could be added to my Army record. I did get a nice citation suitable for framing.

Much more meaningful to me was the send-off I got from my friends at B-32. Colonel Hilling presented me with a plaque thanking me for my work with his people. I have hung it on my wall everywhere I have worked since that time because it is a reminder of our kinship. They were great people to associate with.

So, I had my going-away party at the orphanage on August 17, got shot at over Cambodia on the 18th, had to land in Duc Hoa to fill up with oil on the 20th, and boarded a Freedom Bird on the 29th. It was a World Airways plane destined for home sweet home. I sat down in my assigned seat right next to a guy from Malad, Idaho. He was a helicopter pilot. His name was Thomas James Jones, pretty close to my full name, James Thomas Jones. Small world. I heard that he died in a commercial helicopter crash several years later.

1. Time to get serious about life.

2. Sam in Singapore, May 1969.

3. 175 mm gun, B Battery, Tay Ninh Base Camp.

4. B-32 Special Forces Camp.

5. Catholic Church at Cao Xa village.

6. Sgt. Ingram and ammo dump next to our hooch.

7. With Lt. Tanh at Sector HQ.

8. Cyclos in downtown Tay Ninh.

9. Jim and Captain Thanh, 1969.

10. Dance performance at orphanage.

11. Cao Dai Temple interior.

12. Sector compound after April 11 attack.

13. Jim surveying area after the Sector attack.

14. Summer party at Base Camp.

15. Tay Ninh Base Camp, Nui Ba Dinh in background.

16. Captain Spoor and Jim.

17. Duc Hue SF Camp, south of Angel's Wing

18. B-52 bomb craters northwest of Nui Ba Dinh.

19. B-52 strike in War Zone C.

20. Plowing a rice field.

21. Jim and Tom with Lt. Dinh at his sister's wedding, 1969.

22. Procession to the bride's house.

23. Tet dinner with ARVN rangers, 1969.

24. Do Thi Cung, Kelly, and Jim at Cao Dai Holy See.

9 ● Reflections on the way home

The long flight to Travis Air Force Base gave me a chance to reflect on my 407 days in the Republic of Vietnam. With the anticipation of soon being able to tread again on good old American soil, it was not easy to get any sleep. The guys on the plane exuded a great sense of relief, but there was also a bit of apprehension in the air. We had all heard of the unrest back home over the war and did not know what to expect upon arrival in the U.S.

I was looking forward to reading real newspapers and watching network television. That is not to say that the Armed Forces news outlets were bad or unreliable, but a person got the distinct impression that there was a certain amount of spin. I had not watched a lot of programming on Armed Forces Television during my tour. We did not get TV at Sector and about the only thing I watched back at base camp was the evening news report. It always had coverage of what was going on in-country, as well as what President Johnson and then President Nixon were doing that might affect the war.

Of course, everyone watched Bobbie, the TV weather girl, who reported the weather around Vietnam. She was a blonde-haired, blue-eyed phenomenon, who tended to raise expectations of happy weather each time she reached toward the top of the map in her miniskirt. The weather appeared to be reported in an even-handed manner but one had the abiding feeling that war coverage might be less so. Enemy losses seemed to be played up, while ours were not dwelt upon.

The newspapers we got were also inclined to give a rosy picture of what was happening in the war. We got both the *Army Times* and the *Pacific Stars and Stripes*. Rather than describing the manner in which the war news was reported, as it affected Tay Ninh Province, a review of some of the headlines is instructive.

The following are all from issues of *Stars and Stripes*.

3RD RED DRIVE REPORTED NEAR (Aug. 20, 1968) This article speculated about a new Communist offensive in South Vietnam, based on a flurry of attacks in Tay Ninh Province. It reported 59 enemy killed in the earlier-mentioned attack on Katum SF camp, along with 2 camp defenders. It told of 83 Communists killed at the 25th Division's FSB Buell and another 50 killed by the 25th in a sweep east of Tay Ninh. There was no indication of friendly casualties.

Armor Plows Into Red Regiment (Aug. 21, 1968) The 25th Division kills 101 Communist troops east of Tay Ninh City. This time the paper reports U.S. casualties of 14 killed and 98 wounded.

182 Reds Die Against GI's Wall of Fire (Aug. 22, 1968) The wall of fire was constructed by the 25th Division about 14 miles east of Tay Ninh. According to the report, "U.S. infantrymen raised a dike of firepower against a human wave of Communists, killing 182 attacking Viet Cong and losing only one man themselves." The article speaks of the "Reds swarming into sight" and being "mowed down" by machine-gun fire. It is not clear whether the fire formed a wall or a dike. Of interest, also, is the fact that distances in all of the articles are given in miles, while the military always used kilometers.

U.S. Troops Smash Tay Ninh Attack (Aug. 26, 1968) Troops of the 25th Division "fought off North Vietnamese attackers near Tay

Ninh, killing 62 Communists." The article reported U.S. losses at 8 dead and 45 wounded.

GIs Repel Push on Tay Ninh and Loc Ninh (Sept. 18, 1968) The paper reported 58 Communists killed when the 25th Division "beat back a massive ground attack" at FSB Buell, a couple of miles north of Sector. U.S. casualties were 6 wounded.

REPEL FOE; 358 KILLED (Sept. 29,1968) An all-ARVR force reportedly killed 228 Communists at Phouc Tan Regional Forces outpost about 23 klicks southwest of Tay Ninh, with ARVN casualties of 7 dead and 91 wounded. An additional 130 of Uncle Ho's troops were killed at the previously-mentioned fight at Thien Ngon SF camp.

Viet Irregulars Kill 150 Reds In Rout Northwest of Saigon (Oct. 6,1968) A couple of CIDG battalions took on two NVA battalions near Thien Ngon SF camp, killing at least 150, with no reported friendly casualties. The article also reported the downing of a Huey chopper 18 miles northwest of Tay Ninh, with four killed and one wounded. This would have been in the vicinity of the "rout" but was reported as a separate incident and there is no indication as to the nationality of the casualties, likely U.S.

Why Is Tay Ninh A Prime Target? (Oct. 9, 1968) This article was actually a thoughtful piece, trying to figure out why the Communists had carried out so many attacks in Tay Ninh Province since August 17. They had suffered about 2439 dead in that period. The writer posited that the attacks may have been intended to draw away defensive forces from Saigon, or to draw the Cao Dai Church away from the government, or to win a major military victory for propaganda purposes.

1st Air Cav. Unit Kills 52 Reds (Nov. 27, 1968) The First Cav reportedly killed 52 NVA 21 miles northwest of Tay Ninh, while the 25th Division dispatched another 65 in several skirmishes. Cav casualties were 5 KIA and 10 WIA, but none were disclosed for the 25th.

320 REDS SLAIN ON VIET BORDER (Nov. 30, 1968) In several clashes along the Cambodian border, 25th Division and

First Cav troops killed 320 Commies. The 25th lost 2 Hueys but could not give a number of casualties killed in the crashes. There were 15 other troops killed and 19 wounded in fighting at the landing zone.

1st Cav. Div. Is Keeping 'Em Honest (Dec. 5, 1968) This article speaks of the First Cav's effort to clear out NVA installations on the Vietnam side of the border with Cambodia in the far reaches of War Zone C. The U.S. troops were looking for what they called Hq. R, which obviously was another name for COSVN. They had no luck with that, as the NVA had located it across the border in Cambodia, where it was safe, at least for the time being.

B52 'Engineers' Raze Red Complex (Feb. 4, 1969) Twelve B-52 bombers dropped 720,000 pounds of bombs on a four-square-mile NVA base in War Zone C near the Cambodian border. Infantrymen had turned up 400 bunkers, an underground hospital, 4,500 NVA uniforms and tons of rice, but needed the brute force of the B-52s to destroy it all. This was just a drop in the bucket of the B-52 ordinance dropped on War Zone C.

GIs Hurl Back Charge By N. Viet Battalion (Mar. 10,1969) North Vietnamese regulars attacked the 25th Division's FSB Grant, about 26 klicks northeast of Sector, leaving 77 bodies in and around the wire. Some of the NVA were reportedly using flame throwers. A 122mm mortar round hit the command post, killing the U.S. commander and 3 others. The 25th suffered an additional 7 KIA and 30 WIA.

Red Ambush Kills 30 S. Viet Troops (Mar. 12, 1969) Approximately 1,000 VC troops attacked the village of Ben Soi and then ambushed about 300 ARVN paratroopers coming to the aid of the village. The Communists killed 30 ARVNs and wounded another 105 before withdrawing across the Cambodian border. Ben Soi was 6 km west of the base camp and about 3 klicks from Cao Xa.

Red Ambush Try Fails; GI Escort Kills 76 of Foe (Mar. 14, 1969) A 25th Division supply convoy from Cu Chi to Dau Tieng was ambushed about 11 miles southeast of Tay Ninh, resulting in

76 Communist fatalities and 8 wounded GIs. A First Cav fire base just west of Nui Ba Dinh was also attacked with 62 Communist KIAs and no reported U.S. casualties.

U.S. War Casualties Go Over 250,000 (Apr. 12,1969) The paper reported that "American dead for the war rose to 33,863, while more than 215,000 troops have been wounded, though only about half of them were hospitalized for their injuries. Another 1,318 Americans remain missing or captured." It would not be known for sure until many years later that Richard Nixon had sabotaged promising Vietnam peace talks just before the 1968 election in order to enhance his presidential bid.

Scores of Reds Slain in Clashes With GIs (Apr. 21, 1969) The 11th Armored Cavalry Regiment suffered 7 KIA and 28 WIA in an ambush by NVA troops at Phu Khuong, just east of Nui Ba Dinh. The Communists lost 102 soldiers in two days of fighting.

Red 'Blitzkrieg' Fails, 101 Die in Viet Battle (May 8, 1969) North Vietnamese regulars suffered 101 dead in a desperate fight at the first Cav's FSB Carolyn just 9 klicks north of FSB Barbara. 29 NVA were captured. Nine GIs died and 62 were wounded.

WAR FLARES: 300 REDS DIE (June 8, 1969) Troops of the 25th Division reportedly killed over 300 Communists in two days of fighting in several locations near Tay Ninh City. Eight U.S. troops died and 37 were wounded.

Reds Crushed in Major Battles (June 9, 1969) An estimated 650 NVA troops were killed in two days of fighting in Tay Ninh Province. Allied casualties were 13 dead and 34 wounded. Most of the action took place at FSB Crook, about 12 klicks northwest of the base camp. This was the fight where Captain Kramer of the 25th wished to have firecracker rounds. NVA casualties the first days were tallied at 323 with the assistance of the high explosive rounds I thought were best for the occasion. When Kramer got his wish for the novelty firecracker rounds the second night, enemy casualties were reported to be 76 dead.

Cambodians Reported Battling Reds (June 24, 1969) Informed military sources in Tay Ninh Province reported fighting between

NVA/VC forces and Cambodian troops just across the border. I doubt that I was one of those sources but this coincided with what I observed over in Cambodia while on mortar watch during this timeframe.

C130, Helo Downed; 6 Killed (June 26, 1969) Communist gunners shot down an Air Force C130 transport plane at Katum SF camp, killing 6 Americans and wounding 3. A Huey chopper sent for rescue purposes was also shot down, wounding 3 crew members.

GIs Battle NVA 6 Hours Near Cambodia (June 30, 1969) Sixty-two Communists were killed in several encounters with 25th Division and ARVN troops west of Tay Ninh. Eight U.S. soldiers died.

Battles Focus Attention on Tay Ninh (July 15, 1969) The Reds lost 50 soldiers in several Tay Ninh battles, including 32 in fighting on Nui Ba Dinh. B-52s had bombed the mountain for the first time the day before the fight there. U.S. forces suffered 6 KIAs and 21 WIAs.

Tense Tay Ninh Awaiting Attack (July 21, 1969) The fighting around Nui Ba Dinh continued with 25th Division GIs killing 27 NVA troops. Another 16 NVA were dispatched near the Parrot's Beak. Speculation was that an attack on Tay Ninh was imminent because of an increase in infiltration of NVA forces into the province.

20 B52 Raids in 2 Days Along Cambodian Border (July 31, 1969) B-52s conducted 20 raids in 48 hours on the area around Katum SF camp, while First Cav troops discovered about 70 tons of polished rice, cooking oil, fish sauce and 70 bikes in the area. No indication of whether the party hats were found.

Heavy Battles Flare Throughout S. Vietnam (Aug. 14, 1969) The military reported 447 Communists and 52 Americans killed in 16 battles around the country, including one at Landing Zone Becky located about 7 miles southeast of Katum SF camp. The Becky fight resulted in First Cav losses of 13 dead and 39 wounded, while 59 Communists were reported to have died.

Overall, *Stars and Stripes* did a fairly good job of keeping the troops informed of what was going on in-country, as well as at home. You just had to take the bravado and rosy reporting with a grain of salt. We figured that enemy casualties were generally inflated and friendly casualties were often downplayed. But, I was looking forward to watching the news reporting of Walter Cronkite, Chet Huntley, Edward R. Murrow and their contemporaries. I had grown to like the *Washington Evening Star* during my summers in Washington and was hoping to get back to D.C. to find out from it what was really going on in Vietnam and the rest of the world.

I thought about the Army guys I had worked with and appreciated their dedication to the mission. Whether they were volunteers, draftees or lifers, they went about their jobs in a professional manner. Even the court-martial defendants seemed to take their work seriously, except when they took an occasional detour to the flesh pots of Saigon.

I'd had three NCOs at Sector and they had all performed well. Sergeant Haney did everything that was expected of him workwise and was the best scrounger I ever encountered. If he had just conducted his personal business more on the up-and-up and cut down on bragging about his various exploits, things would have gone better for him. Sergeant Dunn had done a good job except for his shooting-it-up transgression. Sergeant Ingram was the best of the three and a model soldier. He always did the right thing exactly when it needed to be done. He had helped both the province chief and the province chief's kid in their time of need.

Three RTOs had worked in our little group and each had done a good job. They came from Kentucky, Tennessee and New Jersey. None of the three caused any problem, although one assisted Sergeant Dunn with his celebratory gunfire while another provided the battalion surgeon with a unique challenge. The lad had contracted some form of STD that was resistant to ordinary treatment, threatening his ability to return to the States. Word was that you could not rotate back to the States until that type of ailment was cured. The Doc finally figured out how to conquer the infection, expanding the scope of medical knowledge in that particular field of practice—an important one for the soldiers.

The people at the battalion were good and dedicated people, as were the Special Forces guys. Even with his various faults, Billy did a good job of running the battalion. In all, the people I worked with were as good a bunch of soldiers as ever served the country and it pained me to think that they would probably not be regarded as such because their service was in a conflict that much of the American public was coming to hate.

I already missed the South Vietnamese friends I had made, particularly the kids at the orphanage. It was my hope that when peace finally came to this troubled country, I could come back and visit them. Unfortunately, that was not to be.

With the crossing of the International Date Line, our plane landed on August 29 at Travis Air Force Base in California. We had been warned that there were demonstrators at the base who would call us baby killers and all kinds of unflattering words like that. There were some people on hand, but I didn't hear any ugly words. We were bussed to Oakland Army Base where I dropped my fatigues and jungle boots into a trash container, put on some civilian clothes that I had bought at the Base Exchange at Tan Son Nhat Air Base in Vietnam, received $1,400 in mustering-out cash, and boarded a commercial flight to the airport in Twin Falls.

10 ● Home again

My family and some of my friends were at the Twin Falls Airport to welcome me home on August 30. There were no banners or confetti and I hadn't expected anything like that. It was great to be back and to see everyone.

I especially appreciated seeing my folks. They had both been worried to death and I felt kind of bad about having just run off to war. Sometimes you don't think about how that might affect others. My Mom and I had exchanged letters quite often so they knew what I was doing. Back in those days it was not easy to call home. You had to be in a location where there was a real telephone and as I recall you had to have an appointment to make a call. I think I made one call from base camp and a couple while on leave.

Things were not quite the same at home. First of all, it was pretty darn chilly and for a month or so I had to wear a coat. The temperature was in the high eighties or low nineties. You could tell people thought I was a little daft, running around with a coat on in the warm end-of-summer weather. I have to say I did not miss Vietnam's oppressive humidity, though. It took a month or two for my body to re-acclimate. It took about another year and a half for my intestinal tract to stop having periodic attacks of Ho Chi Minh's revenge. Some sort of bacteria or parasite must have accompanied me home.

When I had shipped out for Okinawa about a year and half previously, the newspapers and television were pretty solidly behind the war effort but there was none of that anymore. Events in the war still got coverage but there was no more rah, rah, rah. The coverage was fairly non-committal, tending toward negativity. None of my friends at home had served in the war, although a few had been in the Army. There was not much to share about my Vietnam experience or, for that matter, anyone to share it with. People did not ask a lot of questions and I got to the point of not volunteering anything. For the next several months, my friends and I drank beer, played shuffleboard in the saloons, and did some deer and elk hunting.

After falling in love with flying, I was determined to get a pilot's license. There was a flight instructor at the tiny Jerome Airport so I took lessons there and got my private license. You had to get a flight physical and there just happened to be a doctor in Jerome who was qualified to give one, Dr. Lauren Neher. The doc said the hearing was weak in my left ear, which we agreed was probably from the 175 mm gun going off during my officer of the guard gig. More on that later.

I did put together a slide show of my Vietnam experience, mostly for myself, but for anyone else who was interested. I showed it to my family. The Lions Club in Hazelton invited me to show it and everyone seemed interested in it. Questions from the group were fairly supportive, but I did not get the impression that people were vitally interested in what was going on a world away.

I told people that we were winning the war and I really believed it. That had certainly seemed to be the case in Tay Ninh Province but, of course, I didn't have a lot of information about what was happening in the Mekong Delta or up north along the DMZ. I did read everything I could get my hands on about the war and a lot of it seemed to support my viewpoint if you could read around the negative twist that some of the stories had.

President Nixon's plan to "Vietnamize" the war made sense to me. One of the larger mistakes we made early on was to essentially push the Vietnamese Army aside and take over the conduct of the war. We should have made it clear from the start that the ARVNs were going to have to shoulder the burden of the war, that the U.S. role would be advisory, that we would supply logistic and air support, and that our help depended on the government cleaning up corruption and taking meaningful steps to gain the confidence of the people. We jumped in without recognizing that you can't prevail in an insurgency without winning the hearts and minds of the citizenry, which requires that they be kept safe from harm and protected from corrupt government.

Nevertheless, it appeared that things were moving in a better direction with the U.S. turning back more responsibility to the ARVNs and President Thieu promising various reforms. Among other things, he was proposing a land reform program to buy property from large land owners and put it in the hands of the sharecroppers for free. That was an important step in the right direction.

In any event, I was fairly optimistic that things would work out for the South Vietnamese and that the U.S. effort had been worth it, despite the early miscalculations. At that point it did not seem like there was much to worry about.

One thing I did fret about and needed to decide was what to do about was my relationship with Sam. We had been together 3 times and had corresponded on a weekly basis for over a year. She had been an important part of my life during my time in Vietnam and I felt like I had to either make a commitment or move on. For right or wrong, I did not feel ready to make a commitment, partly because of the distance and partly because I thought I needed to devote my energy to working on a political career. I told her that in what could be characterized as a Dear John letter, which I still look back on as a wretched way to have handled the situation. I was in too much of a hurry to get on with my ambitions. She was a remarkable person and deserved much better from me.

But, having gotten the war behind me, I was charging ahead. I contacted Senator Jordan's Washington office to see about getting a job and was invited to pay a visit. I flew back to Washington, told the Senator about my experiences, and got a job offer to start the first of January, 1970.

During my tour of duty, most of my money went into an Army savings account. Being overseas in a combat zone, I did not have to pay income tax. When I started active duty as a First Lieutenant at the end of November in 1967, my pay was calculated as if I had already served three years. When I went to Vietnam from Okinawa, I started receiving combat pay. When I moved to Sector, I started receiving separate rations pay. When I started doing VR work, I started receiving flight pay. It all combined together in a nice little $10,000 nest egg that the Army was kind enough to pay out before I left for Washington. Back in those days, $10,000 was a fairly tidy sum. Fifty years later, it is more or less pocket change. In any event, it was more than enough to buy a green GTO to ferry me back to Washington, D.C.

When I got to Washington and settled in, I started out doing case work – helping people who had problems with the government, including military personnel and veterans. There were groups of young folks periodically showing up at Capitol Hill offices to protest the war and it was my job to meet and talk with them. The discussions were generally civil at that time and it helped that I knew what was actually happening in the war.

I had been in Washington for just 4 months when President Nixon ordered U.S. troops into Cambodia to attack Communist command and supply bases. The action focused on the across-the-border areas that I had observed from the air all along the northern and western boundaries of Tay Ninh Province. It seemed to me like something we should have done longer ago, so I cheered it on. Flying along the border and knowing there were enemy troops in Cambodia, just waiting to attack into Vietnam at their leisure, had not set well with me. I read in the papers that our troops seized a massive amount of NVA war supplies, but it did not appear we were able to find the elusive COSVN headquarters that was a principal objective of the incursion.

Not long after I got to Washington, I decided to follow up on my love of flying, this time in friendlier skies. The flight bug had bitten me hard and I wanted to get some more advanced ratings. So, I filed for benefits under the G.I. Bill to take lessons for a commercial pilot rating. I did end up getting a commercial license and also bought my own plane—a four-seat Beechcraft Musketeer. Because the weather was often stormy and overcast in the Washington area, there were not many weekends where a person could get up in the air without an instrument rating and a plane with foul weather instrumentation.

One occasion almost ended up in disaster, but for my military training and experience. One weekend, I flew to Pittsburgh to visit a law school roommate, Alby Anderson. When it came time to return to Washington, there was a storm brewing, so I played it safe and took a commercial flight back to D.C. A couple of weekends later, I flew back to Pittsburgh to get the plane. We visited too long and it was getting close to sundown when I got to my Musketeer.

The plane had been sitting there for a couple of weeks and I noticed that the fluid had somehow drained out of the magnetic compass, rendering it inoperable. That did not seem to present a problem since I could just use my radio to follow signals sent out by the ground-based VOR stations on the way to my airport at Gaithersburg, Maryland. The VOR, or visual omnirange navigation system, allows a pilot to navigate to a destination by following the signals transmitted by a series of VOR stations located across the county.

The airfield was little more than a cow pasture so there was no control facility to radio to notify I'd be taking off. So, I did not fire up my radio prior to takeoff, which was shortly after the sky was dark. After getting up in the air, I turned on the radio but it was dead as a door nail. Consequently, the VOR was not working. The directional gyro indicated I was flying east and I knew that Washington was generally southeast of Pittsburgh so I turned a bit south. I came to a river, which I could make out because of the lights reflecting off of the water. I figured it was the Potomac so I followed it as best I could with the various twists and turns of the river, knowing that it would take me near to Gaithersburg. Other than the lights on the ground below, it was a dark night.

Things were not perfect, but it seemed like they were manageable, until I flew into a large cloudbank. There were no longer any stars above or lights below to use as points of reference. It was almost impossible to tell up from down and I knew I was experiencing vertigo. Sometimes when you are flying, you can mistake the cause of a rush of air that you are hearing. It often tells you that the plane is losing altitude and you need to pull back on the yoke to bring up the nose of the plane. If the air rush means that the nose is already up and you pull back on the yoke, you can cause the plane to stall. That is definitely a bad thing.

I could easily have panicked and I have to say I came close. At that time my military experience kicked in and said I had to collect my wits and evaluate the known facts before doing anything rash. Also, my instructors had always said to trust the instruments. The artificial horizon, which shows the attitude of the plane—nose up or nose down—indicated the nose was way up in the air. The turn and bank indicator showed that the plane was in a fairly sharp turn, rather than on the straight course I'd been on before getting into the cloud. It was a dangerous configuration. I lowered the nose, straightened out the course and headed back in the southeasterly direction I'd previously been flying.

Soon, the plane was out of the clouds and I picked up sight of the river again. After a while I saw the beacon from what I thought was probably the Gaithersburg airport. Thank God, it was. Whew!!! It turned out that a diode in the radio had burned out.

Six months into my job, the legislative assistant left to take a job as an administrative law judge dealing with coal mine safety, so I moved into that position. As legislative assistant, I dealt with every possible issue, except those related to natural resources. A nice fellow from Salt Lake City, Ray McGuire, handled issues relating to federal lands, mining, forestry, grazing, and the like. I handled the Senator's work relating to practically everything else, which included military and foreign policy issues.

From time to time the Senator asked me in to discuss the situation in Indochina. It was a hot topic among his colleagues and he seemed to appreciate my perspective. He asked that I prepare a memo on a discussion we had at the end of August so he could share it with some of his Senate friends. This is what my September 2 memo said:

As I said the other day, it appears from North Vietnamese policy pronouncements that their main effort in the near future will be toward conquering Cambodia. This would appear to be an appropriate step to take at this time in order to be in a better position later to maintain their protracted war in the South. Currently they are on the run practically in every area of South Vietnam and making very little headway. It is thought by taking over Cambodia at this time that they can consolidate their position there and later use it as a jumping off point and supply point for operations in South Vietnam.

It is clearly to the advantage of the United States to bomb North Vietnamese positions and supply areas in order to create as much havoc for them as possible. While it would also be helpful to give support to Cambodian troops and to try to support the Lon Nol government, I do not believe that our best interests would be served by this. The Administration is currently walking a sort of tight rope and had best be very careful not to gradually increase its commitment to this government. As Senator McGee pointed out the other day, we do not need a non-communist government in Cambodia. It would be a great help but we do not absolutely need it. Contrary to the Vice President's assertions it would not stop Vietnamization. We would still retain the option of bombing and interdicting supplies headed for the South and of sending in the South Vietnamese to disrupt any would-be sanctuaries. There are no strong policy reasons for making a last ditch stand along with the Cambodian government. At least, as far as the war in South Vietnam goes.

As far as Vietnam goes, I believe that for some months now we have seen the light at the end of the tunnel but have been unable to recognize it. The enemy there has very little capability to launch any type of large scale operation. The North Vietnamese and Viet Cong have been forced into the embarrassing position of reverting to an earlier step in progression for wars of liberation. The enemy is still capable as we have recently seen of conducting terrorist operations. It appears to me, however, that as their control of the population recedes as it has to such a great extent that terrorist activities will become increasingly counterproductive. Instead of just letting the North Vietnamese and VC be, the people will start as they have done already in some provinces to turn in these people to the Government. In Hau Nghia Province, for example, the local citizens turned in practically the entire Viet Cong underground political organization. The Government showed it is capable of protecting them and they turned on the people who had formerly terrorized them with great vengeance.

With regard to the initiative launched by several Senators yesterday on behalf of negotiations and cease fire, I think that they will come to a great disappointment. State Department analysts deem it rather unlikely that the North Vietnamese-Viet Cong will be greatly inclined to negotiate given their present low fortunes. Members of the communist bloc have traditionally balked at negotiating from a position of weakness. Indications are that the North Vietnamese are not inclined to do so unless they can get some kind of outlandish concession. Along this line, I think that President Thieu is a person who speaks very realistically about the Vietnam situation. He is a hard-headed realist in this area, and recognizes that the Viet Cong and North Vietnamese will not come to the bargaining table in good faith unless they are given a great deal of incentive. I do not think that President Thieu is greatly motivated to negotiate because he and his government are in such a position of strength at this time. Even assuming a rapid Vietnamization of the war, it seems to me that it is quite likely that the South Vietnamese can prosecute the war to a successful conclusion. It would not be a military victory won in a decisive conflict, but rather a lengthy rooting out of all the remaining elements of resistance to the government, from the Thieu-Ky regime, to some other type regime, that this process would be carried out.

The really pressing problems currently facing the Vietnamese are on the economic front. This is where the U.S. and the Saigon government should currently be focusing their efforts. The Vietnamese are in great need of an austerity program to combat the high level of inflation in their economy.

Looking back, my assessment was way too optimistic. The fortunes of the NVA and VC had suffered, but that did not take into account their determination to carry on to the bitter end. They regarded setbacks as a normal part of the process. They simply outlasted their opponents.

There was a good deal of discussion in Congress about various ways to wind down or stop the war. Most of them involved cutting off or limiting funds, something that was under the control of Congress. I was skeptical of this idea and was more than happy to share that view with Senator Jordan. Several months after I took over the legislative assistant job, the Senator hired another fellow from Idaho to fill my old job. Lare Eastland had served with the Marines in Vietnam and he turned out to be a vocal supporter of the funding cut-off measures. The Senator did not lack advice on the issue.

As the issue heated up, the number of war protesters visiting Capitol Hill increased dramatically and discussions became testier. A great majority of these visitors were dead set against any further funding, which sometimes did not make for pleasant conversations. I had no problem with people who came in to express their views in a rational manner. They were entitled to do that and they did have a valid viewpoint. What got my dander up was when they morphed into criticizing the troops, calling them "baby killers" and the like.

When the rhetoric got somewhat heated, I would let the visitors know that I had served in the war and had not known of anyone who killed babies or purposely brutalized the population. I was aware of the atrocities at My Lai and knew that it was not particularly an isolated event. Every time something like that happened it was not only a stain on our national honor, but also extremely detrimental to our effort to prevail in the war. You can't win over a civilian population by killing or brutalizing them. You can win over a civilian population by showing them that you are trying to make them safe and that you respect them as human beings. The great number of visitors who wanted to defund the war effort did not want to hear that most of those serving in Vietnam thought they were doing something honorable.

Of the hundreds who visited our office, only one or two had served in Vietnam. I never begrudged any Vietnam veteran for expressing any opinion he had regarding the war. They were brothers and had the right to say what they wished about the conflict.

During that period of time, a couple of my friends from the University of Oregon, Dave and Lynn Walker, were living in Washington. They had been a year behind me in college. When he graduated, Dave initially thought of going to law school but decided to go into the Foreign Service. His first assignment was to Indonesia but later he and Lynn spent a year in Vietnam. The Walkers and I got together frequently to drink beer and discuss the situation in Vietnam. We thought that it could or would turn out well and reinforced each other's beliefs in this regard. Dave and Lynn had actually adopted a baby girl in Vietnam, something that I wish in retrospect that I had tried to do. They said it took a lot of work and the payment of some money to grease the wheels. We kept close track of everything that was going on in Vietnam and it was helpful to get a State Department perspective.

I got a nice surprise in January of 1970. A card arrived from the director of the orphanage. It had been forwarded from my home address. The card had been hand written in Vietnamese, so I asked the Congressional Research Service to translate. This was one of the benefits of working in a senatorial office. It was a heart-warming message. She said: "Xmas is here. The children and us, who like you very much, remember you, our noble benefactor, with melancholy. In February 1970, we received a number of expensive gifts that you sent us; we have incessantly been thinking of you. We sincerely wish that this Xmas and the New Year will bring you and your family many blessings from the Lord Jesus." It was signed by Mrs. Cao Huong Cuong, Directorice of the Orphanage. A couple of days later, a letter arrived from her that was dated two days later than the card. It said much the same thing but it included a hand-written translation. She apparently had an afterthought that I may not have a translator handy. It was a little too generous, but it nevertheless tugged at my heartstrings. It was a nice break from the political world.

Another Vietnam-related break occurred in the summer or fall of 1970. I got a call at Jordan's office from one of my Proud American friends. Captain Caruso, who we nicknamed the Canary (in keeping with our bird theme—the Eagle and the Hawk) called to say hello. I'm not sure how he tracked me down but I was glad he did. He was back from Vietnam and just wanted to chat. He was a good guy. I think he had been the battery commander of our firing battery at the base camp. I'd taken him on a tour of Tay Ninh City and the Cao Dai Church a time or two. His call was the only time I spoke to anyone from the 2/32 from August of 1969 to May of 1990, when I spoke on the phone with Major Painter.

Whenever there was legislation in the works dealing with Indochina, I would prepare a memo for the Senator on the issue. There were a variety of measures to limit or cut off funding for military action in Vietnam, Cambodia, and/or Laos-- the Cooper-Church, McGovern-Hatfield, Church-Case, and several other proposals, either in bill or amendment form--that came forward in the 1970-1971 timeframe. I tried to give a balanced picture of the pros and cons of each proposal but told the Senator I personally believed that the Senate was not well situated to conduct military strategy. An excerpt from a typical memo about the Foreign Assistance Act of 1971, dated October 27, 1971, says:

The following are some comments on the more significant provisions of the bill:

INDO-CHINA *– Section 406, the Cooper-Church Amendment, provides that funds authorized for use by U. S. forces in Indochina shall be used only for the purpose of withdrawing our forces and cannot be used to engage them in hostilities in North or South Vietnam, Cambodia or Laos, except as necessary to protect them against "imminent danger" as they are being withdrawn. This would apply to Air and Naval Forces stationed in other countries and on the high seas.*

The Administration will attempt to strike this provision from the bill because it would hamper the implementation of the Vietnamization program. The Vietnamese have assumed almost the total ground combat role and have been assuming a greater part of the logistics and air support role, but I doubt if they could bear the whole brunt of these latter two roles upon passage of the Foreign Assistance Act.

MANSFIELD AMENDMENT *– Section 407 is a restatement of the Mansfield Amendment declaring it the national policy that U. S. military operations in Indochina should be terminated at the earliest practicable date and that all U. S. forces should be withdrawn not later than six months after the date of enactment, subject to the release of prisoners of war.*

CAMBODIA *– Section 655 provides a spending limitation on Cambodia of $250 million for fiscal year 1972. This limitation applies to all goods and services under every conceivable program. This amounts to a total reduction of $93 million in the amounts tentatively programmed by the Administration for Cambodia.*

Section 655 imposes a ceiling of 200 on the number of U. S. civilians and military personnel who can be present in Cambodia at any time. It imposes a ceiling of 50 on the number of non-Cambodians working in Cambodia whose compensation can be paid in whole or in part by the United States.

The Committee states that these provisions are necessary in order to prevent the steady expansion of aid to Cambodia. The attempt is made to limit outright aid and also backdoor-type spending.

The Administration will contend that the increased aid is necessary in order to enable the Cambodians to have the weapons to fight the communists. Placing a limitation on military and economic aid and, particularly, on arms aid will seriously hamper the effort to build up the Cambodian military.

There have been some unsettling reports that the military plans to provide Cambodia with a more or less U. S. military capability. Reports have surfaced to the effect that semi-sophisticated equipment and weapons will be given to the Cambodians. This would appear to be a mistake and would create some of the same problems which we are confronting in Vietnam. In other words, the Cambodian military should not be prepared to wage hostilities in the same manner that the United States Forces are because they are not technically capable of doing so. It is possible that a dollar limitation on assistance might force military planners to make a better allocation of aid to the Cambodians. However, I would be somewhat hesitant to approve an inflexible limit on the number of U. S. personnel and a limited on the number of non-Cambodian advisors whose compensation can be paid by the United States.

In the fall of 1971, I could tell that Senator Jordan was starting to soften on the funding cut-off proposals. He worked fairly closely with Idaho's other Senator, Frank Church, who was one of the major proponents of cutting off war funding. I knew it was really wearing on him because one morning when I arrived at the office, he was already there and asked that I come in to talk about a funding proposal that was coming up for a vote that morning. I usually got to the office before everyone else, about 5:30 or 6:00 in the morning, and that morning he looked like he had been studying the issue all night. His eyes were red and had noticeable bags under them. There were a lot of materials scattered around his desk that he had obviously been poring over.

A lot of people in the Senate would just take their cue for how to vote on an issue by asking a friend who knew something about it. Jordan did not like that. He told me once that some of these people would walk into the Senate chamber when a vote was called, look at a friend who probably knew something about the issue, get a thumbs-up or thumbs-down signal from their friendly contact, and then vote accordingly. Senator Jordan was an independent-minded guy and spent a good deal of time studying issues on his own to make sure he understood them. I think the negative coverage of the war and the periodic set-backs experienced by our military were really wearing on him.

One morning when I woke up, a great idea popped into my head. I would go to Laos, Cambodia and Thailand on a semi-official trip/vacation, gather some facts for the Senator, and see if I couldn't shore up his support for the war effort. I told the Senator I'd like to go to Southeast Asia on my own dime to see how things were going in the Vietnam neighborhood. He thought that sounded like a good idea so he wrote the Secretaries of Defense and State to ask that they set up an itinerary for me to visit Cambodia and Laos to see what was going there militarily and perhaps to check in on Thailand.

After receiving an itinerary from the two departments, I called Pan Am, my favorite airline, to arrange an around-the-world trip from December 9 to the 31st. One of the former Jordan staffers, Margot Bailey, was living in Spain at the time, so I stopped in Barcelona for a couple of days to visit her. From there I flew to Bangkok and caught a flight on Air Cambodia to Phnom Penh. A State Department employee met me at the airport, whisked me through immigration, and took me to Hotel Le Royal, a wonderful old French colonial hotel where I was to stay. After checking in, he drove me to the residence of Emory Swank, the U.S. Ambassador to Cambodia. I had read in Time magazine how vehicles entering the Ambassador's residence were checked for bombs by using a mirror on a stick that was designed to check the undercarriage of the vehicle. That was done on my arrival. I was ushered in to meet the Ambassador, who was waiting for me behind a dining table spread with an array of good looking food and a couple of bottles of fine wine. We had an enjoyable lunch and a good discussion about the situation in Cambodia.

During my visit, I met with U.S. military personnel, aid workers, and some people that I suspected were CIA operatives. Most of them had served in Vietnam so we had things to talk about. My State Department contact took me around to see the tourist sites and they were remarkable. We visited the Silver Pagoda, Independence Monument, the King's Palace, the King's Burial Temple, Phnom Penh Wat (from which the city got its name), and a monument to Napoleon Bonaparte. As we traveled around town in what was basically a motorized rickshaw – a motorcycle with a two-person bench on the front – I noticed a bit of hostility. One guy displayed his middle finger to us, apparently a universal sign of disrespect. I'd read that Cambodians had mixed feelings about American policy toward Cambodia and I could see why they might be unhappy with us. After all, we were bombing the daylights out of that part of the Ho Chi Minh trail located along Cambodia's eastern border.

I was taken to the Cambodian Army headquarters where a briefing on the military situation had been arranged. A lot of the information at the briefing was stuff I had already read about before I embarked on the trip. There was one hiccup in the briefing.

The State Department folks had provided me information beforehand about practical considerations. Since most of the folks in Cambodia were Buddhists, I was warned not to pat kids on the head and things of that nature. Since they believed in reincarnation, I was warned not to slap mosquitos or otherwise commit violent acts against bugs and animals. At the start of the briefing, I was given a large glass of beer. It was actually pretty good. The problem was that there was a fly that insisted on sitting on the edge of the glass or flying circles inside of it. Rather than slapping at the little varmint and creating a scene, I just gently tried to shoo it away. I was on my best behavior. Unfortunately, while I was trying to politely get rid of the fly, the little critter flew too close to the foam, got caught, crashed, and died in my beer. It was one of those situations where you were trying so hard to do the right thing but things turn out horribly wrong. I burst out in uncontrollable laughter to the amazement of the briefer and the great dismay of the State Department guy. He said, "What are you doing?" Well, I was obviously mourning the passage of the ill-fated fly. The rest of the visit went somewhat better than that.

I enjoyed my visit to Cambodia. Although there were a few people who did not seem to be sold on Americans, most everyone was welcoming and friendly. I judged them to be kind and gentle people. It is hard to fathom how the country could have descended into such horrible genocide just four years later.

After my stay in Phnom Penh, I went back to the airport to catch a Royal Air Lao flight to Vientiane, Laos. When I got to the gate, I saw an old worn-out DC-3 sitting in the assigned space. As I climbed up the access stairs, I immediately noticed the coat closet, which was stacked from floor to ceiling with dried fish. They were big fish. They were all black. They were each about two and half feet long and three inches in diameter. They didn't really stink but, on the other hand, they didn't really smell too good.

As I was climbing up to my seat at the front of the plane (the DC3 is a tail dragger so you gain some altitude as you go toward the front of the plane), I passed a Frenchman who gave off an aroma indicating he had not taken a bath for many a moon. When I got to my seat, I noticed all of the windows in the plane had dozens of stress cracks. A Laotian fellow wearing a pilot cap came out of the cockpit and started speaking with the Frenchman. The French fellow said, "just remember, when you get to the river turn left." That did give me a great deal of comfort because we would be flying over very hostile territory. The Laotian gentleman acknowledged the advice and it looked like we were about ready to go.

I was sitting on the left side of the plane and I heard the left engine getting cranked up. A gigantic cloud of black smoke was emitted from that engine as it coughed and sputtered to life. The same thing happened with the engine on the right. It did not tend to instill a great amount of confidence in the airworthiness of the ancient bird. But, we were soon underway.

After we had flown for an hour or so, the plane went in for what appeared to be an unscheduled landing. I believe it was the air strip at Pakse, Laos. When we deplaned, I saw a neat stack of three bodies on the tarmac just a few feet away. It looked like they had just recently been put there. Then, I heard a noise off to the northwest and saw an old prop-driven Douglas A-1 Skyraider attack aircraft putting in an airstrike on a small hill about a klick from the air strip. I had heard that the Cambodians were fighting with the North Vietnamese and this seemed to confirmed it.

We took off again after a short stop and flew on to Vientiane without further incident. As in Phnom Penh, there was a State Department person there to meet me and whisk me through immigration. A person could get used to that type of treatment. It helped me understand why members of Congress liked to go junketing around the world. Keep in mind, though, that I was paying my own way.

The USAID folks had put together an ambitious program of briefings and visits to various aid projects. They took me to several new villages that had been built specifically for war refugees. The refugees were friendly folks and looked like they were making the best of their circumstances.

I had been hoping that I would be able to meet Pop Buell, a legendary U.S. aid worker in Laos, who was reputed to have CIA connections. He had been written up in the newspapers for the work he was doing and sounded like a great guy to have in that position. He'd just had a heart problem, though, and was recuperating.

The embassy had lined up a Jet Ranger helicopter to take me up-country to see some aid projects. We visited a place called Site

272 or Bon Song, which had a good air strip. I noticed an Air America plane sitting on the runway. It was a Fairchild STOL (short take-off and landing), which I'd read were the workhorse of the CIA on short jungle strips. One of the guys stationed there asked where I was from and when I replied I was an Idahoan, he said he was also. His name was Blaine Jensen and he'd grown up in Pingree, not far from Pocatello. When he said he'd graduated from Utah State in Logan, I told him my brother-in-law, Don McFarland, had gone there also. Turns out they had been in the same class and knew each other.

Blaine allowed as how he worked with Pop Buell and indicated it was just pure old aid work. I asked if he was also involved in covert operations but did not expect him to say so. He didn't. I started thinking this was the kind of work I'd like to do.

We then took off to a place further north where there was going to be an air drop of rice to a Hmong village. It was in hilly country and you could see that large areas of some of the hillsides had had all of the foliage removed. The aid folks said it was slash-and-burn agriculture. The tribe would pick a hillside to plant the year's crop, cut all of the foliage, plant their crop, harvest, and then move on to a new location. It sure seemed like a tough way to live.

The Hmong were getting ready for the new year and everyone was decked out in their best clothes. There were a couple of lines facing each other—young girls with their moms behind them in one line and young boys with their moms behind them in the other. As a kid in one line would throw the ball to a kid in the opposing line, the moms on either side would be discussing dowry issues. It was a ceremony to arrange marriages, I was told. I was asked to join in and was just a little fearful that I may have inadvertently become betrothed by tossing the ball. It was a unique experience. It was pointed out that there were hardly any males in the village between their mid-teens and senior years. The missing able-bodied males were either off fighting or had died in the effort.

We heard a C-130 overhead and were given a heads up since they were ready to do the rice drop. The plane circled over the hilltop several times as bags of rice were kicked out for the Hmong villagers. They were happy to get the new supplies.

Afterwards, the village chief invited us to his home, which was about the size of a backyard storage shed with a dirt floor and thatched roof. He fixed up some tea for us and offered a meal. We drank the tea but begged off on the meal. He would have given us all he had in order to be hospitable. These were truly worthy people who had gotten caught up in a war not of their making.

Our final stop was a village further south where USAID had provided pigs and ducks to the people. The village chief there was also very hospitable. He gave me a bottle of homemade booze as a gift. It looked to be a Johnny Walker bottle but you could not tell because it was wrapped in yellow paper. The aid people called it white lightning and said it was essentially corn whiskey. I brought it home, got yelled at by an airline stewardess (yes, that is what they called them back then) for not having it all the way under the seat in front of me, and didn't get up the courage to drink it until about 5 years later. It wasn't all that bad but might have been better used for stripping paint.

My assessment of Laos was that we were helping the anti-Communists to hold their own for the time being but the long-term outlook was cloudy. We did not appear to be in it for the long game.

My next stop was Khon Kaen, Thailand, where I was to be shown some aid projects supported by the U.S. Government. There were three memorable things from that visit. The water in the bathtub at the best hotel in town ran a less-than-desirable dark brown. There were some dedicated USAID guys who were doing really good aid work, including the construction of a water purification system. The hotel demonstrated the need for that project. Thirdly, I had some of the best Chinese food, ever, at an open-air restaurant that was out in the middle of nowhere.

After the Khon Kaen trip, I went back to Bangkok for a day or two and stewed about whether to try to get in touch with Sam. We had not corresponded for two years but I was still feeling guilty. I thought it would be cowardly to not at least try to contact her so I hired a cab driver to take a message to her that I was in town. The cabbie reported back that he could not find who I was looking for at the address I'd given him. So, that was that.

I flew to Hawaii and had a half-day layover. It was my first visit there so I took a cab to Waikiki Beach. While sitting in a park near the beach, a bird poohed on my foot. That seemed to be a bad omen. My next stop was home, where I spent Christmas, and then back to D.C.

I gave Senator Jordan a full briefing on what I had learned on the trip and he asked me to prepare a summary he could share with some of his Senate friends who were also wavering on the war funding measures. He was particularly interested in the fact that a constituent from Pingree was working in Laos. I told him I was intrigued with the idea of doing that kind of work and asked if he would write a letter to the President recommending me for such a position. He had previously announced that he would be retiring at the end of the year so I needed to move on anyway. He did send a letter to the White House and, although it was politely acknowledged, nothing ever came of it. The Senator was leading an effort to force President Nixon to spend appropriated funds, rather than impounding them, which riled up the President and got the Senator on Nixon's no-favors-for-this-guy list. So, a return to Southeast Asia was nipped in the bud.

On March 30 of 1972, the North Vietnamese launched their Easter Offensive against the South. They attacked in the north along the demilitarized zone, in the Central Highlands, and in the area northwest of Saigon where I had served. I was apprehensive because it was unclear how the ARVNs would stand up to a conventional attack. At the time, I was on vacation in Venezuela and practically went crazy because there was little news available there about what was happening in Vietnam. However, when I learned that the ARVN ground forces, with strong support from

U.S. air power, had beaten the NVA back, it was a great relief. It certainly seemed to illustrate that the ARVNs were on their way to success.

The anti-war demonstrations continued throughout the rest of 1972, the warring parties in Vietnam carried out negotiations on and off through the year, people were abuzz about a break-in at the Watergate complex, I met a woman named Nancy and got married, and my bride and I packed up to move to Idaho. We arrived in Idaho about the time it was announced that the Agreement on Ending the War and Restoring the Peace in Vietnam, also called the Paris Peace Accords, was signed by the parties on January 27, 1973. President Nixon said we had achieved peace with honor. That should have been the end of the story but it wasn't.

11 ● Catastrophe strikes

Our prisoners of war started coming home on February 12, 1973, and all of those who the North Vietnamese acknowledged to be holding had been returned by the end of March. It was great to see them walking off the plane onto American soil. These guys had been through absolute hell.

Among them was John McCain, who could have gone home earlier because of his distinguished parentage but declined to do so because that would have broken the protocol of return by longevity—there were others who had been imprisoned longer. He and the others had stood up in the best tradition of the American military and they were a real inspiration. If anyone deserved the gratitude of the nation, it was them. When McCain passed away in August of 2018, the tributes that came forth from around the world gave a real measure of the man and of what it means to be a true patriot.

There was still a good deal of concern about whether the North Vietnamese had returned everyone they were holding. There was a suspicion that other POWs were being held in Laos or Cambodia. We would not know for many years and may never know the true story.

By the time the POWs returned, I had set up a solo law practice in Jerome. The office had just been vacated by a colorful lawyer who was widely regarded as somewhat shifty. My initial clients were people who came to the office looking for S.A. Kolman, Esq, and just decided to give me a try. Some of them were a bit shifty, too, like the fellow who claimed his pack of dogs could not have killed the neighbor's sheep because only a couple of his dogs had blood on them.

Nancy and I were living in Eden with my parents and planning to build a home on the family farm. Although I had my hands full getting my law practice going, I kept track of what was happening in Washington and overseas with subscriptions to the Congressional Record and Washington Post. My plan was to get involved in politics at the grass roots level and work my way up from there.

The news out of Vietnam was somewhat mixed, although it sounded as if the ARVNs were holding their own against the North Vietnamese. Under the Paris Accords, the parties were to refrain from hostilities but it seemed as if each side was cheating now and then, mostly the NVA. The North Vietnamese were certainly going to make a concerted effort to take over South Vietnam but it seemed as if the ARVNs were taking the necessary steps to survive.

We had given the South Vietnamese a great deal of equipment as part of the enticement to get them to go along with the Paris Accords, but we were starting to get rather stingy with our supply of ammunition and other armaments. There were conflicting reports as to what the U.S. would do to support the South Vietnamese government as time went by. There were some indications that Henry Kissinger had told the North Vietnamese he would be fine if they held off on any major offensives for a couple of years so that it would look like we had gotten things settled. Then, if things went south, it would look like the South Vietnamese had blown it. There were other reports that the President had given the South Vietnamese strong assurances that massive U.S. air support would be forthcoming in the event of a major offensive by the North Vietnamese. It was hard to know exactly what was happening. I didn't lose a lot of sleep over it because I thought the ARVNs were strong enough to hold things together, just as they had during the 1972 Easter Offensive.

When the North Vietnamese launched their Spring Offensive in March of 1975, I was surprised that they were able to take over Ban Me Thout and the Central Highlands so quickly and then to hold onto them. The news outlets started covering the hostilities and reported that we had been overly stingy in providing ammunition since the peace settlement. The ARVNs were short of ammunition and other supplies and, therefore, decided to retreat to the south. The retreat turned out to be a fiasco, which encouraged the North Vietnamese to speed up their offensive and go for Saigon.

What absolutely shocked me is that the U.S. did not lift a finger to help. There was no massive air support, which was beyond baffling. We had been with the ARVNs for years, we had been their partners, many ARVNs had stuck their necks out for us, and this was how we thanked them. This outright betrayal of our friends made me sick.

It was clear that the South Vietnamese were in serious trouble. The people at the American Embassy knew a couple of weeks before the fall of Saigon that the end was at hand and should have been working overtime to extract our friends and supporters. The Embassy did not, apparently under the illusion that a full-out effort would cause panic amongst the general population. There was practically full-out panic anyway.

Operation Babylift brought thousands of children out of Vietnam in the weeks before the collapse. About 100,000 additional Vietnamese nationals, many of whom were in danger of retribution by Communist forces, were extracted by air and sea. However, the number of at-risk Vietnamese—ARVN soldiers, governmental officials, interpreters, and the like—was estimated at well more than ten times the number who were rescued. And, the extraction efforts were chaotic at best. Thanks to dedicated military personnel on the ground, who did the best they could under the dangerous circumstances, at least some of our friends and helpers got out before the Communists captured Saigon.

The U.S. had just turned its back on its former ally. People at home wanted to get on with their lives. Americans had a sour taste in their mouth about the war and wanted to put it out of their minds. Congress essentially washed its hands of the whole thing. President Nixon had resigned just 6 months previously, the government was still in a bit of turmoil, and there was not much appetite to honor any commitments we might have to these people in a far-off land.

When I saw news footage of the Huey lifting off from the American Embassy on April 30, 1975, with an ARVN hanging from the landing skid, it broke my heart. It was absolutely beyond me how my wonderful, honorable country could have so mercilessly betrayed its former friend and ally and so many of its people who had put their lives on the line to side with us. It just did not compute. But there it was, an abject betrayal that I looked at as a great stain on our national honor.

I thought of the more than 58,000 service personnel who had given their lives and it appeared to me that they had done so in vain. Not only that, there were hundreds of thousands who had been wounded, many with grievous permanent injuries, not to mention the hundreds of thousands whose lives had been turned upside down by drug or alcohol abuse, suicide, PTSD, homelessness and the myriad of other problems that veterans always face. And, what about the hundreds of thousands of Vietnamese soldiers and civilians who had suffered or died during the war? None of it mattered a whit to the U.S. Government, which just waltzed away from the whole mess without much of a second thought.

It pained me to think of my friends in Cao Xa Village who were probably being brutalized or killed at that very time. The Cao Dais, who had come around to supporting the government in the last several years, were also in serious trouble. And, my orphans, at least the older ones, were also in jeopardy. The worst thing was that there was nothing I could do about it. There wasn't anything that anyone could do about it.

During the next few years, I kept pretty busy with my law practice. It took a couple of years to get it up and running but then it went a long pretty well. I became a precinct committeeman for the Republican Party in Jerome County and started working my way up in the Jerome County Central Committee. There was not much occasion to speak with anyone regarding my Vietnam experience or what was happening in the country at the time. I do recall one conversation with a friend where mention was made that the South Vietnamese population was probably better off under Communist control. Needless to say, that did not sit well but I won't go into the details.

Although it does not particularly relate to Vietnam, other than to illustrate the events that diverted the public's attention from that lingering conflict in 1974, I feel compelled to comment about the ill-fated jump of the Snake River Canyon that Evel Knievel attempted on September 8, 1974. It may fit in here since Evel was a supporter of Vietnam veterans and revered by many of the troops as a fearless daredevil. I interject it because it was one of the fun highlights of my early legal career.

When Evel's jump flopped, the folks who had paid good money to watch the fiasco got angry and trashed the concession stands at the jump site, which was on the northern outskirts of Twin Falls. The concession stands were destroyed, beer was stolen, and supplies were scattered. A contingent of Hells Angels tried to stop the destruction but to no avail. When asked why he did not try to stop the depredation at the site, the county sheriff said he "withdrew to protect the city." The concessionaires brought suit against Evel, claiming he was responsible for their damages for failing to maintain order at the jump site. Evel's insurance company brought suit against Evel, seeking a court declaration that it was excused from paying the damage claim because of a riot exclusion in the insurance policy.

Jim May, a Twin Falls lawyer who had represented Evel to that point, called to ask if I would defend the insurance company suit because he would need to be a witness in the litigation. Of course, I jumped at the chance to "represent Evel," a punch line I used many times thereafter. It was an interesting case and I learned what many people had been claiming—that Evel didn't like much to pay his bills. Each month I would send my bill for legal services to his manager in Butte, Montana, and each month she would call to say the bill had been received. They never paid a dime, however.

The district court judge, Jim Cunningham, said the riot exclusion applied and let the insurance company off the hook. The Idaho Supreme Court agreed but required the insurance company to pay my fees. It was a great experience and good on-the-job legal training.

One other great experience, which occurred in August 1977, was adopting a beautiful baby girl. Nancy and I picked her up at the hospital when she was a couple of days old and she (Kathy) has been the light of my life since then.

Early in 1978, our incumbent Congressman, George Hansen, received some unfavorable coverage in the Twin Falls Times News. The article dealt with Hansen's conviction on two federal charges of violating campaign finance laws. He had been convicted in 1974 of taking prohibited contributions from corporations. Although he was initially handed a two-month prison sentence, the U.S. District Judge relieved him of that, commenting that he was probably just stupid rather than evil.

At the time, I was Chairman of the Jerome County Republican Central Committee and had gotten to know a few other Republicans. The new publicity about the 1974 convictions caused consternation among some of my fellow Republicans, although others felt that it was not a problem—just another of George's normal indiscretions. To me, it appeared to be an opening for gaining a seat in Congress. I'd never been particularly interested in serving in the House of Representatives, but it was a handy stepping stone to the U.S. Senate.

At the time the article came out in January, I called Senator Jordan to see what he thought about running against George. He cautioned against it, saying George had a hard core of dedicated supporters and it would be difficult to convince them to abandon him. Based on his advice, I decided to wait for some other opportunity.

Four months later, George got some additional unfavorable news coverage regarding his financial situation – whether he had properly reported substantial indebtedness and whether the way funds were raised to pay on the indebtedness had been lawful. This occurred in mid-May, causing me to rethink my decision. For better or for worse, I decided that this was my time to run for Congress. It would not have been a bad idea to devote a bit more thought to the concept. At that time, it was only about two and half months until the August 8 primary election. I was practically unknown outside of Jerome and Twin Falls Counties, although my father, Henry Jones, was well-known among cattlemen and farmers throughout the southern part of the state. Additionally, I am an introvert and at that time was not comfortable when a television camera got anywhere near my vicinity. But, for a young person in too much of a hurry, there did not seem to be any insurmountable hurdles.

On May 26, I announced at the old Twin Falls Holiday Inn that I was throwing my hat in the ring against George. The almost unanimous response from the media was, "Who's Jim Jones?"

Shortly after my announcement, I received a call from KAID, Boise's public television station, asking for an interview. I agreed to sit for an interview in a friend's home in Boise, where something completely unexpected happened. My campaign announcement indicated my service in Vietnam, which I had never downplayed, and during the course of the interview Marc Johnson, the reporter, asked me about my service in Vietnam. Upon the mention of Vietnam, I felt practically speechless, like someone had hit me across the chest with a two-by-four. I could feel my bottom lip quivering and it took a few moments to get to the point where I could speak. I said, "You are not going to use that, are you?" I can't recall what the answer was, but they did use the footage in the story that played on television. I thought it was a blow to my fledgling campaign but it did not actually seem to play out that way. A friend who had watched the program at home told me he thought it made me look human.

I could not explain it then and I'm not sure why I still react in much the same way to the present date. I didn't suffer any trauma in Vietnam and don't have flashbacks, night sweats, or anything of that nature. It may be related to the thought of the 58,220 service members who died in that conflict, or the hundreds of thousands who were injured either physically or psychologically, or the sheer number of innocent Vietnamese who were killed or wounded, or the fact that many of my ARVN friends likely ended up being killed or brutalized in Communist "reeducation camps" or escaping on boats in the South China Sea, or the fate of my orphans, or the drug or alcohol dependence, homelessness, PTSD and suicide that has occurred with Vietnam veterans, or the contempt or indifference that many Vietnam veterans faced when they returned from serving their country, or a combination of all of those factors. Often, when the subject of Vietnam comes up out of the blue, I experience a tightness in the chest, tears in my eyes, and an inability to say anything for a few moments.

The campaign actually went pretty well. It was not so much that I dazzled the voters but that George seemed to keep getting in trouble and not doing much of substance for the people of the Congressional district. After running some third-rate ads right at the start, I put on some pretty good television advertising and got good free publicity for a variety of proposals dealing with state and national problems. We put up about 200 four-by-eight-foot mini-billboards practically overnight and that really caught peoples' attention, as did a white star in the middle of the "O" in the Jones on my campaign material. I threw in over $100,000 of my own money for media advertising and that also helped. During the entire exercise, I always highlighted the fact that I was a Vietnam veteran and that I was proud to have served my country. It isn't clear whether that helped because I think a lot of people still had mixed feelings about the war and Vietnam vets.

Anyway, I worked really hard and covered a lot of ground. For the most part, George ignored me, although it seemed that he started getting concerned during the last couple of weeks of the campaign. The vote tally was not ideal from my standpoint. I got about 44% of the vote while George got all of the rest of it. As is usual in these circumstances, George and I sort of kissed and made up in the interests of party loyalty. Some reporter asked me if I recognized any good qualities in George and I mentioned that he was tall. Over the years, I have gotten a laugh line from audiences by saying that the majority of voters went for George because they wanted a man of convictions, pointing out that he had two federal convictions. I went back to practicing law full time and considering future options.

In the meantime, there was substantial turmoil in Southeast Asia, which resulted in a large outflow of refugees from South Vietnam, starting in about September of 1978. People had been escaping from Vietnam in any way they could since the 1975 downfall of the South, including on rafts, boats, and whatever else would float. However, the fall of 1978 saw a dramatic increase of people fleeing over the waters. It was a real tragedy. Pirates got some of the people, robbing, raping and killing many. A large number of unseaworthy boats capsized or sunk. Those who could get away, went to refugee camps in the surrounding area. America was called upon to give these people refuge and we did to a large extent.

What really burned me up was an increasing chorus of people who spoke out against taking in these beleaguered people, claiming that they would bring disease, crime, political subversion, and all kinds of other horrible things with them. All of that was nonsense. The refugees certainly displayed guts and gumption by risking their lives to try to achieve freedom. They settled in to live the American dream, established businesses, got their kids educated, and became model citizens. That wasn't true for each and every one of the people who came, but it made them just like all of the rest of the immigrant groups who have come to the U.S. The great majority took hold as Americans, just like people from Europe and everywhere else had done in prior years.

Fear of refugees was not new to the country. When people flooded out of Ireland in the mid-nineteenth century because of the potato famine, many Americans had nothing good to say about them. Yet, Irish soldiers continually distinguished themselves fighting to preserve the Union in the Civil War.

Although it didn't deal with refugees, much the same happened in World War II with respect to Japanese-Americans living on the West Coast. Many people in responsible positions claimed that they would subvert the war effort and called for their incarceration or expulsion. President Roosevelt issued an executive order on February 19, 1942, to round them up and put them in what were called "relocation" camps, but which were little more than concentration camps. One of them, the Minidoka Camp, was just about six miles north of where I grew up. Despite the outrageous claims made against these worthy people, many of their sons volunteered to fight the Axis Powers and were sent to Italy and then Germany in the 442nd Infantry Regiment, which became the most highly decorated unit in the war. Members of the 442nd received 21 Congressional Medals of Honor, although many of them were awarded years and years later. William Nakamura, who enlisted from the Minidoka Camp, died in Italy on July 4, 1944, but was not recognized for his conspicuous heroism until 56 years later.

So, the country has a bit of a track record of treating refugees and other immigrants poorly at times, but we have always come to our senses after the fact. More on that later.

In the meantime, I was rethinking my campaign against George. In just a couple of months, I had been able to come within about 6 percentage points of victory and it seemed that if there had been more than just two months of campaigning, the result might have been different. That probably sounds good on paper but it does not always work out that way in actuality. You probably have to assume that the opponent is going to run a different kind of campaign the second time around. Anyway, it seemed like a good idea to be ready for another shot, should there be an opening.

Wouldn't you know it, that opening came shortly after the Shah of Iran was overthrown and the U.S. Embassy in Tehran was seized. While President Carter was trying to figure out what to do, George took matters into his own hands and flew to Tehran in mid-November of 1979 to try to negotiate the release of the Embassy hostages. If there was ever a sign to run another challenge, this seemed to be it. By the end of November, I was making it known that I would likely throw my hat in the ring again. I did not formally announce my candidacy until April of 1980, but kept busy in the meantime lining up support and getting publicity leading up to that. Even though I had more time, got more newspaper endorsements, and ran a better campaign, the result did not turn out as good as the first time around. This time, George put on a campaign of his own, got his supporters out, and ended up getting about 59% of the vote to my 41%. Oh well, live and learn.

After two unsuccessful runs for Congress, it looked like it was time to try something else. It did not take too long for another opportunity to present itself. Idaho's incumbent attorney general, Dave Leroy, announced during the summer of 1981 that he would not seek re-election to that office. Quite frankly, I had not thought about running for attorney general but it seemed to be a reasonable possibility. I checked out the statutory duties of the attorney general and figured it was a job for which I was qualified. That fall, I announced that I would be running for state attorney general.

Not long after it became known that the office was up for grabs, a number of county prosecutors expressed interest in the position, also. On the Democrat side, J.D. Williams of Preston, the Franklin County Prosecutor, indicated that he would throw his hat in the ring. Williams had previously served as a deputy AG in the Tony Park administration. On the Republican side, Jim Harris of Boise, the Ada County Prosecutor, indicated the he would run. Both of them were regarded as having better chances of winning the office than me. It looked like it was going to be a tough fight, in both the primary and general elections.

Running against George Hansen had been quite helpful. I had learned how to shake hands, how to work a room, how to walk a parade, and how to conduct an effective media campaign. My speechifying had improved dramatically and I had learned how to convey my message on television in short little sound bites. I bought an orange Plymouth TC-3 at the former Gettleman Motors in Wendell, drove it all around the State of Idaho for a year, put 100,000 miles on the car, and won both the primary and general elections. Throughout the campaign, I highlighted the fact that I had served my country in Vietnam because I was proud of that fact. It seemed to help a bit in this campaign. The public was warming up to people who had served in Vietnam.

During 1981, I joined my home-town Eden American Legion Post and have been a member ever since. Later on, I joined the Veterans of Foreign Wars Post in Idaho Falls and, again, have been a member ever since. I made a point of visiting posts of both organizations throughout the state and went to conventions of all of the veterans' organizations.

I often heard the older vets comment that Vietnam veterans were a bit standoffish because few joined their organizations. I would mention as how they might feel uncomfortable because the general citizenry did not seem to regard them as having done anything worthwhile for the country. I also said that they would probably come around as time went by.

Another fairly common comment was that Vietnam veterans seemed to have expected to be welcomed home with brass bands and celebrations. My response was that I didn't think they wanted a big thank-you celebration when they returned but that they would have appreciated not being treated with indifference or disrespect. It seemed to me that quite a few people had a hard time separating their distaste for the war and its outcome from their feelings for the people who had served in it.

I didn't begrudge the old soldiers when they expressed slightly critical views of the Vietnam veterans. Most of them had served in World War II and when they went overseas they were there for the duration. Most of us had served for just a year. They did not have as many battlefield conveniences as Vietnam veterans and were not whisked away by medevac helicopters to facilities where their wounds could be treated in good medical facilities. On the other hand, they returned to the embrace of a grateful nation. The fellows who served in Korea had to put up with bitter cold, surging Chinese hordes, and battlefield deprivations. They did not particularly get a heroic welcome home from their largely forgotten war.

For the most part, I enjoyed visiting and campaigning among the veteran groups and I think it was helpful in the final analysis. You do have a camaraderie that brings you together. If I have a choice of two fairly equal candidates and one is a veteran and one is not, I think my choice generally goes to the person who has put his life at potential risk on behalf of his country, even if the wisdom of the war he or she served in is subject to question.

After the November election results came in, I began working with the staff in the AG's office to learn what was going on with the office and what needed to be done to prepare for the 1983 legislative session. The country was going through a recession and I knew that there would be budgetary considerations that had to be dealt with. Little did I know at the time how government financing had such similarity to supply issues I learned about in the Army.

It quickly became apparent that the ASR philosophy applied to government finance. During 1983, my first year in office, government budgets were tight because of the recession. My budget request was modest, asking just for what my office needed. The legislature assumed it was an inflated request because that was the way the game was played. So, they cut down my allocation. I learned, as with the ASR, that you always had to ask for more than you needed because everybody assumed you were inflating your budget request in expectation that it would be trimmed back. Then, when the end of the year arrived, you had to spend all of the remaining amount of your allocation so as to not get cut back for the succeeding year, just like you had to shoot up all of your ammo in Vietnam during any allocation period.

As the only statewide elected official who had served in Vietnam, I was determined to act in a fashion that countered some of the perceptions that a wide segment of the population had developed about Vietnam servicemen. Obviously, there would be no baby killing, torching of villages or any of the other horrible misconceptions that had been burned into the public mindset. Seriously, though, it was important that my office be operated with transparency, honesty, and a realistic view of what could be accomplished. Every public official likes to play up successes but engaging in the type of official puffery that became all too common in the early stages of the war was something to be studiously avoided.

The life experience I gained from my brief military service was invaluable in handling three difficult challenges that presented themselves during my first month in office. One of the largest water rights disputes in state history had been handed to the AG's office by a court decision just before I took over. There was a growing white supremacist threat in northern Idaho that called for a strong state response. The U.S. Supreme Court notified me that a lawsuit a former AG had filed against Oregon and Washington over fishing rights was scheduled for argument at the end of March.

It was clear that there was going to be a very short learning curve. My military experience had been great preparation for dealing with several challenges at the same time, for responding quickly rather than over-thinking each problem, and for having the confidence to handle what I could and delegate the rest. Leadership can't be taught out of a textbook; it requires on-the-job training.

In November of 1982, the Idaho Supreme Court made a head-scratching decision that practically handed the full flow of the Snake River over to Idaho Power Company based on its water right at the Swan Falls Dam south of Boise. At the time, the power company was one of the strongest political powers in the state. The decision touched off a hard-fought, two-year battle between the State and Idaho Power that extended to the Legislature, state and federal agencies, and the courts. The Governor, myself and about half of the Legislature were on one side, trying to regain control of the river, while the power company and the other half of the Legislature were strenuously opposing us.

The fight got very heated with the start of the 1984 legislative session. The power company's chief lobbyist, Logan Lanham, reputed to be the most powerful political influence of his time, was my principal opponent. It got quite ugly and personal. I often joke in recent years that dealing with the Viet Cong was a piece of cake compared with being engaged in verbal combat with Lanham. Although it was a tough fight, I figured it was a war of attrition and that I could outlast the power company. I pounded them mercilessly until it started taking a real toll on their public image. Several years afterward, a CEO of the company told me, "Jim, you really hurt the Company on Swan Falls. You really hurt Idaho Power." It was not my intention to hurt the company for the heck of it, but to get them to the bargaining table. Once that happened, we were able to settle on terms that worked for both parties in what has been characterized as an historic water settlement. Anyone interested in learning the whole story can check out my book, *A Little Dam Problem*, available from Caxton Press or Amazon.

The supremacist problem involved the Aryan Nations hate group that had set up headquarters just north of Hayden, Idaho, in the late seventies. It was gaining notoriety and attracting out-of-state members, including prison alumni, in the early eighties. Marilyn Shuler, then the director of the Idaho Human Rights Commission, called in January to ask for my help in getting malicious harassment legislation unstuck in the Legislature. The bill had been stalled by objections raised by the National Rifle Association, which was usually the death knell for a piece of legislation in Idaho. It was designed to strike a major blow against the Aryans and its failure would be a real setback for human rights.

We were able to work out compromise language and the bill was enacted into law. That episode got me fully engaged in the human rights cause and I thank Marilyn for that. Eventually, the whole of the state government got behind the effort to combat the supremacists and the Aryans retreated into their little compound. The Southern Poverty Law Center filed suit against the organization in 2000, obtained judgment and closed it down for good.

The third challenge was getting ready for argument of a case that Idaho had filed against Washington and Oregon in the mid-seventies, claiming that citizens of those states were catching more than their share of salmon and steelhead runs that originated in Idaho. The case was an original jurisdiction case, which meant that the Supreme Court conducted a fact-finding proceeding, rather than just considering an appeal from a lower court. The fact-finding in this case was performed for the Court by a special master—a hearing officer. The record was voluminous, consisting of about 40 banker boxes. I went to Washington with the boxes, a fish biologist, and deputy AG, two weeks before the argument to get prepared.

We holed up in a hotel near the Court for two weeks, studying the spawning and migrating habits of the various fish runs involved, the upstream and downstream mortality of each run at each of the eight dams between the spawning grounds and the Pacific, and effects of habitat on the fish both in the river and ocean, among many other things. By the time of the argument, I felt that I knew just about everything there was to know about these magnificent creatures. The argument went fairly well, although the very first question from the Court caught me by surprise. Justice White asked, "Mr. Attorney General, how's the fishing out there in Idaho?" The Court's decision was a mixed bag. It held that states sharing a resource were all obligated to care for and enhance the resource and were entitled to an equitable share of the resource, but that the fish runs were too small at the time to set an apportionment formula.

Each of the three challenges turned out alright and I felt comfortable in my new position. The office also gave me a platform to speak out on issues that were important to me. Not long after taking office, I was approached by another Vietnam veteran, Max Brown, who was setting up an organization to help Idaho's Vietnam veterans adjust to civilian life. The Idaho Vietnam Veterans Leadership Program (IVVLP) was funded through a $52,000 grant from Action, a national volunteer agency. The objective was to have veterans who had successfully transitioned to civilian life help those who had not.

I agreed to serve on the Board of Directors, along with Bernie Fisher, an Idaho recipient of the Congressional Medal of Honor, H. Scott Brown, an engineer with Morrison-Knudson, Gary Bermeosolo, the State's Administrator of Veteran Affairs, Mike Brush who represented Governor John Evans, Buhl farmer Ralph Jones and Simplot Company executive Dennis Jones. Our grant was for two years and during that time we were able to carry out a number of programs to highlight the service of Vietnam veterans and to facilitate their entry into the job market.

Working with Bernie Fisher was a wonderful experience. He was a warm, plain-spoken, humble soul. Just chatting with him, you wouldn't necessarily picture Bernie landing his old propeller-driven fighter on a dangerous piece of land to rescue a downed wingman amongst a hail of bullets coming from practically every direction. But that's exactly what Bernie did. He was the first member of the U.S. Air Force to receive the Medal of Honor in the Vietnam War. On March 10, 1966, Bernie and Major D.W. "Jump" Myers were flying their A-1 Skyraiders over the A Shau Valley in support of a Special Forces camp under attack by 2,000 NVA regulars. When Myers crash-landed on the camp's air strip "which was littered with battle debris and parts of an exploded aircraft," Bernie didn't hesitate to act. He landed his plane on the air strip, picked up Major Myers, and, "In the face of the withering groundfire, he applied power and gained enough speed to lift-off at the overrun of the air strip," his citation said. "While effecting a successful rescue of the downed pilot, heavy groundfire was observed, with 19 bullets striking his aircraft." It should be noted that Bernie also received a Silver Star for his bravery the previous day in the same battle. Quite a record for a humble, down-to-the-earth guy from Idaho.

Shortly after the program kicked off with a press conference on May 23, 1983, Vietnam veterans began contacting the office of IVVLP for job referrals. Within three months, the Idaho Department of Employment had placed more than 80 Vietnam vets in jobs. One veteran who got a job said, "I can't say I'm proud to have fought over there. There's nothing to be proud of. But I'm proud to be associated with the guys who were there." The sentiments he expressed were not uncommon for a wide swath of Vietnam veterans, but instead of only helping with jobs we wanted to make them proud of their service.

It probably happened about a year later and I wish I remembered the circumstances because it made a real impression. A young fellow who looked like he had seen some hard times—drugs and the like—approached me and said, "You're Jim Jones, aren't you?" It is the kind of statement/question you sometimes hesitate to answer. He continued, "I served in Vietnam and have never told anybody because I was ashamed of it. I thought it was something to be ashamed about. Then, I saw you say on television that you were a Vietnam veteran and you were proud of it. I started to think it was something to be proud of and now I tell people that I served there. I feel good about it now. Thanks." IVVLP was hoping to bring about this type of attitude adjustment amongst the veteran population.

Members of the IVVLP board took to the speaking circuit to let Vietnam veterans know they had honorably served their country and to let the general citizenry know that they should be respected for having done so. It was not easy because certain stereotypes had set in regarding Vietnam veterans. The most pernicious was the stereotype of the crazed, blood-thirsty Vietnam veteran, as portrayed in an episode of ABC's Matt Houston that aired on

January 20, 1984. That prompted my following letter to ABC headquarters in New York:

In watching the episode of Matt Houston, which was aired on your network on Friday, January 20, 1984, I was appalled by the offensive manner in which a supposed Vietnam veteran was portrayed. A reprehensible villain gleefully related an instance where he had blown up a village in Vietnam, killing 280 people, obviously while a member of the American military forces. As a Vietnam veteran, I must protest this villainous portrayal of the Vietnam veteran. This type of inaccurate and artistically unnecessary portrayal of a Vietnam veteran as a heinous criminal constitutes an unfair blot on all those who served their country in Vietnam. It certainly fosters the image of the Vietnam veteran as some sort of crazy who is living in our society as an uncontrollable time bomb. Most Vietnam veterans have gotten back into the mainstream of American life and are now fulfilling productive roles in our society. A small percentage of those veterans are still encountering difficulties in making their readjustment to society: They deserve our understanding, support and assistance. Neither those who have readjusted nor those who are still encountering difficulties deserve the type of slur contained in the Matt Houston episode. I am hopeful that your network can be more sensitive to this matter in your future programming.

On July 18, 1984, IVVLP brought General William Westmoreland, who commanded American troops in Vietnam from 1964 to 1968, to Boise to speak on behalf of Vietnam veterans. He made an appropriate speech, saying that the war had not been lost on the battlefield but in the political arena. He said Vietnam veterans had done "a heck of a job" and had earned and deserved the respect of their countrymen.

I enjoyed talking to General Westmoreland and thought he had probably done a fairly good job in Vietnam. By the time I got to Vietnam, Westmoreland was gone and General Creighton Abrams had taken over as commander of the war effort. I had never really studied the track record of either commander until many years later. In 2000, a book titled *A Better War* by Lewis Sorley caught my eye in a book store. It was well written and authoritative. The more I read, the more it appeared to me that General Westmoreland had made the mistake of using conventional war concepts in what was essentially an insurgency. We did not start out trying to win over the populace. Rather, we did any number of things to turn Vietnamese civilians against us. Torching huts, destroying foodstuffs, and pursuing conventional war tactics that resulted in unnecessary civilian casualties, is hardly a recipe for winning the hearts of the general population. Those actions were prescribed by the big brass in Vietnam and not dreamed up by the troops in the field. Standing by while the South Vietnamese government forcibly moved people off of their land and engaged in systematic corruption did not help our war effort, either.

When General Abrams took over in June of 1968, things changed much for the better. However, Abrams took over several months after the 1968 Tet Offensive, which was the turning point in the American public's support for the war. Abrams implemented a number of long-needed counter-insurgency measures designed to win the support of the South Vietnamese people. That all probably came too late because the support of the American public and their politicians for the war effort continued to slip away.

Shortly after Westmoreland's visit, IVVLP made plans to send a plane load of Vietnam veterans to a November 11 dedication ceremony at the Vietnam Veteran's Memorial in Washington, D.C. The main Vietnam Veterans' Memorial, the Wall that contained the names of the over 58,000 dead and missing from the war, had been dedicated on Veterans Day in 1982. This ceremony was for a bronze statue of three GIs in combat gear that had recently been built facing the Wall. The Idaho Coors distributors put up over $10,000 to help fund the trip. The plan was to participate in the dedication ceremonies and then make wall rubbings of the names of as many of Idaho's dead and missing as we could fit into the day.

It was a moving ceremony with speeches from President Ronald Reagan and Secretary of Defense Caspar Weinberger. Even more moving was the rubbing of the names of many of Idaho's war casualties. We placed tracing paper over the name of an Idaho veteran and then rubbed it with a charcoal pencil, leaving a dignified impression of the individual war casualty's name. It was good to be working alongside of those good people who had shared the Vietnam experience. We brought the rubbings home for family members of the fallen.

The trip to the Wall pretty much coincided with the end of the IVVLP program. Funding for the program ran out at the end of November so it was shut down at that time. For what was essentially a volunteer effort, I think it did some good, not only in getting jobs for veterans but also in calling attention to the fact that Vietnam veterans were entitled to be respected just like all of America's other veterans.

Shortly after the end of the year, I was contacted by representatives of an Idaho Falls veterans group named the Idaho Freedom Bird. They presented the exciting idea of constructing a state Vietnam veterans memorial in the City of Idaho Falls. I told them I was all in on the project and would help in any way possible. A number of members of the group had served in Vietnam with the 116th Combat Engineer Battalion, which was one of the few National Guard units that had been called up to serve in the Vietnam War. Its members served there with distinction, receiving the Meritorious Unit Commendation for their 1968-1969 service. Six of the battalion's 800 men were killed in Vietnam and 67 were wounded.

The Freedom Bird went about the job in a businesslike fashion, collecting the name and county of origin of each of Idaho's Vietnam war fatalities. It should be noted that the exact number of Idaho fatalities tends to vary depending on how each casualty was counted. Some counts of service personnel used the state of induction, while other used the state of origin. With a mobile population of military-aged people moving in and out of the state, the figures sometimes varied to an extent. When the memorial was later dedicated, it contained the names of 243 dead and missing.

Many people were involved in getting the memorial off of the drawing board, including Ford Burgess, the Freedom Bird President, Tom Chriswell, who served as a Captain for the 116th in Vietnam, Gary George, Roger Scott, Robert Thornley, James Grimm, Lou Valenti, Del Ray John, Harry Vasbinder and John Shaver. Tom Titus of Boise worked hard for the memorial on the western side of the state. Nancy Shamel, who served as a flight attendant on Freedom Bird flights to and from Vietnam, was a driving force in the effort and is still a powerful spokesperson for the women who served in the war.

Tom Chriswell had designed the memorial, a large inverted V, which he said was "the traditional sign of victory turned upside down." It was to have a carbon steel framework overlaid with polished stainless steel. The memorial would face north and be centered on a black polished-rock deck, surrounded by a single-strand black chain fence. The structure would be 24 feet high, contain the names of all of Idaho's dead and missing, and would have a copper-etched map of Southeast Asia and a bronze bas-relief depicting a soldier, a woman and a POW. It sounded very impressive.

The Freedom Bird estimated the cost at $125,000, which they planned to collect in private donations. They prepared a nice brochure, which contained details of the project as well as supporting letters from Idaho office holders.

Having announced plans for the memorial, the Freedom Bird members moved forward with plans for its construction. Most of the construction work was performed by members of the group but once the project got underway local contractors and architects donated their time to the project. The City of Idaho Falls provided the site for the monument in its Freeman Park, overlooking the Snake River. The City also helped with materials and labor.

I helped kick off a fund-raising effort in western Idaho in June of 1987 and had some success with that. Mountain Bell Telephone

Company, which before being gobbled up by a number of other companies (now CenturyLink), was a good corporate citizen at that time and contributed over $10,000. Other companies kicked in to the fund but there was at least one surprising hold-out. I contacted W.J. Deasy, the President of Morrison-Knudson Corporation, thinking that MK would be glad to contribute since it had received about a billion dollars from the Armed Forces for construction work in Vietnam, including the port facilities at Cam Ranh Bay. In the late nineteen-sixties a billion dollars was a lot of money. However, MK stiffed us, saying that "this is a project to be supported by the people of the State who want a memorial, not by the corporations." A couple of years later, I met personally with William Agee, then the CEO of the corporation, to make another pitch for funding. He turned me down flat. Practically every individual in the corporation who had performed work in Vietnam or served in the Armed Forces was behind the project, but the big brass of the company couldn't bring themselves to honor the service personnel who died or went missing in the war. That was a real disappointment. It may be that Agee was devoting his attention to the task of running this venerable Idaho corporation into the ground. He succeeded in that unfortunate endeavor.

During the time that Freedom Bird was raising funds for the memorial, Idahoans were considering whether to amend the State Constitution to allow for a state-run lottery, as well as charitable gaming. One of the lottery proponents got the bright idea of calling for a $200,000 grant to the memorial project out of the first funds received from any state lottery. It looked kind of like a sweetener to enhance the chances of passage for the constitutional amendment, which caused some heartburn for Freedom Bird members. They expressed the belief that the memorial should be financed solely by private contributions and I thought that was an honorable stand.

The lottery amendment did pass, the State established a lottery, and the $200,000 grant from the lottery fund was paid out for the memorial project. As it turned out, the cost of the memorial came close to $275,000, of which $75,000 was from donations and the remainder from the lottery grant.

During its 1987 session, the Idaho Legislature approved Senate Concurrent Resolution No. 101, designating the Freeman Park memorial as the official Vietnam Veterans' Memorial for the State of Idaho. The memorial was dedicated on August 4, 1990, in a moving ceremony. Hundreds of people from around the state were in attendance. A rollcall of the dead and missing was read, I gave the dedicatory speech, Idaho's Adjutant General, Major General Darrell Manning, gave remarks on behalf of Governor Cecil Andrus, and a number of other speakers paid tribute to Idaho's fallen. Nancy Shamel, one of the spark plugs of the Freedom Bird, said of the service personnel she accompanied on Freedom Bird flights to and from Vietnam, "We took boys to Vietnam and brought back men."

We had tried to get former President Richard Nixon to come to Idaho to be our featured speaker at the dedication. I wrote him on November 13, 1989, to extend the invitation. By letter dated December 26, his assistant, John H. Taylor, regretted the invitation based on a conflict with the opening of the Nixon Library and Birthplace at Yorba Linda, California. Mr. Taylor added a P.S., saying that "the former President is sending you a more personal token of his appreciation." Not long afterward, I received a signed copy of his recently-published book, No More Vietnams, with a dandy autograph. It said, "To Jim Jones, With best wishes. From Richard Nixon. 1-1-90" I expect the autograph would bring enough on the open market nowadays to finance the better part of the cost of a grande coffee from Starbucks. At the time the book came, I still felt somewhat charitable toward the former President with regard to his Vietnam policy. That changed years later.

The memorial had the distinction of being the first Vietnam memorial in the country to recognize the contributions of women during the conflict. Estimates of the number of women who served in Vietnam range between 20,000 and 50,000. The number is hard to pin down because no records were kept. Their roles included nurses, Red Cross personnel, flight attendants on Freedom Bird flights, staff positions in headquarter units of military and diplomatic offices, and Donut Dollies who traveled around the country to entertain the troops. We do know that eight female nurses were killed in Vietnam and they and the other nurses who tended the wounded deserve the thanks of their nation.

The Freedom Bird initiated another project during the time that construction was underway on the memorial. It was decided that a memorial book containing biographical information on all of the dead and missing would be prepared, kept at the memorial site and made available for purchase by the public. That turned out to be a large undertaking.

I volunteered to help collect the biographical information, including such items as personal correspondence written by servicemen to families at home, poems, pictures, personal items, and the like. I wrote a letter to the county commission of each of Idaho's 44 counties, listing the dead and missing from their county and asking for any and all information they could find regarding those individuals. I also wrote to every daily, weekly and monthly news publication in the state to ask for the same information. Members of Freedom Bird made similar efforts, including personal contacts with families. We amassed a significant amount of information about the casualties between September of 1988 and the time the memorial was dedicated. Initially, we had hoped to get the project done in time for the dedication, but that was way too optimistic.

With the information at hand, I made a number of attempts, starting in mid-1990, to write the biographies. I recall sitting on the floor of my home with biographical material and mementos scattered all around, trying to dictate some short biographies. It was practically impossible.

It is difficult to think about the 58,220 casualties that were suffered by the U.S. during that ill-fated war. It is an entirely different thing when you are considering the individual life of a service member who was killed or who went missing in action. It then becomes personal. These were your colleagues, even though you may not have known them personally during the war, and it grabs your heart to think of the fate they met, and for what?

I would read the biographical information of each casualty and feel a kinship and then sorrow at their loss. I can't remember how many times I started the work but ended up with a knot in my chest and tears welling from my eyes. Rather than trying to describe the feeling, let me introduce you to some of these remarkable individuals.

Major Lawrence Dale Acre died on October 9, 1969, while leading a classified Special Forces mission in Binh Long Province. He was a 1951 graduate of Coeur d'Alene High School who then went on to graduate from Gonzaga University. He served three one-year tours in Vietnam, as well as four shorter specific missions. His helicopter was downed by enemy fire, killing everyone on board.

Captain Troy R. Oliver, Jr., died on May 19, 1968, in an ambush in Quang Tin Province. Captain Oliver was born in Twin Falls and graduated from Boise High School in 1954. He had been in the service for 14 years and served as the Provost Marshal on General Westmoreland's staff. He requested an assignment as a rifle company commander near the DMZ.

Colonel Mark Lane Stephensen of the 432nd Tactical Recon Wing went missing on April 29, 1967, during a night bombing mission over Hanoi. His weapons systems officer was captured and held prisoner until 1973. Colonel Stephensen's remains were returned in 1988. He had served in the Air Force for 17 years and this was his second tour of duty in Vietnam.

Sergeant Thomas Oliver Ahlberg, a member of the Army's 101st Aviation Battalion, died on May 4, 1970, when his helicopter crashed into another helicopter while they were dropping flairs in Thua Thien Province. Sergeant Ahlberg attended Skyline High School in Idaho Falls but quit to enlist in the Army where he received his GED. He and two of his brothers served in the military in Vietnam.

Master Sergeant William Balt Hunt went missing on November 4, 1966, near Suoi Day in Tay Ninh Province. He had enlisted from Sandpoint and was a member of the Fifth Special Forces Mike Force. He voluntarily left his aircraft to protect a patrol on the ground that was under attack. He was mortally wounded and his remains were never recovered.

Specialist Fourth Class Alberto Quezada Garcia of the 9th Infantry Division died on June 24, 1970, while fighting off an enemy attack on his patrol. He was born in Juarez, Mexico, graduated from a high school in New Jersey, attended Boise State College, and enlisted in the Army in Nampa.

Private First Class Raymond Patrick Finley of the First Marine Division died in Quang Nam Province on October 1, 1967. He graduated from Saint Maries High School in 1966 and joined the Marines. He was a member of the Flat Head Indian Tribe and served as a medicine man for the Coeur d'Alene Tribe.

Sergeant Conn Kay Clark from Rigby was a member of the 116th Combat Engineers Battalion. He got married a month before his deployment. His truck hit an enemy landmine in Lam Dong Province on July 24, 1969. His brother, who was also with the unit, was able to see him before he was evacuated. He was transferred to a hospital in Japan where he died one week later.

First Lieutenant Johnny William Benton, a member of the 11th Armored Cavalry, died on November 25, 1968, in a helicopter crash in Binh Dong Province. He was a 1965 graduate of Jerome High School and had spent a year at Idaho State University. About 20 years later, I attended a remembrance ceremony where a flagpole was dedicated in his honor at the Jerome City Park. It was a moving ceremony. Rest in peace, Johnny.

Corporal Francisco John Flores of Parma was killed in a battle with enemy forces in Quang Nam Province on May 21, 1967. He attended grade school and junior high in Nyssa, Oregon, and worked in the fields with his father. He had been wounded in two previous engagements. He enlisted in the Marines from Parma and served with the First Marine Division.

Major James Herbert Allred was a graduate of Twin Falls High School who died on December 14, 1963. He was a helicopter pilot who flew medivac missions. As he was getting ready to leave on R&R, a request came in for a medivac helicopter and he volunteered for the mission, taking off in his civilian clothes. After picking up the casualties, the helicopter was shot down and crashed in the ocean. He was last seen trying to save a crewman who could not swim.

First Lieutenant Frank S. Reasoner enlisted in the Marines from Kellogg. He was appointed to the U.S. Military Academy (West Point) in 1958 and graduated in 1962. He died on July 12, 1965, while leading a reconnaissance patrol for the Third Reconnaissance Battalion. Frank posthumously received the Congressional Medal of Honor, the second one granted for service in Vietnam, "for conspicuous gallantry and intrepidity at the risk of his life above and beyond the call of duty."

Private First Class Duane Charles Akkerman, a graduate of Lewiston High School, was killed by small arms fire in Quang Tin Province on October 27, 1967. He was a Chippewa Indian from the "Little Shell Tribe." His five brothers all served in the Armed Forces. He was a member of the First Cavalry Division. When he deployed to Vietnam he left behind a two-week-old son.

Chief Warrant Officer Jon Michael Sparks was a graduate of Carey High School, who was drafted into the Army while attending Utah State University. A member of the 48th Assault Helicopter Company, he was listed as missing in action in 1971 and declared killed in action on March 11, 1976. He was captured when his helicopter was shot down over Laos and never seen again.

Lieutenant Commander Roderick L. Mayer, a 1957 graduate of Lewiston High School and 1961 graduate of the University of Idaho was shot down over Hanoi on October 17, 1965. He and his co-pilot both ejected and were taken prisoner. The co-pilot spent 7½ years in prison and was released in 1973. Lieutenant Cdr. Mayer was declared killed in action on October 31, 1977.

Sergeant Louis Craig Emery was a member of the 25th Division who died near Nui Ba Dinh on March 16, 1970. He was killed by a hail of enemy fire when he opened the hatch of his armored personnel carrier to see where he was going. Sergeant Emery was a 1968 graduate of Parma High School and had also attended Boise State College.

Major Jon Keith Bodahl, an Air Force pilot with the 34th Tactical Fighter Squadron, was listed as missing in action on September 12, 1969, and killed in action on May 30, 1974. He was a 1955 graduate of Nampa High School and a 1960 graduate of the University of Idaho. After flying 254 missions, he was shot down by ground fire near Ban Senphan, Laos, while assisting with the rescue of two downed airmen.

Private First Class Jimmy D. Nakayama, a member of the First Cav. Division, died on November 17, 1965. He was one of 234 soldiers that died in three days of fighting in the Ia Drang Valley. Jimmy died when a napalm canister was accidently dropped on his position. The battle was portrayed in the book *We Were Soldiers Once...and Young*, which was made into a Mel Gibson movie in 2002.

I can't think of Jimmy Nakayama's fate without getting choked up. Being practically incinerated by friendly fire is hard to process. The fate of these and all of the other dead and missing was darned hard to deal with, let alone trying to get it down in writing.

Each time I sat down to start working on the biographies, I thought it would be simple enough to breeze on through them but each time I got bogged down thinking about what these amazing people had done for their comrades and how they had died trying to faithfully serve their country. It was a difficult task that did not seem to be going anywhere. Luckily, Nancy Shamel called to say that she had found a woman in Blackfoot who was a good writer and who was willing to take on the job. I gladly handed over all the material to the writer, Marilyn Whyte. She poured a great deal of effort into the book and came up with an outstanding tribute to those Idahoans who died or went missing for their country.

Marilyn Whyte's book, Reasons to Remember: A Tribute to the Unsung Heroes of the Vietnam War, came out in June of 2002 and was well received. It got some good media coverage, but not as much as I thought it deserved. The number of dead and missing ended up at 251. She added quite a bit of additional information that I had not thought about. She put in the age of the casualties at the time they died or were declared to be dead, the number of children left behind by each one, a history of the conflict, and several other thoughtful and appropriate touches. It was really a good piece of work. I was surprised to see a familiar name in the book's acknowledgements. She expressed great appreciation for the "expert advice and input of my good friend and former State Department Foreign Service Officer, Blaine Jensen." I'd had the pleasure of meeting him at Bon Song, Laos, in December, 1971.

Copies of the books were provided to Idaho officials and many of the families. I think it helped a lot of the survivors to obtain some comfort and closure. Unfortunately, there was only the one printing and copies of the book soon became unavailable for purchase, except from some online marketers, including Amazon.

During my tenure as Attorney General, I looked for occasions to stand up for Vietnam veterans or, in the rare case, to address unfavorable stereotypes. One of the latter instances brought me to make two arguments in a murder/death penalty case involving a Vietnam veteran.

Charles Fain, who had served in the 101st Airborne Division in Vietnam, was convicted in November, 1983, for the abduction, rape, and murder of a 9-year-old Nampa girl. News media reports indicated that he was a Vietnam veteran, which played into the crazed murderer stereotype. I was incensed both because of the brutal victimization of a child but also because of his veteran status and decided to personally argue his appeal of the conviction before the Idaho Supreme Court. I made it a practice to argue one or two appellate cases every year to show that the Attorney General was a lawyer and not just a politician.

Leading up to the March 13, 1985 hearing on the appeal, I checked out the evidence that had been introduced at trial. It was a circumstantial evidence case, which included FBI analysis of head and pubic hairs found at the scene of the crime. The FBI lab verified that they were almost identical to Fain's. There were also unique footprint casts that matched the wear pattern on his shoes and the testimony of two jailhouse witnesses. The evidence was not overwhelming but certainly looked to be sufficient to uphold the conviction and death sentence. The Supreme Court did just that.

Several years later, Fain filed an appeal of a post-conviction proceeding in which he had unsuccessfully raised some evidentiary issues as well as a challenge to his death sentence. The second argument occurred on December 2, 1987, and this time the Supreme Court upheld the conviction but vacated the death sentence, sending the case back for resentencing. The District Court subsequently reimposed the death sentence and then Fain proceeded to seek relief in the federal court system, while remaining incarcerated on death row.

When the initial trial took place, DNA testing was in its infancy. The hair samples found at the scene of the crime did not contain enough DNA to effectively analyze at that time. However, Fain was able to have the hair samples reanalyzed in 2001 when DNA technology had greatly improved. It was determined that the DNA in the samples did not match his. The State made the correct decision to release him on August 24, 2001. He had served almost 18 years for a crime he did not commit. I certainly felt bad about that and wondered if the crazed-veteran stereotype had played a part in the jury's decision to convict.

Fred Hoopes, an Idaho Falls attorney, had represented Fain in the appellate proceedings that resulted in his release. I was visiting another attorney in his law firm in the fall of 2004 and happened to notice Fred speaking with a fellow who looked like he had been through hard times. Fred called me over and introduced me to Fain. He said to Fain, "you know Mr. Jones, don't you?" Mr. Fain said that he did, indeed, know who I was. He was very cordial and did not evidence any bitterness. He and Fred had been on the speaking circuit together, telling his story and speaking of the fact that wrongful convictions do occur in this country.

In April of 2015, the FBI made the stunning admission that most of its hair-comparison expert witnesses had regularly skewed their testimony in favor of prosecutors in the eighties and nineties. It was disgusting to learn at that late date that the FBI had given questionable testimony in life or death cases. The questionable testimony in Fain's case resulted in a Vietnam veteran spending a good portion of his life in prison based on a faulty conviction.

Vietnam vets were still experiencing problems related to their service, including medical and psychological issues that the Veterans Administration did not seem interested in addressing. Post-traumatic stress disorder (PTSD) came into the public consciousness in the nineteen-seventies as a result of veterans coming home with a number of symptoms that had been called a variety of other names in previous wars, like shell shock and combat neurosis. It was recognized as a mental disorder by the American Psychiatric Association in 1980, but the Veterans Administration was slow in providing the counseling and other help that veterans needed to cope. There seemed to be an attitude that people should be able to man up and snap out of it. There was also a less than positive VA attitude toward helping veterans with substance abuse problems that had developed overseas and been brought home. It took quite some time for the VA to come around on these issues.

The VA and its hospitals were good in providing medical care for physical injuries. The Boise Veterans Hospital has gotten good marks from veterans of practically every conflict. The problems arose where new types of injuries manifested themselves, like PTSD and Agent Orange.

It is estimated that around 20 million gallons of Agent Orange were sprayed over Southeast Asia during the Vietnam War years. Copious amounts had been dumped on Tay Ninh Province during my time there. I recall seeing a trio of C-123 aircraft spraying the stuff over War Zone C. We also saw pictures of the Ranch Hands, who spread it over the country, covered from head to toe with the dangerous orange brew as they were loading it on the planes.

When veterans started filing claims in the late seventies for illnesses they claimed were linked to Agent Orange exposure, the VA came out against them with all guns blazing. The argument was that the evil substance was harmless and the vets were trying to get medical care they did not deserve. Just being a lay person, it seemed to me that the vets had a good case. At the time the cases arose, the EPA was telling us that dioxin was a carcinogen and seemed to be worried sick about how it posed a danger to aquatic life in the Chesapeake Bay. If it could cause cancer in one place, it sort of made sense that it would be carcinogenic in any other location. Yet, the VA fought the Agent Orange claims tooth and nail for several years. I thought their response should have been to try to find out if the stuff caused cancer and other dread diseases. Congress stepped in to enact the Agent Orange Act in 1991. By 1993, almost 40,000 claims had been filed, but only 486 vets had been compensated.

I never had any personal contact with the VA during the eighties, although a couple of veteran representatives had urged me to file a claim for hearing loss. A friend from the DAV even fixed up some papers for me to sign. My thought was that VA medical care should go to those who were injured in the line of duty. In 2016, when I was having trouble hearing people in court, I thought it might be time to see about getting my hearing checked through the Department of Veterans Affairs. So, I filed a claim online. The form said a person who served in Vietnam need not furnish financial information so I didn't. The response came back that I was in the lowest category and could not expect help since I had not filed any financial information. I sent an appeal saying that I was just seeking approval of a service-connected hearing claim. The response said I had to prove I had served in Vietnam. Apparently, they overlooked that I had sent the proof with my initial application. I think the appeal may still be pending, but I don't intend to pursue it further. It became apparent why some veterans are driven up the wall in dealing with the DVA bureaucracy.

My relationship with the veteran community was a two-way street because the vets helped me in many ways. In fact, I owe a veteran for something that older Idahoans still remember me for more than 30 years later. When I went in for some surgery in March of 2017, a medical technician at the Boise hospital told me that I was still his hero for getting gasoline prices down in the mid-eighties.

Here's the story. Bill Rawlings, who lived at the Veterans' Home in Boise, frequently called the office on issues that concerned him. I told the palace guard to put his calls through since he had served his country. During a call in the late summer of 1986, Bill asked why the gas prices in Idaho were higher than in the surrounding states. I had not given much thought to the issue before that but told him I'd try to find an answer for him.

I wrote a letter to all of the major oil companies doing business in Idaho to pose the question. We furnished a copy of the letter to all of the media outlets. Most of the daily newspapers around the state had headlines the next day, shouting that the AG was investigating high gas prices. Gas prices immediately fell fourteen cents per gallon around the state and another seven cents the following day in eastern Idaho. Everywhere I went in the next couple of weeks people were thanking me profusely for knocking down the gas prices. I could have been elected as king.

During the rest of my term as AG, I carefully followed the price of gas across the state and made some noise when the difference between the wholesale and retail price got over ten cents per gallon. It is the thing people remember the most about my tenure and they have consistently pestered my successors in the AG's office to do likewise. I owed it all to Bill.

Getting back to the quest I had embarked upon in 1961 of becoming a U.S. Senator, just as I was finishing out my seventh year as Attorney General, one of Idaho's Senators, Jim McClure, announced his retirement. Without much hesitation, I threw my hat in the ring. Idaho's First District Congressman, Larry Craig, had received word of the intended retirement ahead of time and had apparently been organizing to make a run for the office, also.

It was a tough race and I gave it my best shot. I had decided years earlier that I was not going to spend any of my own money on any future political race and stuck to that determination in this race. Also, I had developed a strong aversion to asking people for campaign money so I only raised about $39,000 for the race. Larry out-spent me about 10 to 1 and came off as the winner. I ended the enterprise with a $2,000 surplus in the campaign kitty. During the race, I did on occasion compare my military record to Larry's, which did not include Vietnam service, and mentioned the fact that I had volunteered to serve in that conflict. It probably helped a little because the public attitude toward Vietnam veterans was continuing to evolve in a positive fashion. People were beginning to realize that even though the conflict had been bad for the country, Vietnam veterans were entitled to respect for their service. One indicator in this regard was that several high-ranking Idaho politicians privately told me they wished they had served in Vietnam. I did not say it, but I was thinking it would not have been that hard to do. All one had to do is to ask, although I did have to ask twice.

Right before the May primary election, I had a speaking engagement at the Preston Rotary Club and thought it would be nice to see if Major Painter could join me there. After all, he lived just 25 miles away in Logan, Utah. I figured having one of my fellow service members appear with me could not hurt anything, especially since he had been responsible for saving my skin from the blow-up at Sector headquarters. I got his phone number out of the directory (that is the way people got phone numbers back then) and gave him a call. He said he was teaching engineering or something like that at Utah State. He would be busy at the time of the Rotary meeting so he would not be able to join me. It was just as well because the chicken served for lunch was the worst I had ever eaten, or tried to eat. It had the consistency of lumpy oatmeal. My conversation with Major Painter was only the second time ever that I would have contact with a Proud American compatriot after returning home from Vietnam. Incidentally, I carried the vote in Preston and the surrounding area.

Although it did seem like I'd had good support in the election from the veteran community, moral support does not always get you across the finish line. About two months after the election, I ran into three veterans in the lobby of Boise's Morrison Center. We were all there for some kind of performance. They were all happy that I was running for the Senate and each of them told me I had it in the bag. My thought was that none of them had bothered to vote but that it would be impolite to tell them the election had come and gone without the successful outcome they were predicting after the fact. I thanked them for their kind support.

Having gotten the idea of being a Senator out of my head, I was ready to get on with the rest of my life. I had gotten divorced in 1988 and had been single-parenting my daughter since then. I would have more time to spend with her as she entered her teenage years. After leaving office in January of 1991, I reestablished a law practice, this time in Boise. It seemed like I would be able to put Vietnam behind me for good, but it did not work out that way.

12 ● How soon we forget

During the next ten years, nothing out of the ordinary occurred. One memorable event was a Fourth of July parade in Idaho Falls in the early nineties that the city fathers dedicated to Vietnam veterans. I walked through the parade with a group of fellow veterans, including a large contingent from the Freedom Bird, and it was absolutely great. The people along the parade route were standing up and cheering us on. You could absolutely feel the public support in your bones.

Familywise, I took my daughter, Kathy, on a tour of several European countries to see such wonders of the world as Paris, Salzburg, Prague, Amsterdam, and, of course, Euro Disney. It was a great trip, which she realized many years later. In 1994, I got married to a Twin Falls girl, Kelly Florence, who had two kids, Kristi, who was the same age as Kathy, and Jon, who was a couple of years older than the girls. Kelly has become a successful fiction writer and has been very helpful in my writing endeavors.

Workwise, I rented a suite of offices in a building on Broadway Avenue in Boise for my law office and put an ad in the paper saying, "Jones opens on Broadway." Many people said they liked the ad but it did not result in an immediate rush of paying clients into the Broadway office. It was good to get back to private practice and to be able to help individuals resolve their legal problems on a one-on-one basis. The law practice took off pretty well after a couple of slow months. It was a mix of office work, litigation of various types of cases, and a fair amount of pro bono work.

Although I had never pursued a lawsuit against law enforcement for use of excessive force, I decided to take such a case because it involved a Vietnam veteran. Bobby Kessler was a Reserve Deputy for the Payette County Sheriff. When Bobby's daughter reported to the Sheriff's Office that he had sexually assaulted her, the office devised a strategy for placing him under arrest. They were essentially frightened of Bobby because he was a Vietnam veteran, having served in the Third Squadron of the Fifth U.S. Calvary, the "Black Knights." I gathered that Bobby had played up his exploits in Vietnam because the personnel in the Sheriff's Office regarded him as being a scary and lethal force. He was well versed in martial arts and, in fact, taught martial arts in his own dojo in Payette. He was reputed to be armed at all times.

It is not entirely clear why he was employed by the Sheriff's Office if he was so dangerous, but that's the way it was. The Sheriff contacted the Idaho State Police Crisis Response Team (CRT) and requested that it make the arrest. A Deputy Sheriff told CRT members that Bobby was a dangerous individual, would resist arrest, and usually carried weapons. The CRT officers said the Deputy gave them a "Rambo" image of Bobby and said he would "not be taken alive – will shoot it out if he had to – will go after whoever causes his arrest – will not live in cage." This was the typical crazy Vietnam veteran stereotype.

The Sheriff's Office placed a call to Bobby the evening of December 17, 1992, asking that he report for duty at the jail, which was located in the Payette County Courthouse. The CRT team was waiting for him. When he entered the building, he was sprayed with Cap-stun, a cayenne pepper spray, and then mowed down in a hail of bullets. The evidence was conflicting as to whether he reached for his firearm but it is certain that he never fired his gun.

I decided to take the case for Bobby's wife because of the hyped-up Rambo stereotype, which was likely to have led to Bobby's death whether or not he resisted. I filed suit against the Sheriff and the State Police for his widow, seeking damage for his wrongful death.

The District Judge didn't much like the case so he threw in out on summary judgment. It did not particularly help that the courtroom was packed with uniformed State Police Officers when the motion was argued before Judge Weston. I appealed but the Idaho Court of Appeals upheld the dismissal. Not being one to give up easily, I took the case to the Idaho Supreme Court, which reversed the trial court and sent the case back for trial. Anyone interested can check out the case in volume 129 of the Idaho Reports—*Kessler v. Barowsky*, 129 Idaho 647 (1997).

During jury selection, I asked the prospective jurors if they had negative feelings about Vietnam veterans, whether they thought vets were violent people, and similar questions. Most responded that they had no negative stereotypes, but you just don't know. In a small community like Payette, I suspect a lot of people had heard about Bobby and had their own personal feelings about him.

Partway through the trial, some issues came to light that lead to settlement of the case. It is unknown, therefore, what the jury might have concluded about the case or what jury members may really have thought about Vietnam veterans.

During my law practice, I had a chance to get back to what I really enjoyed doing in off-hours – reading history, traveling overseas, and studying ancient cultures. During my high school years, the coach taught history and that consisted of him reading the textbook to the class. The tests generally called upon us to recite back what event happened at what time and who was involved—dates, places and people--pretty dry stuff. There was never much attention given to the interesting part of history—why events occurred. When I got to college, I took a couple of history courses and they opened up a whole new world. It was really interesting stuff and sparked an interest that continues to this day. I'd learned a lot about world history and foreign affairs in Senator Jordan's office and, after leaving the Attorney General's office, there was more time to get back into it. The civilizations I found the most fascinating were ancient Egypt, Mesopotamia, Rome, those along the Silk Road, and Europe generally.

I enjoyed traveling overseas and, in fact, had wanted to travel to every corner of the earth from the time I started collecting stamps in grade school. A lot of the kids' publications in the late nineteen-forties contained ads for scads of foreign stamps. You could send away for packages of hundreds of cancelled stamps from all over the world for just a dollar or two. It was really eye-opening to see all of the stamps from all of the different countries around the world. There were some exotic places with interesting stamps—Rhodesia, China, Japan, Helvetia (Switzerland), Maroc (Morocco), Somalia. I wanted to go to every one of them when I grew up.

My urge to travel was further fueled by a board game I got for Christmas in the early fifties. Pirate and Traveler took you all around the world to important cities and ports and told you what the chief industries were in the countries. It certainly expanded my horizons at that early age.

After I graduated from the University of Oregon in 1964, I attended a summer school of the University of Vienna in Strobl, a small town north of Salzburg, and took courses in European history and foreign relations. That summer, I traveled to East and West Berlin, Prague, Budapest, and the capitols of a number of Western European countries.

In the seventies, I went to Venezuela, Columbia, Russia, and most of the Western European countries. As Attorney General, I took semi-official trips to Japan and Taiwan. In the nineties, Kelly and I went to a number of European countries, Egypt, and China.

During my term as Attorney General, I didn't spend much time studying the Middle East or considering the Israel-Palestine situation. I just assumed that the Israelis were always right and the Palestinians were always wrong because that was pretty much the Republican philosophy. However, somewhere around 1996 I got a copy of Thomas Friedman's book, *From Beirut to Jerusalem*, and found it wasn't that simple. I read some of the books that he referenced, including *The Iron Wall*, by Avi Shlaim and began following the conflict in the *New York Times*, the *Washington*

Post, the U.K. *Guardian*, *Haaretz* in Israel, and the *Daily Star* in Lebanon.

It became clear to me that some of the Israeli leaders were less than perfect. It was also apparent that the Palestinians had suffered from poor leadership. Israel is a valuable friend and ally but you have to draw a distinction between a country and its leaders. It was a tragedy that Yitzhak Rabin was assassinated in 1995 because I believe he had the courage and vision to have successfully achieved peace with the Palestinians. On the other hand, when Benjamin Netanyahu came into office the following year, the prospects for peace disappeared.

My interest in the Israel-Palestine situation expanded to learning more about the history and culture of the entire region, including Egypt, Jordan, and what are now Iraq, Iran, Syria and Lebanon. So much of today's world was formed by events in this region. It was and is fascinating. I went through various phases of historical study—Egyptian, Mesopotamian, Greco-Roman—in that order, and then continuing to present-day happenings in the region.

During the summer of 2001, I arranged a three-week trip for Kelly and me to visit several Middle Eastern countries. We had spent a couple of weeks in Egypt in 1996 but that wasn't enough. I wanted to go back to the Valley of Kings to spend more time than we had had available during a 1996 trip and I also wanted to spend more time in the archeological museum in Cairo. I got in touch with a nice lady named Latifah who operated a travel agency in Damascus and had her arrange for cars and drivers for visits to a variety of sites in Lebanon, Syria, and Jordan. I figured I would handle Egypt on my own. We had all of our tickets and reservations and were set to embark on September 21, 2001. With the destruction of the World Trade Center on September 11, it seemed prudent to call off our trip.

President Bush sent troops into Afghanistan to go after al-Qaeda, which was the right thing to do. The Taliban were knocked out of the picture in fairly short order, but Osama bin Laden and many of his followers managed to get away. It was clear that al-Qaeda was responsible for the twin-towers attack and it should have been the sole focus of our eradication efforts. What was troubling, however, is that the administration started focusing on Iraq as a potential target. In my view, that was sheer folly and I hoped that cooler and smarter heads would prevail.

Vice President Dick Cheney was cheerleading for an invasion of Iraq and the President appeared to be moving in that direction. Based on their public statements, it was fairly obvious they knew very little about the culture of Iraq. Neither seemed to be aware that there were two branches of Islam, that Saddam and his supporters were Sunni, and that the majority of Iraqis were Shiites. The band of neo-cons that was pushing for the war did not seem to know much more about the culture of the country or the fact that it was a great regional counterweight against Iran, which was certainly more hostile to this country than Hussein's Iraq. They all gave the impression that Saddam was in cahoots with bin Laden and may have played a role in taking down the World Trade Center, which was certifiable bunk.

The *New York Times* published a number of stories under Judith Miller's byline in the summer of 2002 that supported the march to war. The stories were built upon questionable facts, apparently supplied by Cheney or his acolytes. They painted a picture of an Iraq bristling with dangerous weapons and an inclination to use them against us, perhaps in league with bin Laden.

George Tenet, who was then the Director of the Central Intelligence Agency, told Congress in late spring that Saddam did not pose a danger to the United States, unless we were to attack him. He never said anything like that again and it is likely that he was told to keep it to himself. There were reports of mobile biological or chemical weapons labs, which was certainly a sinister possibility. However, those reports were debunked by U.N. weapons inspectors. The trucks in question were for weather observation, which made sense. The idea of having mobile biological weapons labs driving around the country did not seem credible in the first place.

There were claims that Saddam had been training terrorists, including al-Qaeda, how to hijack airplanes at Salman Pak, Iraq. That overlooked the elementary fact that Saddam Hussein and Osama bin Laden were mortal enemies. Not to mention the fact that the reports came from a variety of non-credible sources. Cheney was listening to all kinds of baloney from Ahmed Chalabi, who wanted in the worst way for the United States to attack Iraq, but nobody seemed to pay much mind to the fact that Chalabi was a great chum of the leadership in Iran. The neo-cons were listening to scare stories from a guy called Curveball, who German intelligence had essentially determined to be a nutcase. There was talk about Saddam getting yellow cake uranium from Niger, which was debunked to the satisfaction of any impartial observer. Claims that Saddam was importing aluminum tubes to reconstitute a nuclear program were also discredited. It did not seem to occur to anyone in a position of authority that Iran and al-Qaeda were both hoping and praying for the U.S. to depose Saddam. Much of the bogus intelligence that fueled the march to war likely originated from those sources.

In my view, we were headed for catastrophe in Iraq. I wondered why the administration could not see the stupidity of that venture if a guy sitting out in Boise, Idaho, just reading the available newspapers, could see it so clearly. So, I called Chuck Malloy, who was then the editorial page editor at the Statesman, and asked if he would publish a guest opinion on the issue. He said he would happy to do so. I emailed the following guest opinion to him at the end of August 2002:

We need to do some rethinking on this plan to take out Saddam so that we can spread democracy throughout the Middle East. It won't work. It's like using a sledgehammer to smash a gnat sitting on a keg of TNT. Giving Saddam his just deserts might be relatively easy, the aftermath promises to be a costly quagmire.

I come at this from the standpoint of a hawk, having volunteered for combat duty in Vietnam and having supported every U.S. war, intervention, incursion, and the like ever since. This one is different.

America should only resort to war when three conditions are met: (1) Vital interests of the country are at stake; (2) The cost in blood and treasure is outweighed by the anticipated benefits; and (3) There is a strong, informed national consensus behind it. None of these conditions are present here.

There is no doubt that Saddam Hussein is a sadistic, lying, murdering cut-throat. But, there is no credible evidence that he poses a threat to the United States or that he would dare give weapons to terrorists. The CIA said as much to Congress a couple of months ago until it was muzzled. If you are looking for a sadistic, crazy regime that does sell and may use the most dangerous weapons, look no farther than North Korea. We have taken war off the table there. Saddam may pose a threat to some of his neighbors, but we have no business sacrificing American lives to fight somebody else's war.

The cost of this crusade for democracy greatly outweighs any benefit. We have approached this like a bull in a china shop, trying unsuccessfully to build a coalition through threats and the enticement of multi-billion-dollar aid packages. We have systematically damaged relationships with long-time allies and appear to be intent on alienating the entire Muslim world. This kind of conduct will not serve our long-term interests. It will come back to haunt us.

The lives of hundreds or thousands of America's best will be at risk. It isn't worth the price where no substantial national interest is at stake. If our purpose is to remake the Middle East and spread democracy, good luck. Have we done so well in our efforts to bring peace to Palestine that we need to move our efforts to a wider stage?

While we will undoubtedly eliminate Saddam, we'll also have to take responsibility for a chaotic aftermath. It will take many thousands of American troops and a number of years to feed and rebuild the country, to keep the Kurds and Shiites from taking revenge against the Sunnis, to keep the Turks and Iranians out, and to keep instability from spreading to the surrounding countries. And, I don't expect we will be regarded as benevolent conquerors.

The cost of the initial hostilities, including the multi-billion-dollar aid commitments being tossed to the countries in the region, plus the staggering cost of policing and holding Iraq together in the aftermath, will be well over $ 100 billion. The planners refuse to give an estimate. Add this to an already staggering economy, a massive budget deficit and chronic balance of payment deficits and it simply doesn't pencil out. Rome learned that you are only as powerful as the size of your purse.

Then, there is a question of the national consensus. It is shaky at present and would even be more so if the Administration would level with us as to the cost of the long-term post-war commitment. I know what it is to experience a flagging national consensus. When I went to Vietnam, the country was behind us. When I returned, it wasn't—the politicians had all run for cover. Just as we had finally overcome the early mistakes and had the war on a winning track, the U.S. packed its bags and told the government of South Vietnam to take a hike. I carry a deep anger for that breach of faith and a profound grief for my 58,000 comrades whose sacrifice was cheapened as a result. Let's not do it to another generation of America's best and brightest.

We need to focus our efforts on the real target—Al Qaeda and the other terrorists who, unlike Saddam, have nothing to lose and who will stop at nothing to kill Americans. Let's not take our eye off the target. We need to cooperate with our traditional allies to root out and eliminate these people. Each one of them is more dangerous to Americans that Saddam has proven to be. We need to show the world that we will follow through in the aftermath by actually helping to stabilize and rebuild Afghanistan. Going it alone on a diversionary project is simply not helpful.

If the shooting starts, I'll be 100% behind the troops. Until that time, we all have a responsibility to speak out and give the folks in command some pause before they pull the trigger. It just might be that most of the rest of the world has a point.

I probably ought to make two comments here. First, I may have overstated my support for every possible hostile action engaged in by the U.S. since Vietnam. However, I thought it necessary to establish I was not a pacifist so that red-blooded patriots might pay attention to what I said. The point of publishing the piece was to get the attention of our Congressional delegation as they seemed to be inclined toward war. Second, my estimate of the cost of the war was way off of the mark. We squandered at least ten times my estimate and about double that if you figure indirect costs, like the increased prices we paid for gasoline and others fuels as a result of the oil market turmoil caused by the Iraq war, and the greatly increased length and cost of fighting in Afghanistan because of the diversion of critical war resources from that necessary engagement to the unnecessary war in Iraq.

Not long after I sent the guest opinion to Chuck, it was announced that Secretary of State Colin Powell would address the United Nations about Iraq. I thought that Powell was going to bring some sense to the debate so I asked Chuck to hold off publishing the guest opinion. I figured I would see what Powell had to say and go from there.

When Powell finally made his presentation to the U.N., it appeared that there was no point in publishing the opinion piece. As soon as Powell claimed that the weather stations were mobile weapons labs, I figured the fix was in. I lost a great deal of respect for Powell because there was solid information available to him, as well as anybody with access to publicly-available information, that these were not mobile weapons labs. So, we were off to war and practically everything I predicted in my guest opinion came true. We had not learned a damn thing from our Vietnam experience. We were stumbling into a war that was not necessary, we didn't know the culture of the country we were attacking, we did not anticipate the inevitable guerilla war that would ensue, and we were oblivious to the fact that this stupid war would destabilize the entire region for years to come. Heaven help us!

We made short work of Saddam's forces and then set about implementing policies that would almost surely bring about failure of the effort. The person appointed to oversee the aftermath, Paul Bremer, had no idea what he was doing. What he did do is bring in a bunch of know-nothings like himself to dismantle the Iraqi government and military. It apparently did not occur to him that kicking most of the Baath Party members out of those institutions and turning them loose with their guns was not the best idea. The party members, mostly Sunnis, had carried out Saddam's wishes while he was in power and there were certainly some bad actors who needed to pay for their atrocious conduct. However, a great number of them had just joined the party to advance their careers and were not human rights abusers. They could have helped to bring stability to a new government. By tossing them out, Bremer laid the seeds for sectarian conflict and insurgency, somewhat reminiscent of the religious divide in South Vietnam, which caused instability in that country. There, the Catholics, who were a minority but generally in charge, were often at odds with the Buddhist majority. When Buddhist monks began burning themselves to death in public, the self-immolation caused havoc throughout the country.

Bremer apparently had no clue about the Iraqi culture, or the religious fault lines in the country, or how to form a government that would not create unnecessary divisions among the people. This is not the place to delve into the subject in depth but I would suggest a wonderful book that does so—*Imperial Life in the Emerald City* by Rajiv Chandrasekaran, the *Washington Post*'s former Baghdad bureau chief. One of my favorite parts of the book is where a U.S. Army Major describes Bremer's effort to put together an Iraqi government as throwing feathers together, hoping for a duck. That was an apt description.

The U.S. military was also unprepared for the aftermath. Even though the U.S. State Department had put together a viable plan for reconstruction, the administration ignored it. No concrete plans had been drawn up by the military for how to get the country back up and running. The military had waged an effective conventional campaign but was not prepared to deal with the insurgency that was taking shape. It was as if all of the lessons that had been learned in Vietnam had completely disappeared from the military's collective memory. It did not help that the Vice President repeatedly dismissed the possibility that an insurgency was forming, claiming the troubling attacks being carried out against our forces were merely the work of "dead enders."

Again, I will not go into detail about the military's handling of the aftermath but would highly recommend reading *Fiasco: The American Military Adventure in Iraq, 2003 to 2005* by Thomas E. Ricks, the former Pentagon bureau chief for the *Washington Post*. He describes how the military brass had virtually no knowledge of what an insurgency might look like or how to deal with it. General Raymond Odiorno, who commanded the Fourth Division in western Iraq, employed conventional tactics that fueled the insurgency in Anbar Province. During the early part of the war, Odiorno and other commanders used hard-edged tactics against suspected insurgents, substantially more force than was reasonable or necessary, and employed loose rules of engagement that caused excessive civilian casualties. He admitted after the fact that he should have employed counter-insurgency tactics that called for working with the local Sunnis to ensure their safety, both from the Baath Party hard-liners and also from the Shia leadership in Baghdad.

The situation in Iraq seemed to be deteriorating in the fall of 2003 and things did not look any better in Afghanistan. Despite our initial success in Afghanistan, we had shifted our focus to the war in Iraq. Much of the equipment and personnel that were essential to a successful outcome in Afghanistan was shipped off to Iraq. Had we left Iraq alone, as we should have, and focused our attention on Afghanistan, we might have achieved peace there many years ago. But in 2003, we were spread too thin and were struggling in both wars. On August 21, 2003, I wrote to Andy Card, who was then serving as White House Chief of Staff, to make that point. I had met Andy in the eighties, when he was serving as President Reagan's liaison to state elected officials. He often attended meetings of the state attorney general group and seemed to be a reasonable person.

The following guest editorial, which I circulated in Idaho at the same time, sets out the substance of my letter to Andy:

The United States must get serious about stabilizing Iraq and Afghanistan. After eliminating the regimes in both countries, we took on the responsibility of stabilizing those countries, providing security for their people, and getting them back on their feet. We made solemn commitments to carry through with these obligations but have yet to deliver in either case. There are some hopeful signs that Secretary of State Powell and the generals have finally gotten the civilians in the Defense Department to wake up to these facts. We need to make sure they follow through.

The situation in Iraq is extremely perilous and, unless we take immediate and drastic action, it will only get worse. The Defense Department civilians would have us believe we are turning the corner and that we only need to deal with a few Saddam loyalists, foreign trouble makers, and "dead enders." Such rosy assessments are pure hogwash!

It is true that Saddam loyalists are doing their best to create chaos. And, Iraq has become a magnet for foreign extremists looking for easy American targets. But, a growing number of those using our troops for target practice are neither of the above. They are malcontents who are getting fed up with our lack of effective action to honor our optimistic promises to make their lives better and more secure. We have got to apply adequate manpower and resources to address the security concerns of the general populace, get them basic services such as electricity, water, sanitation and medical care, and do something about unemployment. Otherwise, the situation is going to quickly spin out of control. Robbery, car-jacking, factional strife, religious assassinations and, not least, attacks on our troops are all on the rise.

The idea that we can do this job on the cheap is the worst kind of wishful thinking. It is going to take much more manpower on the ground, regardless of nationality, and tens of billions more in U.S. money. We are fast losing the window of opportunity that the Pentagon task force said we might have back in July. It is time to get serious about the situation in Iraq and do something about it.

The same problem exists in a different fashion in Afghanistan. If we are not going to make the Karzai government stronger and expand its influence outside of Kabul, we are just wasting our time there. That government is currently on life support and slowly losing its limited influence in the hinterlands. Unless we act quickly and dramatically, we risk failure there, too.

I grieve for each of our service personnel killed in both countries. As a person who volunteered for combat duty in Vietnam, I know that these folks are willing to pay the price if it makes America more secure. But, America is obliged to follow through with its commitments to ensure their service and sacrifice are not in vain. The thing that hurts Vietnam veterans the most is that our country failed to carry through with its solemn commitment to make their service count for something. If we are too stingy to back up our commitments with adequate resources, too proud to ask other major countries for their help, too short-sighted to see that a failure here will damage America's long-term security interests, and not willing to do the ultimate to protect our troops, let's leave now before it is too late.

It really bothered me that our military personnel were doing their level best to defeat the insurgents in both countries, suffering casualties in the process, and might end up feeling that it had been in vain if we failed in either or both wars. I got a polite acknowledgement in response to my letter but little else.

Almost a year later, I received a letter from Marc Racicot, a former Montana attorney general and governor, seeking funds for the re-election of the Bush-Cheney ticket. As a result of their misguided war policy, I was not much inclined to send any money. It was a form letter and should have just gone into file 13 but I knew Marc through our attorney general connection and thought this would be an opportunity to give some input. So, on May 21, 2004, I send him a letter reading in part:

It is with a good deal of regret that I must decline your request to make a contribution to the Bush-Cheney campaign. In my humble opinion, the Bush-Cheney team has caused substantial damage to the national interest and made the world a more dangerous place for Americans.

History will show the Iraq war to be one of the greatest foreign policy blunders in American history. It has seriously damaged American credibility and will have long-lasting detrimental effects on our vital interests. The war was not necessary as a part of any war on terror or for any other reason. Rather, it has seriously compromised our efforts to combat international terrorism. Indeed, the Bush-Cheney Middle East policy will produce far more anti-American terrorists over time than al Qaeda could ever have produced.

The war has been a tragic series of miscalculations and blunders and is bound to end with a result that will be extremely detrimental to our national interests. There were never enough troops, as the Army generals who weren't afraid to speak out continually said. As a result of continual blunders, we are now begging for the United Nations, which we shunned from the start, to set up some sort of government so that we can hand over the hot potato and hope like hell it doesn't explode before we can get past the November elections. The idea that we were going to shove democracy down the throats of the Iraqis, whether they wanted it or not, was dangerous and naïve. Now, 80% of the Iraqis want us to get out, we have managed to turn Moqtada al-Sadr into a folk hero, a lot of people who were shooting at Americans in Falluja are in charge of the city, the world thinks Americans are brutes because of the interrogation procedures approved by the civilians in the Pentagon and we have the tragic farce playing out with the Neocons' buddy, Chalabi.

Ahmed Chalabi, who had provided bogus intelligence that helped fuel the march to war, was doing his level best to exclude anyone with Baath Party connections from any position of influence in Iraq. Most of them were Sunnis, which helped to stoke religious strife, which strengthened the insurgency. Things had gotten very ugly, in large part because our military leadership had not been made privy to all of the lessons learned, or which should have been learned, from the Vietnam War.

Just six days after I sent my letter to Marc, he replied. Unfortunately, it appeared that he had caught a dread disease that I had been warned against when I was working for Senator Jordan in the summers of 1965 and 1966. Ed Woosley, who was Jordan's natural resources guy at that time, told me not to stay in D.C. too long because I might get Potomac Fever, an affliction that causes you to lose perspective of the wider world. You get sucked into the Washington way of thinking and acting and have a hard time escaping back into the reality of life outside of the Capitol city. Marc responded like so many members of Congress, who often think it a chore to have to respond to pesky letters from constituents:

I have received and carefully reviewed your August 21, 2003 letter regarding the need for changes in the Department of Defense's approach to Iraq and Afghanistan. I appreciate the time it took you to write and share your thoughts and ideas with me. I want to assure you that I will share your ideas at the earliest opportunity with those in the position of authority to act.

At least he did not address the letter to Dear Sir or Madam. Well, what could I expect, he was not serving as an elected representative of the people at the time, being in a private law firm. He was just a good, common-sense fellow from Montana who had succumbed to the Washington way of responding to thoughts or suggestions from beyond the Washington beltway.

There is not much anyone out in the hinterlands could have done to affect what was going on or going wrong in either of the war zones. The die had been cast and things were going to play out however they might. At least General David Petraeus had come to the fore in Iraq and was able to implement an effective counter-insurgency program amongst the Sunni tribes in western Iraq. He met with tribal leaders, learned their concerns, showed that he was intent on working with them to improve the situation for their people and managed to tamp down the insurgency in that area. He had successfully implemented a similar program in Mosul as commander of the 101st Airborne Division shortly after the invasion. Unfortunately, his successors did not follow up on his good groundwork when he left Mosul and the situation there deteriorated. Nouri al-Maliki, who served as Prime Minister of Iraq from 2006-2014, was able to unravel all of the good work Petraeus had done in Anbar Province by cutting the Sunnis out of power in the government and military, leading to the rise of the Islamic State.

Had we heeded the lessons we should have learned from the Vietnam experience, we would not have invaded Iraq in the first place. The claim that Iraq had weapons of mass destruction and an inclination to use them against us was about as solid as the claim that our ships were attacked by the North Vietnamese in the Gulf of Tonkin.

Neither war would have been justified by an objective evaluation of the evidence. When we did invade Iraq, we were clearly unaware of the need to employ counter-insurgency measures to prevent or deal with guerilla war.

However, there was a more important lesson we should have drawn from Vietnam and it seems not to have occurred to those in charge of U.S. military policy even to the present day. One of the main factors that contributed to our failure in Vietnam was public perception, both in the U.S. and around the world. When television reporters can show us what is actually happening on the ground in real time and it does not match up with what the public is being told through official channels, it is a big problem. When people at home can see images from the war on their TV screens that make them shrink back, it can seriously erode public support for a military venture.

When Walter Cronkite told the American public on CBS News after the Tet Offensive that the war was not worth it, that was a turning point in support for the war.

The media should be able to report what is going on in a conflict so long as the coverage does not jeopardize on-going operations. However, the military has to recognize that people around the world are cognizant of what is going on in the war zone. It is no longer a situation where our forces just have to win the hearts and minds of the populace in the area of conflict. We can't succeed if we conduct ourselves in a manner that inflames opinion against us in the wider world. That particularly applies to conflicts in the Middle East.

Many people around the world were angry when we attacked Iraq, but many people in Iraq who had suffered under Saddam's regime were thankful. Some of the thankful people turned against us when we did not take adequate measures to restore order and basic services. Many people became angry when they experienced or saw media reports of heavy-handed measures—kicking down doors, shoving people around, male soldiers searching the person of female suspects. They became inflamed when they learned of suspects being waterboarded at CIA black sites, of indiscriminate shooting of civilians by U.S. Government contractors, of the brutal treatment of prisoners at Abu Ghraib Prison, and of the perpetual imprisonment, without trial, of suspects at Guantanamo Bay.

These are all things that could and should have been avoided, without adversely affecting the mission.

All of our actions are being played out on the world stage and we need to comport ourselves in a fashion that wins the hearts and minds of that broader population. For instance, the unnecessary mistreatment of prisoners at Abu Ghraib caused many people in Iraq and around the world to think we were brutal hypocrites. It was used by jihadis around the world as a handy recruitment tool, claiming we had it in for all Muslims. Many American casualties likely resulted from the reaction caused by that fiasco. Likewise, the imprisonment, without end, of suspects at Guantanamo has helped terrorists to recruit many followers. We could have incarcerated those people in maximum security prisons in the U.S. and would likely have been able to process them through our civilian court system years ago. The military is still trying to figure out how to handle the prosecutions and it is a continuing black mark for our country.

The Muslim ban implemented in 2017, limiting travel to the U.S. by citizens of several Muslim countries, is a continuing thorn in the side of our country. We are allied with numerous Muslim-majority countries whose support is critical to our national security. It does not make sense to target these countries, especially since none of the 9-11 attackers came from the affected countries. The ban is an unnecessary impediment to our national security objectives.

There is one thing that came out of the Vietnam experience that was very positive.

As people reflected upon the war, I believe many of them came to think that the troops who served in Vietnam were not all that bad. After all, they served their country, even if it may not have been in an ideal war. With that in the background, when the wars in Iraq and Afghanistan were underway, it really warmed my heart to see the respect and thanks the troops got from people across the spectrum. Folks were generally supportive of the war in Afghanistan, at least until it stretched past the first decade. There were fewer people who supported the war in Iraq, thinking that it was not necessary.

Nevertheless, people were able to separate their feelings about the conflict from their feelings about our service men and women. It was great to see folks go up to those in uniform and thank them for their service. Welcome home.

13 ● Benched, then uncorked

In addition to speaking out about Iraq and Afghanistan, I continued to write opinion pieces and letters to Congress regarding flawed U.S. policy toward Israel and Palestine. Sometimes the members of the Idaho Congressional delegation would write back in response to my letters, thanking me for taking the time to write and giving assurances that they would give serious consideration to whatever it was that I had written about. Back when I was working for Senator Jordan, that type of non-response was reserved only for those who sent mimeographed form letters to the Senator. When a constituent sent a letter expressing their own views in their own words, I always prepared a reasoned response for Jordan's review.

My 1990 campaign for the Senate had pretty much satisfied my ambition to serve in that body. It was becoming increasingly partisan and my views on many issues were diverging from Republican orthodoxy. When I first decided that the Senate was a worthy goal back in the early sixties, really remarkable people were serving in the Senate in both parties. They were their own people, not merely the agents of big business or big labor. Both parties had members whose philosophies diverged in some respects from their party platforms. In subsequent years, each party began retreating into group think, a trend that intensified in the nineties.

Middle Eastern policy in the George W. Bush administration was particularly galling. Speaking out against the administration's actions may not have done any good, but at least it gave me a sense that I had tried to make a difference. It is good to get it off of your chest when you see the country's policy going off of the rails. However, I made a decision in October of 2003 that affected my ability to speak out on the issues. Wayne Kidwell, who was then serving on the Idaho Supreme Court, gave notice that he would not run for reelection when his term expired at the end of 2004. That meant his successor on the Court would be selected at the May primary election in 2004. The day after Wayne's announcement, I was meeting with Al Lance on an issue affecting a shared client. In addition to talking about our client's issues, we discussed Wayne's decision to retire from the Court. Wayne had served a term as Attorney General before me, from 1975 to 1979, and Al had served two terms after me, from 1995 to 2003. Al asked if I was going to throw my hat in the ring for Wayne's position and I told him he was crazy.

When I got home that evening, I started thinking about serving on the Court. The more I thought about it, the less crazy it sounded. I had done a good deal of appellate work since starting my law practice in Jerome. The Attorney General handles all civil and criminal appeals for the State of Idaho and I had argued one or two cases on behalf of the state each year during my eight-year tenure, including three in front of the U.S. Supreme Court. It was interesting work and the idea of doing appellate work from behind the bench started to sound pretty good. I ran the idea past Kelly and she thought it might be alright, so long as it did not entail a big campaign.

I set out to organize a campaign committee of people from across the state, representing a wide range of views and interests. My thought was to discourage any challengers and the plan worked quite nicely. There was no competition in the May primary, so I was elected to the job with a start date of January, 2005.

It became apparent early on in that endeavor that I would have to put a cork in my public discussion of political issues. That was a bit of a downer, but it was an essential component of the job. Therefore, I pretty much maintained silence on issues that I often felt strongly about for the next 12 years.

In addition to the frustrations of the Bush administration's Middle East policy and its inattention to the worsening situation in Afghanistan, there was dangerous fallout from the instability caused by the Iraq War. The insurgency there resulted in a massive flood of refugees into Syria. Extremists from there and other nations had flocked to both Afghanistan and Iraq to fight American forces and our policy in Iraq was fueling extremism throughout the area. At the same time, democracy advocates in Egypt, Syria and other Arab countries were demanding freedom from their repressive dictators. When the Arab Spring broke out in March of 2011, the seeds were sewn for potential disaster. The Egyptians got rid of their oppressive leader, Hosni Mubarak, the Libyans got rid of their odious dictator, Muammar Gaddafi, and the Syrians tried to get out from under the thumb of their dictator, Bashar al-Assad.

But for the fact that I was essentially muzzled because of my job, I would have admonished President Obama for not putting more effort into trying to stabilize Libya after helping to knock out Gaddafi. It might have been better to stay out of that fight altogether, except for the fact that it looked like Gaddafi was getting ready to wage a bloodbath against his own people. The NATO intervention was probably the right thing to do but it should have been followed up with substantial effort to get the country back up and running. It was hard to just sit on the sidelines and not throw in my two bits worth on this one.

It was even harder to keep quiet about the political firestorm that arose over the death of Chris Stevens, the U.S. Ambassador to Libya, at Benghazi on September 11, 2012. The Republicans in Congress used his death as a bludgeon to hit Hillary Clinton over the head in the lead-up to the 2016 presidential election. The State Department could and should have taken steps to protect the U.S.

compound at Benghazi, but Chris was undoubtedly aware of security concerns in that volatile city. He also knew that he nevertheless had an important job to do there.

I don't recall that I ever met Chris, but his father, Jan Stevens, was a good friend. He had been a judge in California, but when I got to know him he worked as a Deputy Attorney General for the State of California. He was an accomplished attorney in the natural resources field and a wonderful human being. We had gotten acquainted in working on multi-state resource issues and social events at meetings of the Conference of Western Attorneys General in the nineteen-eighties. At a meeting in Sedona, Arizona, my daughter, Kathy, had been befriended by some of Jan's children, which might have included Chris. Kathy enjoyed their friendship, particularly that of Jan's daughter, Hillary. They were really good people.

The grief they had to live with because of the vicious political warfare over Chris' death was beyond the pale. In my estimation, Chris had served his country honorably and way beyond the call of duty. The people of Benghazi obviously revered him, as was made clear from news reports from the city after he was killed. He was working effectively for his country in an important part of Libya, under dangerous conditions. Rather than turning him into a political football, Congress should have given him high honors for his extraordinary service. I wrote a couple of letters to the editor in that regard but had to put them in the wastebasket because of my judicial position.

It was also difficult not to voice concern about the situation in Syria. We certainly encouraged the Syrian dissidents and correctly called for the removal of Assad but didn't do much at all to help those who were yearning for freedom and democracy. This has been somewhat of a recurring theme in American foreign policy. That is, we urge oppressed populations to throw off the yoke of their oppressors, building expectations that we will help when they do, but we often fail to come to their aid when they do rise up.

I recall back to the Hungarian Uprising in 1956, which we heard a lot about on the radio at the time. Voice of America had been urging the oppressed people in Hungry and other Eastern European countries to rise up for freedom from the USSR and the Hungarians apparently took that as a sign we would help. They did rise up in 1956, we did not lift a finger to help, and they were brutally suppressed by their Soviet overlords.

Much the same thing happened in Czechoslovakia during the Prague Spring in 1968. We encouraged the Czechs to support liberal reforms in their country. When they rose up in support of the reform movement, the Soviets invading to put a stop to it. We did not step forward to help the reformers as their movement was being crushed.

You have to be careful about raising the expectations of a suppressed population. If you are not going to come to their aid, you must make that fact explicitly clear. When people in Syria took to the streets and were met with brutality, they responded with armed insurrection, partly based on encouragement from our government. We then had an obligation to give them a hand. Sitting in my office at the Supreme Court, it was hard not to say something and I almost felt like joining the insurrection. When the insurgents were able to plant a bomb in military headquarters that did away with a few top Syrian leaders, it looked like the insurgency might be successful. Had we taken action at that time to support the people who were truly seeking democratic reforms, it may well have paid off. By dithering around, undecided as to what to do or who to support, the situation slipped into chaos. It was fertile ground for the rise of the Islamic State, which was primarily the project of Saddam loyalists, many of whom were graduates of our failed efforts early on to stabilize Anbar Province. Al-Qaeda also got into the act, making the Syrian revolution a many-sided war that simply got out of hand.

Limited early involvement in the Syrian uprising would have served America's interests. This was a popular revolt against a repressive government that was a thorn in the side of Israel and Lebanon. Assad was also a major backer of Hezbollah, which participated in the bombing of the U.S. Marine barracks in Beirut in 1983 that killed 241 American servicemen. We should have provided support to the Syrian citizens' uprising. It was hard to keep my mouth shut on this travesty, although it was unlikely speaking out would have made any difference.

In August of 2006, I attended the 40-year reunion of Kelly's high school class—the Twin Falls High School Class of 1966. The class had taken on the project of refurbishing a memorial at the City Park for the 17 Twin Falls County residents who died in the Vietnam War. The memorial was dedicated on Memorial Day in 1967 and was the first Vietnam memorial in the state. Kelly introduced me to a former classmate, James Peterson, who had served with the Special Forces in Vietnam—with B-32 at Tay Ninh, A camps at Thien Ngon and Trang Sup, and B-36 MGF (Mobile Guerrilla Force). James was rotating back to the States near the time I arrived in-country. He knew all about Thien Ngon, Katum and all of the other places out in War Zone C that I had flown over. He had been on the ground and we were able to compare notes.

I told James about the NVA facilities our intelligence people had identified over the border in Cambodia and of my skepticism about their accuracy—the hospital and R&R center north of Katum and the base camp southwest of Thien Ngon. He indicated that those facilities were indeed located just over the border. So, our intel people were better than I had thought. I told him about the bridge I had collapsed just before leaving Vietnam, whereupon he excused himself and went to rummage around in the trunk of his car. When James came back, he showed me an album with pictures of the area where he had served. Much to my amazement, the album contained a photo of that very same bridge.

Class members decided the high school needed a plaque honoring alumni who had served and died in Vietnam. The project was completed and the plaque dedicated in May of 2007. It was a moving ceremony. Those who were honored by the memorial plaque were a remarkable group of people, just as their many comrades in arms who gave their lives in that conflict.

There is one other thing that deserves mention about my time on the court. For those twelve years, the Idaho Supreme Court had two Vietnam veterans. Dan Eismann was elected to the Court in 2000 and left after I did. Dan served in Vietnam as a door gunner on a Huey gunship and received two Purple Hearts. It was good to have someone on the Court who shared that experience, although we did not talk about it all that much. Dan had been exposed to Agent Orange and grappled with a difficult case of non-Hodgkins lymphoma, which he eventually overcame. He then had to deal with melanoma. He showed a lot of courage during those struggles, which is not surprising given his war record.

As I started my 12th year on the Supreme Court, I was itching to get back into the public arena and to have a general change of scenery. The number of interesting appeals had fallen off in the last several years and the job did not have the same challenges as when I had started 11 years earlier. I announced in March that I would serve out the rest of my term but not seek reelection in the May primary. I decided not to take senior status – that is, to stay on as a member of the judiciary and be available to sit in on cases when one of the Court members was recused on a case or otherwise unavailable to participate – so that I could do some legal work and take part in public discourse. There was an increasing political divide in the country, particularly when the presidential race shaped up as a contest between Hillary Clinton and Donald Trump, and it was hard to resist making public comment on the issues upon which the two repeatedly clashed. I was looking forward to shedding my robe, along the restraints that it placed on my ability speak my mind.

Despite wanting to move on, I have to say that being able to serve on the Court was a great honor. For the most part, it was challenging and rewarding work. During my 12 years, the Court made some really important decisions, particularly in the area of water rights and water management, and it was exciting to be part of that. The other members of the Court were all fine individuals who were dedicated to the rule of law. Roger Burdick, the fellow who preceded me as Chief Justice and then succeeded me in that position when I retired, is an outstanding jurist and dear friend. I do miss them but don't regret my decision to leave.

My last day on the Court was December 30. My Swan Falls book had been released earlier in December and I wanted to get out to promote it right away—something that would have been difficult as a member of the Court. I already had some speaking engagements lined up. It did not work out quite like I planned, though. I'd had some discomfort in my left side a couple of times in the previous weeks and had gone in for an MRI and then a CT scan. Both showed a suspicious blob on my pancreas so my doctor ordered an ultrasound. On Friday the 13th, just two weeks after my last work day, Dr. Akshay Gupta, who had done the ultrasound, called to say he had bad news. He said the blob was a pancreatic cancer tumor. It was not particularly what I had expected of retirement.

Anyway, the tumor and surrounding tissues were removed by Dr. Joshua Barton, one of the best pancreas/liver surgeons around, with the assistance of the Da Vinci mechanical operating system at St. Luke's Hospital. Then, there were 6 months of chemotherapy by Dr. Dan Zuckerman, a skilled Boise oncologist, with the help of some wonderful people at the Mountain States Tumor Institute. The cancer went into remission, which has allowed me to get on with my life.

When I got the diagnosis, I did what we all do for any ailment from hangnail to heart attack—consult with the real expert, Mr. Google, who advised that the chances of recovering from pancreatic cancer were pretty iffy, anywhere from 3% to 30%. At least it was not hopeless.

The cancer news caused some rethinking about my plans for this book. Writing about Vietnam had been on my mind for years but it is easier to think about such a project than to get it going. It looked like the project would have to get kicked into high gear if it was going to be completed before it was too late. So, there was finally some incentive to get going and I did just that.

One thing that puzzled me was what could have caused the cancer. I started thinking about the large area of War Zone C that had been sprayed with Agent Orange. Although I had not tramped through the jungle, there was a good likelihood that evaporation into the air contained traces of dioxin. That air drifted over Tay Ninh City and we regularly flew through it on VR missions. It also occurred to me that the Tay Ninh Canal, which was fairly close to our hooch, was downstream from War Zone C and in its drainage area. It could be that the putrid-smelling water in our shower contained amounts of dioxin. So, there were several sources of dioxin in the vicinity.

Several people commented online that they or a family member had contracted pancreatic cancer as a result of exposure to Agent Orange. It was not a cancer that was recognized by the DVA as being linked to Agent Orange, but I'm not sure that means much, given the agency's track record of resisting Agent Orange claims.

Another possible cause surfaced when I was exchanging emails with another Vietnam vet who mentioned a Belgium beer festival that was going to be held somewhere along the Saigon River in the summer of 2017. I responded that it was odd for the Vietnamese to be boosting beer from Belgium when they probably still made Tiger Beer and Export 33. He claimed that the Vietnamese beers had contained formaldehyde, which struck me as unlikely. The internet told me in no uncertain terms that Tiger Beer contained formaldehyde, that Export 33 probably did, and that just about all of the beer shipped over to the troops from the U.S. also did. It was added to preserve the beer in the hot climate. It can't be good for a person to ingest the stuff and I had probably drunk more than my share. It has been linked to nose and throat cancer, leukemia, and who knows what else. On the bright side, it might help to preserve a person in the event of an untimely death.

Whatever caused the cancer is probably beside the point. I was lucky to have good health insurance so there is really no reason for trying to pinpoint a cause. But, it leaves one to wonder whether it might be another carry-over effect of service in Vietnam.

Despite the bad health news, it was a good feeling to be able once again to speak my mind. Having shed the judicial robe, I was liberated and the shackles were off. I did not let any grass grow under my feet. Earlier, I had scheduled a speech at the Twin Falls Rotary Club for January 18 and decided to use the opportunity to address the refugee issue that had arisen in that community. The College of Southern Idaho's refugee program was under attack by some local folks, as well as a number of less-than-credible outside media sources. My presentation was along the lines of the following press release I sent out that day:

Former Attorney General and Supreme Court Justice Jim Jones said today that "Idaho has a moral responsibility to welcome Middle Eastern refugees into our good-hearted state." In post-retirement remarks to the Twin Falls Rotary Club, Jones said the obligation arose because the United States helped initiate the refugee crisis by invading Iraq and creating great instability in the Middle East. Jones emphasized that the remarks were his own and that he no longer spoke for the Idaho court system.

"The invasion of Iraq set off a chain of events that resulted in the Syrian Civil War, which produced the greatest refugee crisis in recent history. Since the United States was a large contributor to the refugee crisis in the Middle East, we can't simply turn our backs on these unfortunate people. We have a moral responsibility to take in some of the people we helped to misplace."

Jones said "a number of so-called news organizations have engaged in fear-mongering in order to portray refugees, and particularly those from Syria, as a danger to our country. Breitbart News, World Net Daily and others have played fast and loose with the truth and should not be regarded as credible. They have unfairly attacked the College of Southern Idaho refugee program, Twin Falls government officials, and Chobani, which has been a wonderful addition to the community. We should not tolerate this type of conduct by outsiders."

Jones commended the CSI Refugee Center for its work in settling refugees in the Magic Valley. "I have gotten to know some of the people who were settled here and found them to be good patriotic people with a strong work ethic." Jones said the chance of Syrian refugees being disguised terrorist is almost nonexistent. "If a terrorist wanted to get into this country, he could do it much quicker and with less vetting by getting a tourist or student visa. Refugees from all countries, and particularly those from Syria, are subjected to careful screening. If one would take the time to get to know our refugee community, it would become clear that they just want what we all do—to live and raise their families in a safe environment. Many of the Syrian refugees have been subjected to unspeakable horrors—constant shelling by the Assad regime or the Russians, murder of their family members, or torture. The United States and Idaho should step forward to give these people refuge."

Jones, who served a tour of duty with the US Army in Vietnam in 1968-1969, said he had lived and worked with South Vietnamese soldiers who were refugees from North Vietnam. "They were good human beings. When South Vietnam fell in 1975 and waves of Vietnam refugees sought shelter in America, we heard dire and misplaced warnings of the woe that they would bring to our country. Those warnings are similar to those that Breitbart and others are spewing out today about Middle East refugees. The Vietnamese refugees have been a credit to our country and so will those people who are now seeking refuge here."

Jones noted that the U.S. has taken in less than 20,000 Syrian refugees to date. Turkey has admitted about 2.7 million, Lebanon over 1 million, Jordan around 1 million, Iraqi Kurdistan about 1.4 million. "Based on the role the U. S. played in destabilizing the Middle East, we have done very little to protect these unfortunate people."

The Rotary Club was friendly and I think the message was well received. Several members who had served in Vietnam came up to express their thanks. However, my sentiments apparently did not filter upward to the President-elect, who was inaugurated two days later. On January 27, he signed his first executive order barring admission of refugees into the country, as well as all citizens of seven Muslim-majority countries. The next day, the Idaho Statesman published the following guest opinion that I pretty much whipped up on the spot:

President Donald Trump's executive order on refugees diminishes America and makes Americans less safe.

Overall, the order is a serious impediment to our fight against ISIS and other radical groups. It neatly fits into their long-standing narrative that the U.S. is an enemy of Islam and must be attacked. As with our invasion of Iraq, the jihadi groups will use this as a recruitment tool to enlist terrorists to kill Americans. Coupled with the President's recent musings that we should have taken Iraq's oil, and still might, it will discourage the Muslim allies we are working with to defeat ISIS in Iraq and Syria.

The order imposes a temporary ban on visas for people from Iraq, Libya, Yemen, Somalia, Iran, Syria, and Sudan. Who would want to build a hotel in any of those places at present? Strangely, the order does not apply to the counties that produced the 9-11 terrorists — Saudi Arabia, the United Arab Emirates, Egypt, and Lebanon. Better countries for hotels?

Section 5(c) of the order proclaims that the "entry of nationals of Syria as refugees is detrimental to the interests of the United States." That is simply wrong. Candidate Trump acknowledged that the U.S. invasion of Iraq led to the rise of ISIS. That group, together with the Assad regime, created the massive flow of refugees out of Syria. It is irresponsible to deny refuge to the victims of the crisis we helped to create. Further, we are relying on the Syrian Muslims to combat ISIS. We have troops embedded with those allied forces. It is a kick in their teeth for America to turn away their countrymen who are fleeing Assad and ISIS for their very lives. It is certainly not helpful to the safety of our embedded troops.

The order calls for changes in the vetting process for Syrian refugees, despite the fact that the U.S. has the strictest and most lengthy refugee screening process around the globe, particularly for Syrians. Most of the Syrian refugees are women and children and there do not appear to be any instances where Syrian refugees have engaged in conduct detrimental to U.S. interests.

Section 5(d) of the order limits the entry of refugees from all countries to a total of 50,000. This is a 50% reduction. This will seriously impede the entry of Iraqis and Afghans who risked their lives to help American forces. We have already been shamefully stingy with visas for these people. Many have been murdered by those who consider them collaborators. We are morally obligated to give them refuge.

The order proposes to grant priority to refugees who claim to be Christians. Christians have undoubtedly been horribly persecuted but ISIS appears to brutalize people of all faiths. It may be that Shiite Muslims suffer even more at the hands of the ISIS butchers. This country has not been about religious tests in the past and should not be in the future. We became a haven for people of all faiths who were persecuted in their homelands. That is one basis upon which we base our claim of exceptionalism. Are we ready to forfeit our claim of moral superiority?

Congress has the authority to undo the provisions of the executive order that are most detrimental to the interests of our country. Knowing our Congressional delegation's past opposition to lawmaking by executive order, our representatives should be willing to step in. Let's call on them to act and keep America a great nation.

My surgery took place on January 31, so that put me out of commission for several days. Nevertheless, I gave a talk to the Idaho Association of Counties on February 8 and a speech to a water conference in Burley on February 16.

After getting back on my feet, I joined a law firm in Boise as an "of counsel" member, which meant that people did not expect me to go to work every day or to bring in lots of money for the firm. The good folks at Parsons Behle & Latimer were wise not to have great expectations in either regard. They did agree to provide a nice office with a view of the Idaho Capitol, secretarial help for my personal writing, and a reserved parking space.

I took to the speaking circuit over the next year, often addressing refugee and immigrations issues—a variety of service clubs, the Boise and Idaho Falls City Clubs, the Herrett Lecture at the College of Southern Idaho and the two law schools in Boise. My experience with refugees in Vietnam always played a part in my talks.

For a number of years before retirement, I had harbored the thought of being a newspaper columnist. It was not the best timing because newspapers were shedding columnists right and left to save money. The money angle was not an issue for me as I did not intend to charge for the privilege of inflicting my opinions on others. It seemed like the best way to go about it was to just send the columns to all of the Idaho dailies and see what happened.

By mid-spring I was sending out an opinion piece every week to most of the daily newspapers in the state and having some luck in getting them printed. The columns dealt with a wide range of subjects, including judicial appointments (get the politics out), climate change (recognize the danger and do something about it), medical care (make it more available), the rule of law (respect our legal system). There are several recurring themes related directly to my service in Vietnam—maintaining America's moral leadership in the world, countering Russian aggression, respecting our allies, helping refugees, and honoring veterans. President Trump provided quite a bit of fodder for opinion pieces so there has never been a shortage of things to write about.

One thing of great concern was the country's failure to continue the long-standing U.S. policy of speaking up for human rights around the world. It has been a principal facet of American foreign policy since the Second World War and has gained great admiration and support for our country from foreign democracies, as well as peoples yearning for freedom and dignity. It has helped keep our country safe. Unfortunately, America's moral standing is in decline. I sent this column out in June of 2017 shortly after the President had a jovial meeting in the White House with two top-level Russian officials:

Ever since World War II, the United States of America has been the champion of democracy and human rights throughout the globe. We have stood up to dictatorial governments and demanded that their citizens be allowed to live free of fear and oppression. Presidents of both parties have pursued that policy. It has been the cornerstone of our national security and has made our country the envy of other nations. Our country has decidedly strayed from that policy in recent months, heartening autocratic nations and causing concern amongst our steadfast allies.

As the world rose from the ashes of World War II, the U.S. embarked on a policy of building alliances with European and Asian nations to counter the Communist countries. We formed the North Atlantic Treaty Organization (NATO) and the Southeast Asia Treaty Organization (SEATO) as bulwarks against the totalitarian countries. Although SEATO eventually withered away, we have maintained strong bonds with democracies in Asia, which act as a mainstay of our national defense in that part of the world. In Europe, we have based our security on democracies that are united through NATO and the European Union. The policy has served America well.

We have supported and encouraged democracy throughout the world, believing that democratic nations are less likely to resort to force of arms to resolve disputes. We have believed that autocratic governments which deny their citizens basic human rights can produce violence, either against the people or by the people. In order to promote human rights, the U.S. State Department annually scores nations on their human rights record. We have engrafted advancement of human rights into our foreign policy.

President Trump has taken another direction in dealing with democracies and autocrats. Although Russia gobbled up Crimea, has maintained a thinly veiled proxy war in Ukraine, and launched a serious attack on our election process, he has declined to utter a harsh word about Vladimir Putin. Former FBI Director Comey says Russian hackers have attempted to hack into hundreds of governmental and business networks to find exploitable weaknesses. Our allies around the world have had similar experiences and they must be mystified by the President's silence. Rather, they have seen the Russian videos of the President yukking it up with the Russian foreign minister and ambassador in the White House. Then, he publicly criticized our European friends and pointedly refused to recommit to the mutual defense article of the NATO Treaty, something that had to seriously disturb our friends, but greatly please Mr. Putin.

During the President's trip to Saudi Arabia, he informed the Saudis and other Middle East despots that they need not worry about the U.S. pestering them about providing basic human rights for their subjects. As long as they do business with America and buy our "beautiful weapons," all will be good. The Saudis will be able to continue indiscriminate bombing in Yemen without our interference, despite the fact that this will fuel even more rage amongst the civilian population there and elsewhere against the U.S.

President Erdogan of Turkey has been warmly received by the President even as Erdogan expands his powers and tramples on the rights of his citizens. Same with President Sisi of Egypt. President Duterte of the Philippines is graciously treated despite his overseeing of 7,000, and counting, extra-judicial killings. These leaders all show up on the rogues' gallery of the State Department's human rights score sheets but we apparently no longer expect nations to treat their populations humanely in order to gain our favor. That encourages the despots and greatly diminishes America's standing in the world, as well as our nation's security.

The President's infatuation with Vladimir Putin has also been a continuing subject of great concern. It was hard to comprehend why he did not come down hard on Russia for attacking our 2016 election. It is also difficult to understand why the Republican Congress has not demanded tough action. When I was growing up in the Republican Party, the Soviet Union was considered by the Party to be a mortal enemy. The USSR furnished scads of weapons to the North Vietnamese forces for the purpose of killing American troops. The Russians were all in against America in the Vietnam War.

I'd gotten a taste of the Soviet way of doing things during the summer of 1964 and didn't much like it. While I was attending the summer school in Austria, I was able to take short trips to East Germany, Czechoslovakia and Hungary.

It was clear that fear ruled almost every aspect of life in East Berlin. Very few people would look at you and none would speak. While a person could move around the city, you felt you were being observed at all times. The city still had extensive war damage and was littered with anti-American propaganda. There was a war museum full of exhibits claiming the U.S. to be guilty of all kinds of war crimes and any number of atrocious actions. There was poverty and squalor as far as the eye could see. U.S. guards at Check Point Charley, where people moved back and forth between the free and Soviet sectors, spoke of people being killed by East German guards as they tried to escape their giant prison through rows of barbed wire, traps, machine gun emplacements and the Berlin Wall. The Communist guards were decidedly menacing and made passage as unpleasant and time consuming as possible.

Czechoslovakia was not much better. Entering the country on the train, you observed armed guards with machine guns and vicious-looking German Shepherds inspecting every inch outside and then hassling travelers on the inside. Prague, which had been a proud and vibrant city, was drab and dirty with soot. There did not appear to be much joy in the streets. Four years later the people would rise up in the Prague Spring, only to have their hopes crushed by a Soviet invasion.

After the fall of the USSR, there was hope that Russian aggression would dissipate and it did until Putin insinuated himself into power. His plan was to recreate the Soviet state and its former glory. We should certainly talk with the Russian Federation on issues of mutual concern but we have to recognize it as one of our main enemies in the world. Appeasement will not work. This situation was one of the primary targets of my opinion pieces. In November of 2017, just after the Trump-Putin meeting in Vietnam, I wrote an op-ed taking the President to task for failing to confront Putin for meddling in the 2016 election. Several months later, I wrote a column criticizing administration officials and members of Congress for not forcefully speaking out about U.S. inaction in the face of Russian aggression. Many more such columns followed.

Another subject of great importance to me, and a frequent topic of columns, was the need for the United States to continue to be a leader in refugee resettlement. We have a clear moral responsibility to do so since we have been responsible for creating much of the refugee problem in the world in the current century.

It is probably because of my speaking on refugee issues that I was asked to join the board of directors of Jannus, Inc., a social service organization that operates as Idaho's refugee resettlement administrator. The organization dates back to 1974 and has gone through a number of organizational changes since then. It operated under the name of Mountain States Group from 1993 until 2015, when it became Jannus. It operates a number of programs besides refugee-related ones, such as the Suicide Prevention Hotline, Early Head Start in the Idaho Panhandle, Nutrition Works, and the Idaho Center for Fiscal Policy.

The President's hostility toward refugees had a detrimental effect on the work of Jannus, as well as refugee resettlement agencies across the country. In late April of 2018, about a year after joining the board, I sent out an article expressing concern about the direction the new administration was taking on refugees and other immigrants:

Ever since the Statue of Liberty raised her torch in New York Harbor, she has welcomed the "homeless, tempest-tossed" masses from foreign shores. Those masses have played a central role in making America the powerful nation it is and the moral beacon it was. America's government has decided to pull up the welcome mat to foreigners and relinquish its role as moral leader of the world.

With ever-increasing intensity, the Trump administration has been closing America's door to refugees and asylum seekers; clamping down on immigration; and working to eject non-citizens. The administration's Muslim ban, which was argued in the U.S. Supreme Court on April 25, has drawn a good deal of public attention but it is just the tip of the iceberg. The government is conducting a full court press against foreigners.

With regard to refugees, the administration has capped the number that can be admitted to the country at 45,000, which is less than half of the yearly average taken in by the U.S. since 1980. However, we will likely give refuge to less than half of the cap because the administration is slow-walking the admission process. For example, Idaho received 1,118 refugees in fiscal year (FY) 2016, but only 629 in FY 2017 and we will be lucky to get 300 in FY 2018.

Do we have a responsibility to give safe harbor to refugees? These are people who were brutalized by their governments and had to flee for their very lives. The U.S. has played a major role in creating the massive refugee flow from Iraq, Syria, Afghanistan, Somalia, and Yemen by wars we have started or supported. We certainly have some responsibility to provide refuge to at least a few of the victims of those wars.

With regard to people seeking asylum, particularly those fleeing terrible violence in Central American countries, we have pretty much turned a blind eye. When parents arrive at the border with their minor children to ask for asylum, the kids are often taken and detained separately from the parents--more than 700 since October of 2017. John Kelly had suggested the policy as a deterrent for asylum seekers. On another front, Jeff Sessions wants to eliminate domestic abuse as a ground for obtaining asylum.

Much is happening on the immigration front. The President wants to reduce legal immigration by half and eject many people who are presently here, legally or not.

Many people who were admitted to the country on a temporary basis because of calamities at home are set to be removed from the country. That includes about 200,000 Salvadorans who came to the U.S. following a couple of 2001 earthquakes. Even though their status was initially expected to be temporary, these folks have established roots in the country and have been contributing. Now they have been notified to leave. The same has happened to Haitians, Liberians, and Hondurans, among others.

The DACA issue has gotten a good deal of coverage and it is not clear what the administration intends to do with these individuals who were brought to the country as minors and are now in jeopardy of being deported. The signals coming from the President continue to be conflicting. What does seem to be clear is that Dreamers are being held hostage as bargaining fodder for funding to build a costly and ineffective border wall and legislation to substantially restrict legal immigration.

Much more has been and is being done to make the United States a hostile environment for foreigners. It is contrary to our very being and will come back to haunt us in future years. Please, Lady Liberty, save us from ourselves.

When Public Television broadcast the Vietnam series by Ken Burns and Lynn Novick, I was saddened and outraged by the cynical calculation demonstrated by Nixon and Kissinger on the White House tapes. I thought back to all of the American and ARVN service personnel, not to mention innocent civilians, who were killed, wounded and scarred because of the political machinations of these two scoundrels. The fact that we did not make a concerted effort to rescue the South Vietnamese who helped and befriended American troops was particularly galling. Our more recent refusal to take in the Iraqis who put their lives was a similar cowardly betrayal of former allies. I put out a column about that in September:

Now that Ken Burns and Lynn Novick have told the Vietnam story from their viewpoint, I'd like to add my two bits. I thought the PBS series was very well done, particularly the taped quotes of the Presidents and others in charge of the war. I had been aware of it before, but it was extremely distressing to hear the cynicism pouring from the mouths of President Nixon and Henry Kissinger. Their war decisions were based on politics, not upon honesty. They were willing to dump South Vietnam like a hot rock without letting that country know what they were up to.

I certainly didn't disagree with the withdrawal of American troops, but we should have clearly advised the South Vietnamese that we would not provide combat air support to repel a future North Vietnamese attack. Indeed, Nixon told them we would have their back. It is hard to tell how many South Vietnamese soldiers, interpreters, and others who worked with American forces lost their lives or spent years in brutal "re-education camps" because they trusted us and believed Nixon's words. I believe some of my friends were among them. Had we been honest, many of those people might have chosen to leave the country and we should have offered them safe harbor in America.

When the communist forces were moving on Saigon in April of 1975, U.S. intelligence knew the country was on the verge of falling and urged that we organize an evacuation of those who had helped us and were in danger of retribution. We did not act until it was too late and then we were slow to open our doors to the many thousands of South Vietnamese who risked their lives in flimsy boats, seeking refuge in America. It was a sad chapter in our history.

Now, there are about 50,000 Iraqis who stuck their necks out by helping U.S. forces in the Iraq war and who are awaiting entrance into our country as refugees. They rightfully believed we would provide them protection from retribution for helping us. Many Afghans are in the same boat, although they still have the benefit of a special visa program. We destabilized the Middle East with our unnecessary invasion of Iraq, contributing to the massive refugee crisis, but seem to think we have no responsibility to give comfort to the refugees we helped to create.

The President has now capped refugee admissions to 45,000 for the coming year, the lowest level in decades. This is a massive evasion of responsibility. We were a major cause of the refugee problem but are unwilling to make a meaningful effort to solve it. So much for owning up to our moral responsibility. Both Admiral Michael Mullen, former Chairman of the Joint Chiefs of Staff, and Michael Chertoff, George W. Bush's Secretary of Homeland Security, have recently stated that a larger refugee ceiling is in America's national security interests and they are absolutely right.

These things do not happen in a vacuum. Our unwillingness to shoulder our responsibility plays out in front of the world community. Governmental leaders of many nations, including our close allies, see how the U.S. either meets or shirks its moral duties. If we are not willing to own up to what we are honor-bound to do, which countries are going to be inclined to help America when we may need them? America needs to be a country that owns up to its responsibilities, that honors its commitments, and that acts as a moral beacon to the world. We can't be great if we are not good.

When my law school roommate, Alby Anderson, learned that I had turned into a would-be columnist, he suggested that I set up a blog. Not having the slightest idea of how one would do that, I initially declined. He insisted and actually set one up for me. It can be found at htpps://JJCommonTater.com. The "tater" theme was thought to be appropriate for a common guy who grew up on an Idaho potato farm.

JJCommonTater tries to keep from being overly repetitive, but it does dwell on some common themes. A primary and recurring one is that we should always show appreciation for the service and sacrifice of our military personnel, regardless of the popularity of the conflict in which they served. I took the opportunity to say so in my column on Veterans Day in 2017:

When I was getting ready in August of 1969 to return home from my tour of duty in Vietnam, I bought some civilian clothes in Saigon. Word was that many people in the U.S. took unkindly to persons in military uniform. When I mustered out at the Oakland Army Base, I tossed my fatigues and boots into a trash can, put on my civvies, and caught a plane to Twin Falls. Although I don't recall anyone being hostile because of my Vietnam service, many returning vets did experience hostility. Things have changed.

I'm glad that people appreciate the service of men and women in uniform nowadays. It means a lot when you let them know you are thankful for their service. A couple of years ago, a highly respected judge from out of state who had served as a Marine at Khe Sanh, but rarely talked about it, told me, "Welcome home and thanks for your service." I was genuinely touched.

But we should do more than just thanking veterans and active duty personnel for serving their country. While we generally provide good medical treatment for their obvious physical injuries, the country can and should do much more to treat their less obvious injuries, such as PTSD, exposure to toxic substances, and the like. The high rates of suicide, substance abuse, and related problems are clear indicators that we are not living up to our responsibility to provide veterans and active duty personnel the mental health support and treatment they need and deserve. War is, as they say, hell and it takes a real toll on the psychological wellbeing of many of them.

We also owe it to the people who protect our nation to see that they receive proper treatment for ailments caused by exposure to toxic substances. After the Vietnam war, it was maddening to see the government deny treatment to returning veterans who suffered serious illnesses as a result of exposure to Agent Orange. Veterans of the First Gulf War and the war in Iraq received similar shabby treatment when they returned with strange symptoms related to exposure to dangerous substances. They deserved better.

The deaths of four servicemen in Niger [in October of 2017] pointed to another problem. Most Americans had little idea the U.S. had troops in harm's way there. I believe that is partly because only a tiny minority of the population is exposed to serving this country in dangerous places. It is easy for the rest of us to put it out of our minds. There is not a culture anymore that expects everyone of military age to do some type of service to this great country. It hurts me to hear about service personnel doing 4, 5, and 6 tours of duty in Iraq and Afghanistan. Some may thrive on it, but I'm sure it is a strain on many others, as well as their families.

When discussion started after Vietnam about an all-volunteer military, I had some misgivings. The idea of having greater professionalism and better pay made sense, but it seemed to me that we were going to get away from the idea that all citizens should have some skin in the game--that all young people should have the opportunity to serve their country in a meaningful way. When everyone is exposed to serving the country, I think we pay more attention to what the country is doing overseas. It certainly worked that way in the Vietnam era. Now, the country comfortably goes about its normal life while a small minority of dedicated citizens regularly faces danger in foreign places, largely unacknowledged by the country until some of them are shipped home in body bags. Instead of just thanking our veterans and service personnel, maybe we, as a country, should start thinking about how we can all help to serve the country.

In my estimation, young Americans should have an opportunity to provide meaningful service to their country. I would not advocate reinstitution of the draft but, rather, programs that would provide stipends for young men and women to provide public service in communities, national forests, assistance programs beyond our border and the like--service that would build up our country both at home and abroad. It would broaden the horizons of those young people and demonstrate that we can all work together for the common good.

During my speaking tour of service clubs in Idaho in the year and a half after retirement, I was surprised at the number of grey hairs in the various audiences who told me they had served in the military, including in Vietnam. Military service was sort of a rite of passage. Although not everyone did it, enough did that it was almost expected of young men back in the fifties and sixties. It provided experience in leadership, as well as maturity and a sense of a broader community of shared interest as Americans. We ought to provide that kind of opportunity for our young men and women coming of age today.

I know that I would not be the same person today had I not had the chance to serve in the military. The service, particularly in Vietnam, left a lasting mark on me and I am much the better for it.

Epilogue: Returning

As our plane was descending to land at Hanoi International Airport on January 17, 2018, I remembered back to my first landing in Vietnam 50 years earlier. That time, the World Airways plane made a rapid and steep descent into Tan Son Nhat Airport in Saigon so as to reduce its exposure to ground fire. Looking out of the window then, I saw bomb craters and other evidence of the fighting in the vicinity of the airport that had taken place during the Tet Offensive just five months earlier. This time the descent was normal, but it felt odd to be landing in a place that I had wanted to be blown off of the face of the earth in 1968--an unfortunate thought, but that was the way it was then.

My wife, Kelly, and I enjoyed our interaction with the Vietnamese people we met in Hanoi. It is hard to believe they were bitter enemies not so long ago. One person we met brushed off the "American War" as just an interruption in the long history of Vietnam.

We made the obligatory visit to Hoa Lo Prison, also known as the Hanoi Hilton, the old French prison where American POWs were held and brutally mistreated during the war. I was disappointed that about 90% of the compound had been demolished to make way for a commercial building. Seems like it should have been maintained as a memorial. One thing that gave great offense at the facility was the propaganda claim that

American prisoners had been humanely treated. Ho Chi Minh may have been a nationalist, but he was also a brutal dictator who approved of the mistreatment of American POWs. Yet, you can't hold that against the people living there now. The majority of the country's population was born after the war.

We also stopped to pay a visit to Ho in his mausoleum. I'm not sure why the Communists thought it was a good idea to embalm their leaders and put them on public display. I had seen both Lenin and Stalin when they were laid out for public viewing in Red Square in the nineteen-seventies. Lenin had looked a bit waxy but in fairly good shape, while Stalin looked somewhat freezer-burned. He was removed from view shortly after I saw him. Kelly and I had opted not to take a peek at Mao Zedong when we were in Beijing in the nineties—the line was too long. The wait to see Ho was rather short because people were hurried along. He had that waxy look, also. That look is probably hard to avoid after just laying around dead for such a long time.

We arrived in Hue, the old imperial capital of Vietnam, on January 21. It is a wonderful city. The main attraction is the Citadel where Vietnam's emperors lived and ruled through the nineteenth century and well into the twentieth. Much of the Citadel was destroyed during the 1968 Tet Offensive when Hue suffered the most intense urban fighting of the Vietnam War.

The Communist forces attacked and overran Hue during a truce that had been called to celebrate the Lunar New Year. It took a month of brutal, close-in combat to dislodge them. South Vietnamese troops fought well, suffering 452 killed and 2,132 wounded. U.S. forces sustained 1,584 wounded and 216 killed in action. Well over 5,000 Vietnamese civilians died, more than half of whom were executed by the Communists.

The government has restored a good deal of the damage but much more work lies ahead. You can see large areas where bullet holes were plastered over but many still remain there and elsewhere around the city. After all the mayhem, it does not seem right that a red flag with a yellow star should fly over the Citadel but that's just the way it is.

The Communists expected the citizens of Hue to rise up in support of the offensive, but they did not. Many citizens were traumatized by the mass executions. Maybe I read too much into it, but many of the older folk who were likely in Hue during the offensive would return a nod or smile to me on the streets. Could it be they had formed a warm spot in their hearts for Americans in those tragic days?

During our visit in January, the Vietnamese were gearing up to celebrate Tet, with Happy New Year signs wherever one looked. It was also the 50-year celebration of the Tet Offensive, which is often cited as the psychological turning point in the Vietnam War. When I returned from my tour of duty in August of 1969, I thought we were on our way to winning the war. It did not turn out that way and that still causes me great pain. However, I think Vietnam is moving on a positive track and has a bright future.

The South Vietnamese people I got to know during the war were wonderful people and I carry fond memories of them. During three weeks in Vietnam almost five decades later, I encountered many people just like them from Hanoi to Saigon and points in between. They were friendly, welcoming and often went out of their way to make a visitor feel at home. When we had to catch an early flight from Dalat to Saigon, the hotel opened breakfast service early to accommodate us.

One of the remarkable things was the courtesy the people showed to one another, as well as to foreigners. For instance, the streets of the larger cities were swarming with motor bikes. You would think that a pedestrian would be risking his or her life by trying to cross a crowded street. But, if you could get up the nerve to cross through the traffic, riders gave way so that you felt like Moses must have when the Red Sea parted.

The food was great, the service was friendly and helpful and people were quick to show a genuine smile. My wife and I greatly enjoyed our interactions with the Vietnamese people. We were in

Hanoi when Vietnam beat Iraq in the regional soccer semi-finals. Young people took to the streets in a lengthy and noisy, flag-waving procession through the city streets to celebrate. When the team won their next game with Qatar during our visit to Hoi An, the same thing happened. They were proud of their country and we were cheering with them.

We watched the soccer final with Uzbekistan at our hotel in Dalat. There we met a bright young man who attributed his almost perfect English to having spent 3 high school years in Boston. He will go far. China is making a play for the affections of Vietnam and people like him. Because of a long history of thorny relations between those countries, Vietnam would like to strengthen its relationship with us. I hope America's recent inward turn does not push them away. We need friends is this region.

The country is not perfect because the people still are unable to exercise some of the freedoms that Americans take for granted. That does not take anything away from the people, who are genuine good folks. We certainly have reason to know that because the Vietnamese who came to the U.S. as refugees after the war have been great additions to the American landscape.

Saigon (even though it was renamed Ho Chi Minh City in 1975, most locals still call it Saigon) has grown into a real metropolis, boasting a population of about 12 million people and 8 million motorbikes. While Hanoi has about 5 relatively tall buildings, Saigon has dozens and more are under construction or in the planning stage. Wages are rising and people are optimistic about the future. Although the government is still reluctant to allow political freedom and dwells on the past with anti-U.S. propaganda at historic sites, the people everywhere in the country are welcoming and friendly to Americans. The country is up and coming.

We made a point of visiting the War Remnants Museum, which was originally named the Museum of Chinese and American War Crimes. Although the name was changed, the tenor of the exhibits has not. There is still a strong propaganda flavor in the museum, but it does not represent the view of the present-day citizenry. The museum had a 175mm gun with an information plaque that I found of interest. It said the 175s had "caused numberless destruction" in Vietnam. The person who composed the message was apparently unaware of the marked inaccuracy of this particular weapon.

One of my trip objectives was to find some of the kids from the Cao Dai Orphanage. When Kelly and I arrived at our hotel in Tay Ninh, the interpreter I'd hired told us the orphanage had been closed by the Communists when they took over in 1975. However, she said her grandmother had worked in the orphanage and remembered me.

We met with grandma, Do Thi Cung, a delightful 78-year-old, on February 2. (photo #24) When she had worked in the orphanage in the late sixties and early seventies, she had been an employee of the Cao Dai Church. When the Communists took over and closed the orphanage, she stayed on in another capacity and was still working for the church. She remembered me because I'd handed out umbrellas to the orphanage staff during the Christmas party in 1968. I was the "umbrella Guy." She told us she had lost touch with the kids but she knew that some of them had ended up in America. Meeting with her was a real highlight of the trip.

The Cao Dai Great Divine Temple and Holy See were about the only things that remained as I remembered them. The ornate temple is one of the two attractions that bring tourists to Tay Ninh and it is well worth a visit. The other attraction is Nui Ba Dinh, the extinct volcano that towers over the rather flat province. Fifty years ago, it was dangerous territory but now it has a gondola that takes visitors about halfway to the top. I remember directing artillery fire against parts of the mountain back in the day.

I was not able to find any of the ARVNs with whom I had served but I did not really expect that they would still be around. Most of them had been Catholics from Cao Xa village. The name of the village had been changed and the church with its tall bell tower was no longer there. I expect my friends had either been killed, gone to prison camps or fled the country.

A guide who took us on a river trip south from Saigon told us he grew up in Binh Long Province, which bordered the east side of Tay Ninh Province. He said that the Communists executed about 78 ARVN troops and dumped them in a mass grave when they took over a town there in 1975. About ten years ago, the government exhumed the bodies and gave them a respectful burial.

The guide also related an interesting family story that illustrated the conflicting loyalties that the war brought about. He said his mother had been a Communist sympathizer and was in love with the local leader of the Viet Cong. She had to marry the guide's father in an arranged marriage. The groom was an ARVN soldier and his family supported the South Vietnamese Government. When the Communists won the war, the VC leader asked if she wanted him to kill the husband and his ARVN comrades. She said no, so the husband was able to get off with two and a half years in a re-education (prison) camp.

I wanted to find out if the elusive COSVN headquarters actually existed in the northern part of War Zone C. We had arranged for a car, driver and interpreter to drive us to the northern border with Cambodia. The drive was a real revelation. The area all of the way to the old Thien Ngon SF Camp was settled with residences, shops and businesses. There were farms growing all sorts of crops, including peanuts, vegetables, and rice, as well as rubber plantations and a national park. All of that area had been uninhabited jungle during the late nineteen-sixties. There was a war relic monument at the site of the SF camp.

As we traveled north along the Cambodian border, we came to a location about 11 klicks north of Thien Ngon that was designated on our tourist map as an early COSVN nerve center. About 5 klicks further, in the northernmost bulge of Vietnam into Cambodia, there was a memorial to the Viet Cong's headquarters for South Vietnam. (Map # 1) I had seen a picture and plaque about this location in the War Remnants Museum. A short distance east, which was about 16 klicks north and 10 klicks east of Thien Ngon, we reached what was claimed to be the COSVN headquarters. (Map # 1) There was a large patriotic mural of the Communist forces struggling to ultimate victory against tough odds. One person in the mural held a sign equating President Johnson to Adolf Hitler. The location also had a preserved crater created by a bomb from a B-52. The road into this area was still covered by triple canopy jungle for a distance of about five klicks, which would have concealed it from the air.

I had some doubts that COSVN was actually located on the Vietnamese side of the border, despite the claims onsite and in the tourist brochures. It would not have made sense to conduct business inside of a free-fire zone that was frequently the beneficiary of B-52 raids when there was essentially a King's X zone just over the border in Cambodia. However, from a propaganda standpoint, I can see why they would claim the headquarters was in Vietnam.

On our way back to Tay Ninh, we drove around the east side of Nui Ba Dinh. When I last saw it in 1969, that area looked like swiss cheese from the air because of the hundreds of bomb craters left by the B-52s. (photo #18) You can't see any of them nowadays. The whole area is now cultivated and intensively farmed. There are pineapple trees and all sorts of produce being grown on that formerly embattled ground.

Despite the dark years the people of South Vietnam suffered after the war, things are looking brighter and I feel better about how things have worked out for them. The price we and they paid for the conflict was way too high, but the young people of the country seem to be doing relatively well. Who could have predicted this outcome back in the late sixties?

Because of our history of ugly conflict with the Communists, it felt a bit odd to be well received by almost everyone we met. I'm pleased we are able to get along now and I hope our two countries can strengthen our bonds, as each has strategic interests in doing so. One can't help but wonder whether the resort to war those many years ago was really necessary. Rather than struggling with that question, I think it is best to draw as many lessons from that experience as is possible and actually apply that knowledge as we move forward. I certainly won't forget the experience because Vietnam is engrafted deep into my soul.

Acknowledgements

There are many people who deserve great thanks for making this book possible, going back to my parents, Henry and Eunice Jones who were the absolute best. President John Kennedy inspired me, as well as many others of my generation, to pursue satisfaction in public service. Senator Len Jordan gave me an opportunity to get my feet wet in the public arena, both before and after law school, and was one of the finest people I have ever known.

The U.S. Army and all those with whom I served have helped set the course of my life. The friends I made in the South Vietnamese Army and the Vietnamese civilians, including the wonderful kids at the Cao Dai Orphanage, have enriched my life. I wish they had been able to have the good lives that we thought we could help provide.

I am grateful to the people of Idaho for giving me the opportunity to serve, both as Attorney General and as a member of the Supreme Court. Both experiences have greatly shaped the person I am. During my journey from private practitioner to my retirement from the Court, my legal assistant and good friend, Tresha Griffiths, stuck with me for 40 years. My daughter, Kathy, also put in 40+ years of help and support along the way. She is a great kid.

These last 24 years, my dear wife, Kelly, has given me love, support, and advice on my writing ventures that has been extremely helpful. She read my manuscript a couple of times and gave great input. I incorporated almost all of it. My friend from high school days, Marjorie Langton, was kind enough to give her thoughts about the book. James Peterson, a friend who served with the Special Forces in Vietnam just before I got there and in many of the same places, provided valuable input. My long-time political and personal friend, Lydia Justice Edwards, the finest State Treasurer to ever safeguard Idaho's cash also helped with the book.

Cathy Pontak, my legal assistant at the law firm where I am "of counsel," has graciously helped me get my thoughts down on paper and I owe her a great debt of gratitude. I appreciate my firm, Parsons Behle & Latimer, allowing me to use their facilities for working on the book.

In addition to the book, I have been writing a weekly column on state and national issues, which has sharpened up my writing. Kelly tells me I have been improving and I think it is because a variety of publications has been willing to give voice to my opinions. Two that regularly publish my stuff are Randy Stapilus at Ridenbaugh Press and LaVarr Webb at Idaho Politics Weekly. Thanks guys.

Idaho's daily papers have soldiered on despite headwinds resulting from digitization of news media and I appreciate their support—Pun-loving Mike Patrick at the Coeur d'Alene *Press* in Coeur d'Alene, Alison Smith at the *Times News* in Twin Falls, Ian Fennell at the *Idaho State Journal* in Pocatello, Monte La Orange at the *Post Register* in Idaho Falls, Marty Trillhaase at the *Lewiston Morning Tribune*, Devin Rokyta at the Moscow-Pullman *Daily News*, Caroline Lobsinger at the Bonner County *Daily Bee*, Scott McIntosh at the *Idaho Press Tribune* or *Idaho Press* in Caldwell-Nampa, and my friend Bill Manny formerly of the *Idaho Statesman* in Boise. Please support your local newspapers. They are a vital ingredient of a healthy democracy, especially when they print my opinions.

Thanks also go to Tom and Marcia Fulham, who accompanied Kelly and me on our 2018 trip to Vietnam. They were great traveling companions. And, thanks to Alby Anderson for setting up the JJCommonTater website.

Ridenbaugh Press has made this process very easy for me. I appreciate everything Randy Stapilus and Linda Watkins have done to get this book into print. They have really done creditable work in getting the book published.

My brother-in-law, Brian Florence, is a talented graphic artist. He did a great job on the front cover of the book and in preparing and labeling Maps # 1 and 2. Map # 1 was difficult to assemble. The righthand side was a composite of 8 Army Corps of Engineer maps from the 1960s. There were no maps available for the left side, which was along the Cambodian border, so I had to take photos of the map book I used for my visual reconnaissance flights. It was not easy to match them up to the right scale and it did not help that 50 years had caused the maps to warp and the tape to deteriorate. But, it worked out well enough to give a picture of the lay of the land.

Finally, I want to thank Kathy's daughter, Kylee, for her interest in my Vietnam story. I hope the book gives her and her brother, Cameron, an understanding of what grandpa did in that war. I hope for their sake and for our other kids and grandkids, the United States can avoid unnecessary wars in the future. Love to Jon, Becca, Dillon, Christopher, and Miriam, and to Dave, Kristi, Corbin, Jaden, and Ellie. Love, also, to my brother, Calvin, and to my sisters, Renie and Carol.

JIM JONES grew up on his family's farm in Eden, Idaho. He graduated from the University of Oregon in 1964 with a BA degree in Political Science and a Second Lieutenant commission in the U.S. Army. He received a law degree from Northwestern University School of Law in 1967.

Jim served as an artillery officer in the U.S. Army, including a 13-month tour in Vietnam. He was honorably discharged as a Captain in August, 1969. Jim received an Army Commendation Medal for his civic action work with an orphanage run by the Cao Dai Church in Tay Ninh Province, Vietnam, as well as a Bronze Star and five Air Medals.

Jim served as legislative assistant to former U.S. Senator Len B. Jordan for three years (1970-1972). He practiced law in Jerome, Idaho, from 1973 until he was elected as Idaho Attorney General in 1982. Jim served eight years as Attorney General. He practiced law in Boise from 1991 until being elected to the Idaho Supreme Court in 2004. He served twelve years on the Court.

Jim's earlier book, *A Little Dam Problem: How Idaho almost lost control of the Snake River*, was released in 2016. The book garnered him the Outstanding Achievement in the Humanities Award from the Idaho Humanities Council in 2017. He is now a would-be columnist, writing about military affairs, foreign and domestic policy, immigrants, refugees, climate change and a wide variety of other state and national topics. His columns can be found at https://JJCommonTater.com.

Jim is married to Boise author Kelly Jones. They have three children and eight grandchildren.